PRAISE FOR *CULTURE*

"This book is many things: a deep scientific study, an impressive roadmap for the understanding of corporate cultures, a manual for effective behavioural interventions and a demonstration of great wisdom and practical experience in helping corporations to be become better places for people."
Professor Guido Palazzo, Professor of Business Ethics, University of Lausanne

"This book is a detailed guide in measuring and connecting the *what* with the *how* and the *where*. It is an essential advancement in applied behavioural science and connected analytics and will change the way we drive business success."
William Ingham, Chief People Officer, OURO, and former SVP HR Visa, Europe

"This book is a masterpiece and is an essential read for anyone seeking to understand the complex interplay between cultural patterns and data science. The author brilliantly demystifies complex analytical techniques, offering profound insights into cultural trends and patterns. A must-read for scholars and practitioners alike looking to understand and leverage the power of cultural data. This book beautifully summarizes decades of practical experience, knowledge and invaluable contribution to behavioural and impact driven culture studies for valuable insights including analysing cultural patterns though the practical use of predictive analytics and its importance for the entire organizational culture journey to drive desired outcomes."
Ashish Sinha, Senior Partner, EMEA practice lead, People Analytics & AI, Korn Ferry

"Even the greatest organizations simply do not survive the test of time without a deliberate focus on their workplace culture. It is a pleasure to read this book which articulates a powerful approach for organizational culture measurement, using behavioural science and predictive analytics to scientifically measure and embed desired culture to achieve chosen business outcomes and thereby harness the true power of culture. A must-read for leaders that want to tangibly measure, improve and transform their workplace culture."
Miguel Ángel Rodriguez Sola, Senior Advisor to Boston Consulting Group

"A thought-provoking book which combines grounded research with insightful reflection. As leaders we continue to wrestle with what culture really means and how we measure it – this book provides new perspectives and challenges our beliefs."
Melanie Richards, non-executive director, UK

"It is a joy to read a book which brings hard data, deep analysis and real insight to culture in organizations. It is a book which will make you think and think again."
Jo Owen, author of *How to Lead* and *Smart Thinking*

"Whilst AI will undoubtedly transform many aspects of society, culture will continue to play a vital role in shaping how we develop, use and co-exist with it. This book provides an amazing insight into the power of data, how to interpret and analyse it and, more importantly, apply it in a cultural context with practical behavioural changes. The extensive range of models and techniques are thought provoking in themselves, but this book isn't just about statistics and their application, it's about the future of organizations. It's a must read for anyone who is interested in organizational and people effectiveness and wants to be a cultural hero."
Dave Millner, author and Founder of HR Curator

"More than just a world-class expert, the author is an amiable and plain-speaking guide. He illustrates each theoretical framework with relatable, how-to, applied practical examples. It's rare and welcome to find an analyst in any field who can bring together the interests of scholars and practitioners so neatly. While most mere mortals get a headache from even considering how to quantify cultural phenomena, Hani Nabeel presents a stress-free introduction that's full of valuable tools and methodologies. I'll be keeping this book close at hand as the prime source on framing and tracking the elusive dynamics of culture."
Roger Miles, behavioural risk researcher; Head of Faculty and Co-Founder, Conduct Leadership Academy at UK Finance

Culture Analytics

An evidence-based approach to company culture

Hani Nabeel

Publisher's note

Every possible effort has been made to ensure that the information contained in this book is accurate at the time of going to press, and the publishers and authors cannot accept responsibility for any errors or omissions, however caused. No responsibility for loss or damage occasioned to any person acting, or refraining from action, as a result of the material in this publication can be accepted by the editor, the publisher or the author.

First published in Great Britain and the United States in 2025 by Kogan Page Limited

Apart from any fair dealing for the purposes of research or private study, or criticism or review, as permitted under the Copyright, Designs and Patents Act 1988, this publication may only be reproduced, stored or transmitted, in any form or by any means, with the prior permission in writing of the publishers, or in the case of reprographic reproduction in accordance with the terms and licences issued by the CLA. Enquiries concerning reproduction outside these terms should be sent to the publishers at the undermentioned addresses:

2nd Floor, 45 Gee Street
London
EC1V 3RS
United Kingdom

8 W 38th Street, Suite 902
New York, NY 10018
USA

www.koganpage.com

Kogan Page books are printed on paper from sustainable forests.

© Hani Nabeel 2025

The right of Hani Nabeel to be identified as the author of this work has been asserted by her in accordance with the Copyright, Designs and Patents Act 1988.

All trademarks, service marks, and company names are the property of their respective owners.

ISBNs

Hardback   978 1 3986 1747 6
Paperback 978 1 3986 1744 5
Ebook   978 1 3986 1748 3

British Library Cataloguing-in-Publication Data

A CIP record for this book is available from the British Library.

Library of Congress Control Number

2024035275

Typeset by Integra Software Services, Pondicherry
Print production managed by Jellyfish
Printed and bound by CPI Group (UK) Ltd, Croydon, CR0 4YY

CONTENTS

List of figures and tables x
Acknowledgements xviii

PART ONE

1 **Building clarity: Redefining culture and values** 3
   Leaders are the custodian of culture, but every employee is accountable for culture 6
   The symbiotic relationship 7
   Notes 9

2 **Let's talk behaviours and demystify behavioural science!** 10
   What is behavioural science? 10
   Behavioural science for workplace culture 13
   Notes 17

3 **The differences between behaviours and outcomes** 18
   Behaviours: the foundation of actions 18
   Outcomes: the consequences of actions 19
   Lagging and leading indicators 20
   Path analysis 22

4 **Understanding cultural dimensions** 24
   Behavioural measurement 26
   Mapping behaviours to organizational values/frameworks 30
   Notes 34

5 **Data analytics concepts for actionable insights** 35

6   **The link between organizational culture and its impact on outcomes** 43

Defining key statistical terms 43
Notes 53

7   **Applying predictive analytics to culture metrics** 54

8   **You have to know the 'why' before you get to the 'how' and where'** 62

9   **Leveraging leading indicators** 67

10 **Understanding and applying path analysis as the roadmap for driving change** 73

Steps for developing a path analysis using SEM modelling 76

11 **Simplifying the actionable insights and understanding ROI** 102

Odds ratio 104

12 **Cultural types** 121

Culture type – primary behavioural clusters 121
Culture type – secondary behavioural clusters 124
Workplace culture tensions 129

13 **Applying behavioural interventions** 135

Stage 1: Behavioural selection and context 136
Stage 2: Design the intervention 140
Stages 3 and 4: Plan the interventions and implement 142
Stage 5: Validate 148

14 **The impact of growth on organizational culture** 149

The role of workplace culture in mergers and acquisitions as a strategy for growth 150

15 Cultural navigation in the digital age 154

The impact of the digital age on workplace culture 154
The opportunity for connected data to provide actionable workplace culture analytics 155
Ethical considerations for using employee data for workplace culture analytics 158

PART TWO

16 Gaining predictive insight into employee sentiment through behavioural science and analytics 163

Background 164
Context 166
How we crunched the numbers 176
Notes 177

17 Driving organizational change through workplace culture and behavioural analytics 180

Part 1: Do your change champions have what it really takes to effect change? 181
Part 2: Sizing the 'ask' of your organization when you ask it to change 188
Part 3: Building a behavioural roadmap to drive effective change 194
Notes 202

18 Are your HR processes supporting alignment between culture and strategy? 205

Notes 214

19 Going beyond diversity metrics to actionable insights on DE&I 215

What's the elephant still in the room? Maybe it's real commitment to DE&I programmes! 217
Seven behaviours of a DE&I-friendly workplace culture 218
The context for the case study 219
Insights generated 221

What actions were taken? 237
So, did the needle move? 239
So what? What about the outcome? 240
Implications for the research approach focused on inclusion 241
Notes 242

20 A tale of two organizations: Why innovation needs the letter 'C' 245

It's not just about smarts and process: Why the letter 'C' is important 246
Context and methodology 247
The seven behaviours defining the innovation index 248
The traditional bank (TB) 249
The challenger bank (CB) 254
Do we need the letter 'C' in Innovate? 260
Notes 260

21 Safety culture and risk management 262

Context 263
The generated actionable insights 264
Path analysis 271
Notes 278

22 What about agile culture? Does that need the letter 'C'? 279

Context 283
Analytics and actionable insights 287
Path analysis 291
Note 296

23 The crucial role that workplace culture plays in shaping employee wellbeing 297

Context 298
Analytics and actionable insights 299
Path analysis for wellbeing 301
Intervention design and planning 306
Note 324

24 Can we make organizational culture the hero it deserves to be? 325

1. To drive success, stop focusing on results alone and focus on the behaviours that drive these 326
2. Off-the-shelf models and values do not work 327
3. Leaders are the custodian of organizational culture, but every employee is accountable for it 328

Index 333

LIST OF FIGURES AND TABLES

FIGURES

Figure 2.1	How to drive behaviour change	16
Figure 2.2	The five-step approach	17
Figure 3.1	Path analysis example	23
Figure 5.1	The behavioural factors scale interpretation	38
Figure 5.2	The dichotomous behavioural factor pairs and the scale	39
Figure 5.3	A connected data approach to provide behaviour-first or outcome-first analytics for insights	40
Figure 5.4	The 'where' of behaviour presence or absence using the quadrant dispersion method	41
Figure 6.1	A graph showing the β coefficient	47
Figure 6.2	Correlational effect size benchmarks	51
Figure 6.3	The predictive relationship between the nested five behaviours and performance rating	52
Figure 7.1	Heatmap results for the five behaviours that drive performance workplace culture	55
Figure 7.2	Quadrant distribution diagram showing where the five behaviours driving performance are present	56
Figure 7.3	Line graph showing performance grade against the five behaviours	59
Figure 8.1	Quadrant distribution graph showing behavioural alignment vs employee engagement scores	64
Figure 9.1	Example of one set of behavioural data measurement, a leading indicator to many thematic outcomes	70
Figure 10.1	The first two outcomes in the risk path analysis	84
Figure 10.2	The sequence of how the three outcomes should manifest in the risk path analysis	88
Figure 10.3	The sequence of how the four outcomes should manifest in the risk path analysis	88
Figure 10.4	The sequence of how the five outcomes should manifest in the risk path analysis	91
Figure 10.5	The outcome sequence for the second developing path	96
Figure 10.6	The sequence of the second developing path for the outcomes	96
Figure 10.7	The outcome sequence for the second full path	96

Figure 10.8	The outcome sequence for the third path	98
Figure 10.9	The first path with the behaviours now included	98
Figure 10.10	The second path with the behaviours now included	98
Figure 10.11	The third path with the behaviours now included	99
Figure 10.12	The behavioural leading indicators and the outcomes they drive over the three paths	100
Figure 11.1	The odds ratio per behavioural quartile vs likelihood of outcome occurrence	107
Figure 11.2	The odds ratio for Living our Values outcome vs behaviour presence	108
Figure 11.3	The odds ratio for the Recognition outcome vs behaviour presence	109
Figure 11.4	The odds ratio for the Purpose outcome vs behaviour presence	110
Figure 11.5	The odds ratio for the Resilience outcome vs behaviour presence	111
Figure 11.6	The odds ratio for the Psychological Safety outcome vs behaviour presence	112
Figure 11.7	The odds ratio for the Development for the Future outcome vs behaviour presence	113
Figure 11.8	The odds ratio for driving the Taking Ownership of Risk outcome vs behaviour presence	114
Figure 11.9	The odds ratio for driving the Collaborate for Managing Risk outcome vs behaviour presence	115
Figure 11.10	The odds ratio for driving the Risk Anticipation outcome vs behaviour presence	116
Figure 11.11	The odds ratio for driving the Risk Avoidance outcome vs behaviour presence	117
Figure 11.12	The odds ratio for driving Proactive Learning for Risk outcome vs behaviour presence	118
Figure 11.13	The behavioural leading indicators and the outcomes they drive as well as the likelihood of outcome manifesting over the three paths	119
Figure 12.1	The behaviours and related culture type for a behavioural cluster	122
Figure 12.2	The culture types with the present and targeted behaviours marked	123
Figure 12.3	Consider First vs Act First culture types	124
Figure 12.4	Question and Listen vs Define the Answer culture types	125

Figure 12.5   Ensure Safety vs Navigate Possibility culture types 126
Figure 12.6   The Consider First vs Act First secondary culture types 127
Figure 12.7   The Question and Listen vs Define the Answer secondary culture types 128
Figure 12.8   The Navigate Possibility vs Ensure Safety secondary culture types 129
Figure 12.9   The percentage behavioural tension as alignment or misalignment between Place and People 133
Figure 13.1   Intervention time plan implementation 145
Figure 13.2   Example behavioural interventions time and resource plan 146
Figure 14.1   Steps involved in the workplace cultural integration of two independent companies 152
Figure 15.1   The big data digital approach to culture analytics 156
Figure 16.1   Path model for employee voice for this organization 169
Figure 16.2   Direct impact of the Place on employee wellbeing 170
Figure 16.3   Direct impact of the People and the Place on trust 170
Figure 16.4   Direct impact of the Place on employee voice 171
Figure 16.5   The six behaviours that drive trust, wellbeing and employee voice 174
Figure 17.1   Behaviours metrics versus probability of change 185
Figure 17.2   The behaviours for the change metric 186
Figure 17.3   The three organizational change pillars versus behavioural alignment 191
Figure 17.4   The profiles of the eight clusters and the alignment by pillar 193
Figure 17.5   Combining the insight of the Place defining the size of the ask vs the People defining the propensity for change 198
Figure 17.6   The eight-cluster mapping analysis within the size of the ask (Place) vs propensity for change (People) metrics 199
Figure 17.7   The translation of target clusters as the starting point of the change programme into the three pillar benchmarks 201
Figure 18.1   The behavioural defined alignment categorization zones 207
Figure 18.2   Multiple countries analysis hiring against the targeted five behaviours 209
Figure 18.3   Employee demographic insights versus the alignment zones and the likelihood of occurrence 210
Figure 18.4   The tenure odds ratio for five behaviours: Disenfranchise, Delivery Focus, Collective, Consolidate and Conformity 212

LIST OF FIGURES AND TABLES   xiii

Figure 19.1 Radar graph and inclusion index for the whole organization, organizational behaviours 224
Figure 19.2 Radar graph and inclusion index for Front Office, organizational behaviours 225
Figure 19.3 Radar graph for Front Office, personal behaviours 226
Figure 19.4 Radar graph showing the organization (Place) behavioural differences and the inclusion index for different ethnic groups for the whole organization 227
Figure 19.5 Regression analysis odds ratio for the first outcome, employees being valued by the organization 229
Figure 19.6 Regression analysis odds ratio for the second outcome, employees being valued by their team 230
Figure 19.7 Gender behavioural radar graph and inclusion index for model one outcome, employees valued at the organization 232
Figure 19.8 Gender behavioural radar graph and inclusion index for model two outcome, employees valued by their teams 233
Figure 19.9 Ethnicity behavioural radar graph and inclusion index for model one outcome, employees valued at the organization 234
Figure 19.10 Ethnicity behavioural radar graph and inclusion index for model two outcome, employees valued by their teams 235
Figure 19.11 Quadrant distribution of the three targeted behaviours: Conformity, Team Focus and Expressive 236
Figure 19.12 Behavioural quadrant alignment matrix and descriptions per quadrant 238
Figure 20.1 Power and hierarchy theme 250
Figure 20.2 Importance of internal risk management theme 251
Figure 20.3 External moderators to innovation theme 252
Figure 20.4 The innovation index indicator and a radar graph for the seven behaviours that drive it for the Place 253
Figure 20.5 The innovation index indicator and a radar graph for the seven behaviours that drive it for the Place and the People – traditional bank 255
Figure 20.6 Creating the best customer experience theme 256
Figure 20.7 Importance of collegial relationships theme 257
Figure 20.8 External perceptions theme 258
Figure 20.9 The innovation index indicator and a radar graph for the seven behaviours that drive it for the Place and the People – challenger bank 259
Figure 21.1 The odds ratio for Psychological Safety where Active Learning, Standardized, Collective and Sequential behaviours are present 265

Figure 21.2   The odds ratio for Inclusion at work where Active Learning, Conformity, Relationship and People Focus behaviours are present 266

Figure 21.3   The odds ratio for Questioning Attitude at work where Active Learning, Conformity, Sequential and Team Focus behaviours are present 267

Figure 21.4   The odds ratio for Safety Communication outcomes at work where Standardized, Sequential, Relationship and Team Focus behaviours are present 268

Figure 21.5   The odds ratio for driving a Continuous Learning culture at work where Active Learning, Strategic, Team Focus, Sequential and People Focus behaviours are present 269

Figure 21.6   The odds ratio for driving a culture for Accountability at work where Strategic, Conformity, Team Focus and Sequential behaviours are present 270

Figure 21.7   The Accountability path, also showing the behaviours' presence needed to drive that path 271

Figure 21.8   The full outcome details for the Accountability path and the R value illustrating the strength of the relationship between the outcomes 272

Figure 21.9   The Proactive Safety Management path, also showing the behaviours' presence needed to drive that path 272

Figure 21.10   The full outcome details for the Proactive Safety Management path and the R value illustrating the strength of the relationship between the outcomes 273

Figure 21.11   The behaviours that need intervention design, planning and implementation as well as the odds ratio for impacting the outcomes' return on investment 274

Figure 21.12   Quadrant distribution for the entire sample size for the seven absent behaviours, Conformity, Team Focus, Collective, Relationship, Outer Focus, People Focus and Empower 277

Figure 22.1   The odds ratio for the transparency outcome where Team Focus, Conformity, Empower and People Focus behaviours are present 288

Figure 22.2   The odds ratio for the growth mindset outcome where Active Learning, Team Focus, Conformity and Strategic behaviours are present 289

Figure 22.3   The odds ratio for the driving effectiveness outcome where Active Learning, Conformity, Strategic and outer Focus behaviours are present 290

Figure 22.4	The odds ratio for the psychological safety outcome where Conformity, Expressive and People Focus behaviours are present 291
Figure 22.5	The full agile path analysis with the leading behavioural indicators 292
Figure 22.6	The three-stage sequential intervention plan and the odds ratio likelihood for the return on investment 295
Figure 23.1	The odds ratio for applying the standards outcome where Conformity and Team Focus behaviours are present 300
Figure 23.2	The odds ratio for supporting employee wellbeing outcome where Conformity, Team Focus and Strategic behaviours are present 301
Figure 23.3	The first established path for Psychological Safety along with the behavioural leading indicators 303
Figure 23.4	The second established path for Wellbeing outcomes as well as the behavioural leading indicators 304
Figure 23.5	The absent behaviours, and the proposed behavioural intervention stages for the Psychological Safety and Wellbeing paths as well as the return-on-investment likelihood 305
Figure 23.6	The quadrant distribution for the Expressive behaviour functionally across the organization 308
Figure 23.7	Quadrant distribution for the Team Focus behaviour functionally across the organization 310
Figure 23.8	Quadrant distribution for the People Focus behaviour functionally across the organization 311
Figure 23.9	Quadrant distribution for the Conformity behaviour functionally across the organization 312
Figure 23.10	Workshop output for the Expressive behaviour 313
Figure 23.11	Workshop output for the Team Focus behaviour 314
Figure 23.12	Workshop output for the People Focus behaviour 315
Figure 23.13	Workshop output for the Conformity behaviour 316
Figure 23.14	The interventions implementation time plan 323

TABLES

Table 4.1	CultureScope behavioural dimensions 26
Table 4.2	Full behavioural factors descriptors 31
Table 4.3	Mapping example 32
Table 4.4	Full mapping 32

Table 4.5	Cluster values behavioural mapping	33
Table 5.1	A values-based heatmap	35
Table 5.2	The presence or absence of the behaviour factors driving the three organizational values	36
Table 5.3	A numeric heatmap for the presence or absence of the behaviour factors driving the three organizational values	37
Table 5.4	The targeted behaviour factors and the type of intervention needed	39
Table 6.1	Regression summary output	46
Table 6.2	Secondary regression output: Analysis of Variance (ANOVA)	46
Table 6.3	Regression component analysis	48
Table 6.4	Regression results key components	50
Table 7.1	Comparison between the organizational values behavioural mapping and predictive performance culture	59
Table 7.2	Behavioural mapping for Positivity	60
Table 7.3	Changed values wording and relevant behavioural mapping	61
Table 9.1	The eight behaviours mapped to all five themes	71
Table 10.1	Correlation analysis for all provided outcomes	78
Table 10.2	Correlation analysis with the mean for each outcome calculated and ranked	80
Table 10.3	Correlation analysis with all values less than 0.2 eliminated	81
Table 10.4	Correlation analysis with values less than the column mean removed	82
Table 10.5	The computed average mean correlations and rankings	83
Table 10.6	The path starting point outcome that has the highest corresponding correlation coefficient to another outcome	85
Table 10.7	Risk Avoidance is our next outcome in the path analysis as it has the highest correlation coefficient with Risk Anticipation	86
Table 10.8	The highest corresponding correlation coefficient outcome to Risk Avoidance is Collaboration	87
Table 10.9	The highest corresponding correlation coefficient outcome to Collaboration is Proactive Learning	89
Table 10.10	Our first path has come to a dead end	90
Table 10.11	The computed average mean correlations and rankings, now with the first path outcomes removed	92

Table 10.12	The highest corresponding correlation coefficient outcome to Psychological Safety is Recognition 93
Table 10.13	The highest corresponding correlation coefficient outcome to Recognition is Resilience 94
Table 10.14	The highest corresponding correlation coefficient outcomes have both been already used in the path 95
Table 10.15	The computed average mean correlations and rankings, now with the first and second path outcomes removed 97
Table 11.1	The number of best and least outcome vs behavioural quartiles 106
Table 12.1	Culture types and behaviours for the Risk Tension 130
Table 12.2	Culture types and behaviours for the Progressive Tension 131
Table 12.3	Culture types and behaviours for the Independence Tension 132
Table 13.1	Template to be completed as a team exercise to show the current and future shift for each targeted behaviour 137
Table 13.2	Exercise showing the current and future shift for the Empower behaviour 137
Table 13.3	Example extract for Empower behaviour analysis post-workshop 139
Table 13.4	The COM-B function labelled with the behavioural inhibitors for Empower 141
Table 13.5	Intervention design for an executive committee 142
Table 13.6	Intervention design for leadership team 143
Table 19.1	The two outcomes comparison before and after interventions by gender and ethnicity demographics 240
Table 22.1	The resulting behavioural map for agile organizational characteristics 281
Table 22.2	The sample size per county targeted for the agile methodology 283
Table 22.3	The organizational current state vs the target agile characteristics 284
Table 22.4	The behavioural mapping for both the current organizational state as well as the targeted agile state 285
Table 22.5	The behavioural mapping for the current organizational state as well as the targeted agile state 293
Table 23.1	The starting point behavioural distribution per functional area with the organization 307
Table 23.2	All intervention designs 317

ACKNOWLEDGEMENTS

Writing this book was a wonderful trip down memory lane, remembering all the special people and moments that inspired my research journey in the quest of making organizational culture the hero it deserves to be. To all of you I say a heartfelt thank you.

A special thank you to Bharat Shah, who has dedicated himself completely to what became our joint mission in escalating workplace culture measurement and design, as the key focus for all organizational leaders and board members.

I also fondly remember and thank Eugene Burke. His deep knowledge in psychometrics, behavioural science and people analytics was not just inspirational, but transformative in how I bring culture insights to life.

As I also reflect back on the Neural Computing design for predictive analytics, I thank my son Joe Nabeel and Charlie Levi both for their amazing scientific data modelling and design, and for the awesome work by the talented software engineers at Future Processing in bringing all the design work to life.

My sincere appreciation goes to my colleague Michelle Renecle, a whirlwind combination of behavioural research excellence and actionable insights, who has and will always be a constant source of inspiration.

To family – without their constant support (and sometimes tolerance!), I would not have been able to dedicate myself to this quest.

PART ONE

1

Building clarity: Redefining culture and values

> Culture is like the wind: blowing in your direction, it makes for smooth sailing; blowing against you, everything is more difficult.

We hear so much about organizational culture, organizational values and 'what we stand for', countless articles, books, documentaries, white papers, research studies, etc – all for the sake of addressing this crucial topic.

It is universally recognized that corporate culture is one of the most critical levers for driving organizational success and creating stakeholder value. When organizations successfully align strategy with culture and talent, they elevate performance and minimize risk. Yet, culture is the one element that most organizations fail to empirically measure and track, and therefore they underutilize this important lever. Further, organizational culture is often the 'villain' when it goes all wrong, but there are many great stories out there where culture has been the 'hero' for an organization.

Many organizations of all shapes and sizes battle with answering many significant questions as part of their journey. As an example of a non-exhaustive list:

- What is the current culture of the organization and how aligned is it with our strategy?
- What are the behavioural changes required to drive culture change to achieve our strategy?
- How do we consider culture in our talent management strategy to attract, develop and retain talent?
- What is the gap between our current and desired culture?
- How well do our organizational structure and practices support our ideal culture and minimize risk?
- Will our current culture support our growth plans?

For organizations that are on a significant organic growth path, and have a great current culture, the oddity is that such growth could be the enemy of culture. In fact, culture is key in driving 'how' growth is sustained. As you grow and add people or even suppliers to your team, your culture is at risk. After all, the more people involved, the greater the opportunity for dilution.

So, let's start with some definitions. Perhaps Richard Perrin's concept of organizational culture as 'the sum of values and rituals which serve as glue to integrate the members of the organization', which suggests that organizational culture is present in structures, routines and actions. Or Edgar Schein's model which suggests that organizational culture has three components:

1 Overt elements that are apparent to outsiders (colours, fonts, furniture, dress code, etc).

2 A distinguishable set of declared values and norms that affect how members interact.

3 Basic assumptions which are beliefs and behaviours so deeply embedded that they can sometimes go unnoticed.[1]

Nevertheless, basic assumptions are the bedrock of organizational culture and problems can arise when they do not align with the most evident elements.

Organizational culture refers to the shared beliefs, values, attitudes, norms and behaviours that exist within an organization. It represents the way things are done in the organization and shapes the overall working environment. Organizational culture outcomes can be observed through various elements such as dress code, communication patterns, leadership style, decision-making processes, risk management, performance and employee engagement.

On the other hand, organizational values are the guiding principles or core beliefs that drive the behaviour and actions of individuals within the organization. These values reflect what the organization stands for and what it considers important. Organizational values can influence decision-making, goal-setting, performance evaluations and overall workplace behaviour.

While culture describes *how* things are done, values represent *why* they are done. Culture is more about the collective behaviour and mindset of the organization, whereas values are the underlying principles that guide that behaviour. In fact, if the organizational values do not manifest in behaviours, it renders them empty words that take up space on a website or wall, as one key piece of evidence of 'living the values' is behaviours.

Understanding organizational culture and values is crucial for several reasons:

- **Employee alignment**: Knowing and understanding the culture and values of an organization helps employees align themselves with the overall goals and mission. It gives them a sense of purpose and direction, and a feeling that they are a part of something bigger.
- **Decision-making**: By understanding the culture and values, employees can make decisions that are in line with the organization's goals and principles.
- **Employee engagement**: Driving motivation and commitment to perform high-quality work and contribute to organizational success. Engaged employees exemplify eagerness to perform well, accomplish their tasks and positively impact their organization.
- **Recruitment and retention**: Individuals who align with the culture and values are more likely to be successful and satisfied in their roles. It also helps in retaining employees as they are more likely to stay in an organization that reflects their personal values.
- **Organizational performance**: A strong organizational culture and values can positively impact the overall performance of an organization. When employees are aligned with the culture and values, they work collaboratively, communicate effectively and strive towards achieving organizational goals.
- **Effective risk management**: While rules and regulations are important, culture is your best and most effective ally for risk and reputational management.

It is common knowledge that nurturing a positive organizational culture is essential for creating a healthy and successful work environment. It helps to shape employee behaviour, hence to improve performance, manage risk and drive the overall success of the organization. In fact, if you are in a leadership role, one of the most critical responsibilities you have is to create the intended organizational culture. That means that you are responsible for creating the 'workplace' environment for the intended culture to fully manifest, including role-modelling – that is, own behaviour, peer behaviour, policies, processes, procedures, performance management, governance, organizational design and even physical office design. All these factors work on behaviours and can be great allies in driving desired behaviours and organizational culture.

This is critical to remember: later I will revisit this aspect by referring to it as the 'Place' and the 'People', and I will re-emphasize the definitions later as well. This is probably why we often hear the famous Peter Drucker quote 'Culture eats strategy for breakfast'.[2] I would go further by saying: let culture be your best ally in achieving your strategy!

Another interesting quote by Peter Drucker is, 'If you can't measure it, you can't change it'. Again, I am going to go further with this by adding: if you can't measure it, then you can't change it, fix it, sustain it, evolve it or even repeat it! These few words ignited my seven-year extensive and dedicated research into behaviours and workplace culture… but more about that later.

Leaders are the custodian of culture, but every employee is accountable for culture

In any organization, leaders undeniably hold a pivotal role. They're often seen as the architects, crafting vision and shaping strategic direction. In the sphere of organizational culture, they emerge as its custodians. They set the tone and guiding principles, and delineate the values that become the pillars. Yet, while they initiate and nurture this culture, its true essence thrives on collective ownership.

Leaders: steering the ship

As custodians, leaders are responsible for setting clear expectations and exemplifying the behaviours they wish to see. Their actions, decisions and communications shape perceptions and establish norms. This idea of establishing the 'tone from the top' or role-modelling the desired culture and behaviours is well documented and understood by most leaders, but it is often over-relied on as the only method through which cultural norms are established.

Although leaders are the torchbearers, illuminating the path for the rest to follow, a torchbearer alone doesn't light up the entire landscape. That's where every employee comes into play.

Employees: the keepers of the flame

While leaders set the stage, it's the collective everyday actions of employees that bring culture to life. Think of culture as a living organism, pulsating and evolving with every interaction, decision and process. Each employee, in their daily duties and interactions, either reinforces or challenges the established cultural norms. Thus, while leaders are the custodians, every individual is accountable for nurturing and sustaining the cultural fabric.

For instance, consider a company that values open communication and expressiveness. While the leadership can champion this through town halls and transparent discussions, it truly comes to life when an entry-level employee feels empowered to voice their opinion in a team meeting or when colleagues actively listen and respond to each other's perspectives.

The symbiotic relationship

There exists a symbiotic relationship between leadership and the broader employee base when it comes to culture. While leaders lay the foundations and uphold the standards, continuous reinforcement from every corner of the organization ensures that the desired, targeting culture is embedded. The greater the size and complexity of the organization, the more difficult it is for leader role-modelling and the 'tone from the top' to consistently help illuminate culture, and the more critical employees' roles are in nurturing and driving that culture.

Therefore, this duality means that:

- Leaders must ensure that their actions mirror their words, creating an environment of trust and setting the standard.
- Every employee should recognize their influence. Whether in team meetings, client interactions or casual coffee breaks, their behaviours contribute to the organizational culture's mosaic.

To truly foster a thriving organizational culture, it's essential to embrace this dual responsibility. Leaders must cultivate, employees must nurture, and together they sculpt a culture that resonates, evolves and drives success.

Let me demonstrate by sharing with you a quick story. A CEO of a promising new start-up excitedly explained his company's core values which he had come to through a combination of following what he'd read in the latest bestselling business book and copying values he knew worked for his most successful competitors. Six months later, he had rampant turnover and couldn't keep his best people. Why? Because the values, while impressive on paper, didn't work for his unique strategy, context and employees.

In another company, a medium-sized financial services organization, the head of HR shared the results of their recent engagement survey – vibrant charts, impressive infographics and enthusiastic comments. And yet she admitted with a sigh, 'It tells us that people are disengaged and have issues with psychological safety, but it doesn't answer the most pertinent question: **why**? It's as if we've taken a selfie. Lovely to look at, momentarily insightful, but we don't really know what's going on in the background.' The survey had captured sentiments, not the actions driving them.

Then there was the case of a fast-growing FMCG organization. Its leadership team was often caught in a dilemma – despite booming sales, internal conflicts and low morale were rampant. They were in the dark about how the company's cultural nuances were influencing these outcomes, for better or worse.

Now think further about the so many other stories where culture has brought large organizations to their knees: Boeing, where the 'culture of concealment' and cost-cutting led to two fatal crashes of 737 Max aircraft claiming 346 lives; the Volkswagen emissions scandal – also known as 'emissionsgate' and 'dieselgate' – which started in September 2015, when the US Environmental Protection Agency (EPA) announced that it believed VW had cheated the emissions tests. Also Wells Fargo's toxic sales culture which created minimal accountability for the questionable practice of taking unfair advantage of customers to meet challenging sales targets, Enron, BP, Facebook, Lehman Brothers… I'd better stop now.

So, what's the common thread here? The cardinal misconceptions in understanding and managing organizational culture: *adopting* values that sound right or mimicking successful peers, *assuming* engagement surveys or qualitative deep dives are accurate measures of your organizational culture, and *acting* to enhance organizational outcomes you care about (sales, well-being, engagement, risk management) in the absence of understanding how your culture drives these outcomes.

No leader wakes up in the morning thinking, 'I can't wait to get to work and do everything I can to drive the most toxic, ineffective culture possible for my company'. Yet, due to these three cardinal errors, many leaders get caught out by the wrong behaviours becoming dominant in their organization, and some of them end up unintentionally harming employees, customers or communities, which results in shutdowns, lawsuits and media scandals.

While well-intentioned, leaders often wade through these murky waters of culture ill-equipped as they have been poorly served regarding how to understand and effectively manage organizational culture.

In this book, I will share my learnings with you and offer practical insights and recommendations on how to successfully identify, measure and embed the right culture to enable your organization to achieve great things and stay out of trouble.

Before we move on, another thought-provoking idea is that growth can be the enemy of organizational culture, as demonstrated in the above examples. Why? Well, it's about not leaving workplace culture to chance! I will cover this idea in detail in Chapter 14.

Notes

1 E Schein (2016) *Organizational Culture and Leadership* (5th edn), Jossey-Bass
2 S Hyken. Drucker said 'Culture eats strategy for breakfast' and Enterprise Rent-A-Car proves it, Forbes, 5 December 2015, www.forbes.com/sites/shephyken/2015/12/05/drucker-said-culture-eats-strategy-for-breakfast-and-enterprise-rent-a-car-proves-it/ (archived at https://perma.cc/VDM5-NDMW)

2

Let's talk behaviours and demystify behavioural science!

Understanding human behaviour: The art and science of behavioural science

Human behaviour is a complex amalgamation of genetics, culture (country, organizational or both), environment and individual experiences. It shapes our interaction with the world, influences our decision-making and ultimately defines who we are as individuals and as a society. The field of behavioural science offers a systematic approach to understanding human behaviour, shedding light on the underlying mechanisms and providing valuable insights into the way we think, feel and act.

The above is a myth-bust – that behaviour is the pure result of personality types.

What is behavioural science?

Behavioural science is an interdisciplinary field that combines knowledge and insights from various disciplines such as psychology, sociology, anthropology, economics and neuroscience to study human behaviour. It explores the factors that influence our actions, motivations, beliefs, attitudes and emotions, often employing scientific methodologies to gain a deeper understanding of the complexities within the human mind.

Quantitative behavioural science builds on traditional behavioural science by adding a research and statistical lens to the study of human behaviour. This involves the collection, description, analysis and inference of conclusions about human behaviour from quantitative data. The mathematical theories behind statistics rely heavily on differential and integral calculus, linear algebra and probability theory. This theory will later come to life to explain powerful actionable insights for driving workplace culture.

Key concepts and theories

The behavioural science research of the renowned psychologist Daniel Kahneman helped us articulate that human behaviour is driven by two independent systems: System 1 and System 2:[1]

- System 1: Our brains' fast, automatic, unconscious and emotional responses to situations and stimuli. It handles our more familiar tasks.
- System 2: The slow, effortful and logical mode in which our brains operate when solving more complicated problems.

On average we all have about 35,000 decisions to make each day.[2] These differ in difficulty and importance. It could be you taking a step to your left or right when walking, or deciding whether to take the stairs or the elevator. If you had to consciously process all these decisions, your brain would crash. Your automatic System 1's primary task is to protect your deliberate System 2 thinking. It helps you prevent cognitive overload – but System 1 is susceptible to bias.

There are a few ways in which our automatic system lightens the load for our deliberate system. First of all, it takes care of our familiar tasks by turning them into autopilot routines, known as habits. But what your System 1 is primarily doing is rapidly sifting through information and ideas, without you even noticing it – prioritizing whatever seems relevant, and filtering out the rest by taking shortcuts.

So, can we change daily behaviours to become embedded in System 1? If so, how? The answer is yes, we can. The theories behind that process are as follows:

- **Classical conditioning**: One of the fundamental theories in behavioural science is classical conditioning, proposed by Ivan Pavlov, a Russian and Soviet experimental neurologist and physiologist. It explores how individuals learn to associate certain stimuli with specific responses, shaping their behaviour.

- **Operant conditioning**: Developed by B F Skinner, an American psychologist, behaviourist, inventor and social philosopher. Operant conditioning focuses on how reinforcement and punishment can affect behaviour. Positive reinforcement encourages desirable behaviours by offering rewards, while punishment discourages negative behaviours through unpleasant consequences. This theory highlights the influence of consequences on human actions.
- **Social learning theory**: Proposed by Albert Bandura, a Canadian-American psychologist who was responsible for contributions to the fields of social cognitive theory, therapy and personality psychology, and the transition between behaviourism and cognitive psychology. Social learning theory suggests that we learn by observing and imitating the behaviour of others. This theory emphasizes the impact of role models, peer influence and observational learning in shaping our behaviour.
- **Cognitive behavioural therapy (CBT)**: A therapeutic approach derived from behavioural science, CBT focuses on understanding the relationship between thoughts, feelings and behaviours. It helps individuals identify negative thought patterns and replace them with healthier and more constructive ones, ultimately leading to positive behaviour changes.

Biases vs nudges

Before we move on, let's address the difference between biases and nudges.

A **bias** is a mental shortcut used to solve a particular problem; it is a quick, automatic and intuitive algorithm your brain uses to generate an approximate answer to make a judgement. Biases describe at a high level how the majority of people will behave under specific circumstances.

If you want to drive a behaviour from System 2 to System 1, then you need to explain and train it. For example, to drive a bias towards recycling (System 1), you need to first address System 2 by considering why we need to recycle. The benefits of this become the 'normal' way of thinking.

A **nudge** is a corresponding set of stimuli for each bias that becomes the tactics to actively harness the bias and change behaviour. For example, providing recycling bins in many locations, posters reminding us to recycle, and so on.

Practical applications

Behavioural science has numerous practical applications across various domains, making it a valuable tool for understanding and influencing human behaviour. Here are a few examples:

- **Behavioural economics:** Behavioural science plays a vital role in understanding economic decision-making. By examining the biases, heuristics and cognitive processes that affect how individuals make choices, economists can design more effective policies and interventions to promote healthy financial behaviours.
- **Public health:** Behavioural science has proven instrumental in designing interventions to promote healthy behaviours, such as smoking cessation programmes, dietary interventions and encouraging physical activity. By understanding the factors that drive behaviour, public health practitioners can develop targeted interventions to improve overall health outcomes.
- **Organizational behaviour:** By applying behavioural science principles, organizations can create work environments that foster employee engagement, productivity and satisfaction. Understanding the motivations, biases and dynamics of individuals and groups within an organization can inform leadership strategies, team dynamics and organizational policies.

Needless to say, this last practical use case will be the main focus of this book, which will include many cases across many organizational culture themes.

Behavioural science provides us with a powerful lens to understand, predict and influence human behaviour. By uncovering the complex interplay of biological, psychological, social and environmental factors, behavioural science helps us gain new perspectives on the intricacies of being human. From creating effective public policies to improving individual wellbeing, the insights gleaned from behavioural science enable us to design strategies that align with our innate human tendencies and create positive change.

Behavioural science for workplace culture

Now for the critical bit for workplace culture: how do we drive effective change? I would like to introduce you to the COM-B model of behaviour change.

The COM-B model is widely used to identify what needs to change for a behaviour change intervention to be effective. It identifies three factors that need to be present for any behaviour to occur: *capability*, *opportunity* and *motivation*. These factors interact over time so that behaviour can be seen as part of a dynamic system with positive and negative feedback loops.

Capability is an attribute of a person; it is all about the 'People'. Are they capable of behaving in a certain way? Do they have the knowledge, skills and abilities required to engage in a particular behaviour? Its two components are:

- psychological capability: our knowledge/psychological strength, skills, decision process, memory, stamina or behavioural regulation
- physical capability: our physical strength, skills, stamina or proficiencies acquired through practice

Opportunity is an attribute of an environmental system; it is all about the 'Place'. Does our workplace provide the opportunity for a behaviour to happen? Its two components are:

- physical opportunity: opportunities provided by the environment, such as time, location and resources
- social opportunity: opportunities as a result of social factors, such as cultural norms and social cues and pressures, social comparisons and leadership

Motivation is also an attribute of an environmental system; it is a mental process that energizes and directs a behaviour. Its two components are:

- automatic motivation (System 1): automatic processes, such as our desires, impulses and inhibitions, incentives, rewards and punishment
- reflective motivation (System 2): reflective processes, such as making plans and evaluating things that have already happened, beliefs about consequences, goals, roles, intentions and identity

So, capability is about the People, whereas opportunity and motivation are about the Place. For a behaviour to be possible or fully manifest, it is very important to have alignment between People and Place. Of course, this is true whether you want to drive or inhibit a behaviour.

You may remember in Chapter 1 we discussed how organizational values, beliefs and even mindset will also affect culture – so how can we connect that to the behaviour systems and COM-B? This is where good design is essential and connecting the dots becomes important. Organizational values are the first layer that should drive 'what' (capability), 'how' (opportunity) and 'why' (motivation). During organizational values design, you can start with the type of culture you are targeting and the behaviours you are targeting to enable the intended culture to fully manifest. You can now design the values statement.

This design method is reliant on the ability to typify the intended culture, something that I will visit in the next chapter. Figure 2.1 brings the entire system together.

The imperative for alignment between People and Place to drive culture change is also a critical aspect for measurement.

How do we go about transforming organizational culture using these behavioural science principles? What does an entire project for culture change look like? I will now introduce a simple five-step approach that is an end-to-end process, as follows:

1 **Define**: what do you want to achieve, and what is your purpose for doing so? Connecting culture to strategy is an obvious first step for most, but it is rarely done with the rigour and precision that is required. Start by reviewing your organizational strategy and mission, highlighting key objectives and goals. Ask questions like 'What tangible results are we aiming for in the next year?', 'What employee or customer experiences do we want to drive?' and 'What do we want to control and minimize around risk, disruption and change?' From this, outline and populate the specific outcomes you wish to achieve, such as increased sales, improved psychological safety, enhanced customer satisfaction or high compliance with safety processes.

2 **Measure**: this measurement is split into three:
    o behaviour measurement of the People
    o behaviour measurement of the Place
    o the intended or targeted outcomes measurement

3 **Actionable insights**: which behaviours you must focus on to achieve your outcomes. To be actionable, insights must explain the 'why' for the outcomes, 'why' the targeted outcomes happen (or not), 'how' to improve and the return on your investment. Additionally, insights must deliver 'where' in the organization you can learn from and 'where' to drive interventions.

4 **Culture by Design:** This ties all the previous steps together. Ultimately, it's now about using the COM-B model to achieve culture change.

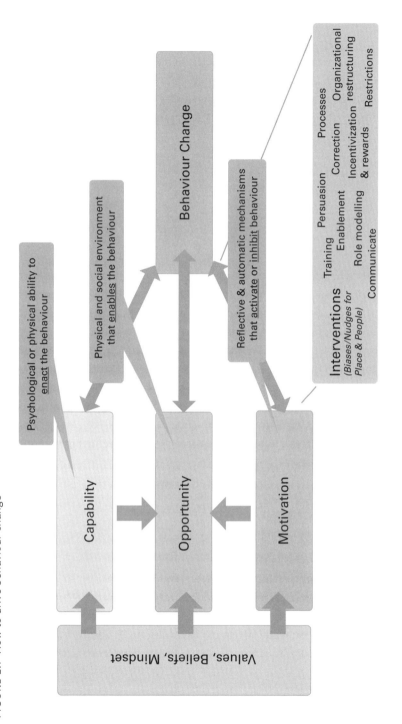

FIGURE 2.1 How to drive behaviour change

FIGURE 2.2 The five-step approach

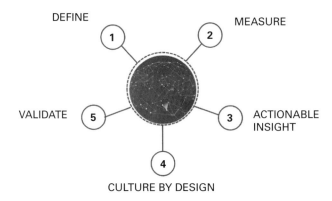

5   **Validate:** This is your feedback loop, Re-measure the impact of the inventions taken to drive behavioural change. The three measurements must be repeated – behaviours of the People, the Place and the outcomes. This should happen within six to nine months of the first intervention deployment.

Figure 2.2 gives a quick summary of the five-step approach.

You may be wondering why I called the behaviour intervention, planning and implementation 'Culture by Design'. Well, you tend to design all other parts of your organization, like your financial systems, your operation models and IT infrastructure, so why would you not work on designing the most critical aspect of your organization, your culture? Hence the name.

This approach will be used for all the thematic case studies presented later in this book.

Notes

1   D Kahneman (2011) *Thinking, Fast and Slow*, Allen Lane
2   A Reill. A simple way to make better decisions, Harvard Business Review, 5 December 2023, https://hbr.org/2023/12/a-simple-way-to-make-better-decisions (archived at https://perma.cc/U4DA-N2MF)

3

The differences between behaviours and outcomes

Understanding the distinction between behaviours and outcomes is a key component for managing and developing workplace culture, and one that is so often misused or even misunderstood.

In our daily lives, we often become preoccupied with the outcome of our actions, striving for favourable results. However, it's important to recognize that behaviours and outcomes are distinct concepts. While outcomes are the end results we desire, behaviours are the actions we take to achieve those outcomes. Understanding the differences between these two pillars can help you develop a more comprehensive approach to managing and developing workplace culture.

Behaviours: the foundation of actions

Behaviours refer to the actions and choices we make in pursuing a particular outcome. These encompass a wide range of tangible actions, such as expressiveness, following the rules, being fair, etc. Our behaviours can be a reflection of our values, beliefs and mental models, shaping our interactions and determining how we navigate the challenges and opportunities we encounter. However, we also know that environmental factors (which I have referred to as 'Place' in prior chapters, defined as leadership behaviours and role modelling, peer behaviour, policies, processes, procedures, governance and physical office design) and situations will also impact how we behave.

Key characteristics of behaviours:

- **Within our sphere of control**: Unlike outcomes, which may vary due to external factors beyond our control, behaviours are fully within our realm of influence. We have the power to shape and improve our behaviours through intentional effort and self-reflection.

- **Observable:** Behaviours are observable by others or even by ourselves, e.g. whether we act ethically, communicate openly, adapt to change or take the initiative.
- **Impact on outcomes:** Behaviours have a direct influence on the outcomes we strive for. Consistency in behaviours will increase the likelihood of achieving our desired results. This will be regularly demonstrated in the many thematic case studies later.

Outcomes: the consequences of actions

Outcomes are the results that follow our behaviours. They can be either positive or negative, depending on various factors, including external circumstances, luck, timing and the actions of others. Outcomes are often measured in terms of accomplishments, incidents, financial gains, recognition or formed opinions. While outcomes are important indicators of success, relying solely on them to evaluate our efforts can lead to an incomplete understanding of actions and hinder potential.

Key characteristics of outcomes:

- **Influenced by many factors:** Outcomes are often influenced by many factors, including behaviours, events and other outcomes.
- **Subjective interpretation:** Outcomes can be perceived differently by different individuals. What one person may consider a success, another might view as a failure. It's essential to avoid solely defining oneself by outcomes and consider the broader context of behaviours when evaluating success or progress.
- **Learning opportunities:** Regardless of the outcome, every action provides an opportunity for learning. Outcomes, whether favourable or not, must lead us to evaluate behaviours, refine our approach and pursue corrected behaviours to achieve the desired results.

Let's now illustrate the difference between behaviours and outcomes using simple everyday examples. You get in the car with your colleague, and you observe that they are putting on their seatbelt and asking you to do the same. They check their seat to make sure that they are in the correct position and have full view of the rearview and side mirrors, and they indicate and check all mirrors before they carefully drive out.

You have just observed outcomes. The behaviours that facilitate these outcomes are: 1) being consistent in following processes, and 2) obeying the rules.

Now think further; such behaviours will also mean that your colleague will take care crossing the road. This illustrates the power of behaviours as they affect multiple outcomes. Now to stretch your thinking even further; the outcomes above will also impact other outcomes like the reduced likelihood of an accident. Now you see the power of a few behaviours impacting a multilateral chain of outcomes. This insight will be significantly demonstrated in the case studies in Part 2 of this book.

Embracing the balance

While the driving force behind our actions is the desired outcomes, understanding the distinction between behaviours and outcomes allows us to adopt a more holistic approach. Focusing solely on outcomes may lead to shortcuts, unethical behaviours or neglecting the importance of the journey itself. In contrast, placing excessive emphasis on behaviours without considering outcomes may result in lack of accountability or reduced motivation.

Striking a balance by aligning our behaviours with desired outcomes enables you to navigate challenges, adapt to evolving circumstances and condition your workplace culture.

Lagging and leading indicators

Leading and lagging indicators are two types of measurements used when assessing performance in a business or organization. A leading indicator is a predictive measurement; for example, the percentage of people wearing hard hats on a building site is a leading safety indicator. A lagging indicator is an output measurement; for example, the number of accidents on a building site is a lagging safety indicator. The difference between the two is that a leading indicator can influence change, and a lagging indicator can only record what has happened.

All too often we concentrate on measuring results, outputs and outcomes. Why? Because they are easy to measure and they are accurate. If we want to know how many sales have been made this month, we simply count them. If we want to know how many accidents have occurred on the factory floor, we consult the accident log. These are lagging indicators. They are an after-the-event measurement, essential for charting progress but useless when attempting to influence the future.

A different type of measurement is required to influence the future, one that is predictive rather than a result. For example, if we want to increase sales, a predictive measure could be to make more sales calls or run more marketing campaigns. If we wanted to decrease accidents on the factory floor, we could make safety training mandatory for all employees. Measuring these activities provides us with a set of leading indicators. They are in-process measures and are predictive.

Leading indicators are always more challenging to determine than lagging indicators. They are predictive and, therefore, do not guarantee success. This not only makes it difficult to decide which leading indicators to use, but also tends to cause heated debate as to the validity of the measure at all. To fuel the debate further, leading indicators frequently require investment to implement an initiative before a lagging indicator sees a result.

When developing a business performance management strategy, using a combination of leading and lagging indicators is always good practice. The reason for this is obvious; a lagging indicator without a leading indicator will not reveal how a result will be achieved and provide no early warnings about tracking towards a strategic goal.

Equally important, however, a leading indicator without a lagging indicator may make you feel good about keeping busy with many activities. Still, it will not confirm that a business result has been achieved.

There is a cause-and-effect chain between leading and lagging indicators; both are important when selecting measures to track towards your business goals. Traditionally, we tend to settle for lagging indicators; however, we do not underestimate the importance of leading indicators.

A health warning here: do not assume that the behaviours that predict outcomes in one organization will be the same for another organization. Remember that earlier we discussed that the organizational environment would be different for different organizations, like the processes, procedures, operating model, etc… hence the danger of borrowing off-the-shelf frameworks and assuming that such frameworks will simply work for you. If you delve into any leading management book, white paper or keynote speech, you'll likely stumble upon models or values presented as the universal remedy for organizational challenges. They draw you in with promises such as 'Follow these steps and you'll see transformation'.

The realm of organizational behaviour, leadership and culture often suggests the existence of universal truths. These are solutions that, when applied across the board, promise to lead to outcomes every leader dreams of – soaring sales, unwavering resilience, a loyal consumer base and so forth. As our research commenced, we held a glimmer of hope. A hope that within the myriad data points and diverse organizations spread across 61 countries, we'd find these universal keys to success or uncover a template for organizational thriving.

Yet the reality that emerged was sobering: every organization's behavioural blueprint to drive success was different. Well, that does make sense, as we know that organizational culture is unique and it's a key asset for any organization. You can replicate products and services, but it's very hard to replicate workplace culture.

By understanding and consciously aligning behaviours with desired outcomes, you can enhance your chances of success. Ultimately, it is the combination of the behaviours and the lessons you derive from outcomes that paves the way for continual improvement and a fulfilling journey towards your culture goals.

Path analysis

Path analysis uses is a powerful statistical technique for investigating complex causal relationships among variables. It provides a comprehensive framework to test hypotheses, explore direct and indirect effects and refine models. So, how will this help us in understanding relationships between behaviours and multiple outcomes?

Let me demonstrate using one of our above examples: wearing hard hats on a building site. The behaviours that lead to this outcome 'always wearing hard hats' are being consistent and closely following rules and procedures. That outcome of 'hard-hat wearing' itself becomes a leading safety indicator, and the outcome of 'safety indicator' becomes the leading indicator of low number of injuries, etc. With this simple example we have established the starting point behaviours, their impact on multiple outcomes and the sequence in which those outcomes would happen.

You can go further and add events to the developed path to test its robustness. For example, what are the events that can happen that can be better managed with the hard hats on or off? Is there any likely event that has a better outcome if the hard hats are off?

Figure 3.1 shows the path.

If you are interested in the maths for quantitative behavioural science, I can further explain that path analysis is established using a technique called **structural equation modelling (SEM)**. It is a statistical analytical approach that allows researchers to analyse complex causal relationships among

FIGURE 3.1 Path analysis example

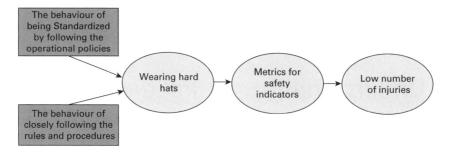

multiple variables. Path analysis using SEM provides a rigorous framework for testing hypotheses and exploring the interplay between variables in a larger model.

Structural equation modelling is a multivariate statistical technique that combines factor analysis and multiple regression analysis to examine the relationships between measured variables and behaviours. It enables researchers to investigate both direct and indirect relationships in a comprehensive way. However, path analysis goes further, as it helps you interpret the relationships between variables, providing valuable insights into causal pathways and mediating effects.

The advantages of path analysis using SEM are numerous. First, it allows researchers to examine complex relationships with multiple variables simultaneously, providing a more comprehensive understanding of the underlying mechanisms. Second, it helps to identify direct and indirect effects, thereby allowing for a better understanding of the contribution of each variable to the overall outcome. Third, it enables researchers to test competing hypotheses and compare alternative models, facilitating development and refinement.

Furthermore, path analysis using SEM can also account for measurement error, which enhances the accuracy of the estimates and reduces bias. It is particularly useful when dealing with latent constructs that are not directly observed and may be measured incorrectly. By accounting for this, path analysis using SEM provides more reliable and valid estimates of the relationships between variables.

Many of the examples offered in Part 2 of this book will use this approach to help you establish its practical yet powerful applications.

4

Understanding cultural dimensions

We have already covered the importance of measurement for organizational culture insights and how measuring leading indicators can be more complex, in particular, when the leading indicators are behaviours that are a critical and actionable component of managing and evolving your workplace culture. So, the two important questions are: which behaviours, and how do we measure these behaviours?

Those were exactly the questions that ignited my seven-year research. It was to become the most extensive quantitative behavioural research study on organizational behaviour and culture to date, in which I studied over 51,000 employees across 60 diverse organizations in 61 countries. This was not a venture into abstract theories or transient sentiments, but an in-depth exploration of over 350 million data points to uncover tangible behaviours that form the bedrock of organizational cultures.

Before we discuss the outcomes of that research and by way of background, my earlier research started in airliner cockpits, having observed many pilots and crew members to better understand human factors and how they manifest in behaviours. The flight deck is a very 'clinical' place to conduct such research, as skill and knowledge are somewhat a given, so you are left with the behavioural aspects.

Whenever you board a flight, it's safe to assume that whichever airline you have chosen, all pilots know their 'stick and rudder stuff'; the skill of flying and what all the buttons and gauges do. What you don't know is how are they going to behaviourally conduct the flight. Suddenly behaviours become a significant leading indicator of outcomes, and of how the crew respond to critical or somewhat benign situations.

Back to the seven-year organizational study. The below is a quick brief on the methodology.

Research dimensions: n = 51,236 – 60 diverse organizations – 61 countries – 229 behaviours – 350 million data points.

There were six key stages of research, as follows:

1. **Principal Component Analysis (PCA)** for valid item selection, scale construction and factorial definitions. The purpose of this study was to identify a robust set of dimensions to define a working structure for the CultureScope diagnostic tool. After eliminating items/dimensions with insufficient variances, initial scales were refined through an iterative sequence of internal consistency and principal component analysis.
2. **Factorial analysis with orthogonal rotation** (Varimax rotation) to examine variability for final dimensions selection, to investigate the interrelations between a set of behaviour variables and explain them in terms of their latent common dimensions, called factors. It is a technique of information reduction that does not consider the variables as dependent or independent, since all are considered simultaneously.
3. **Test-retest for diagnostic reliability** to measure reliability (or internal consistency).
4. **Multi-Traits Multi-Methods (MTMM)** to examine construct validity.
5. **Multivariate Analysis of Variance (MANOVA)** to examine inter-organizational variability and consensual validity.
6. **Predictive analytics validity**, to examine how well the leading indicators impact outcomes as the lagging indicators using multi-level modelling, regression analysis, multiplicity and odds ratio. By way of a definition: multiple regression is a statistical technique that can be used to analyse the relationship between a single dependent variable and several independent variables. The objective of multiple regression analysis is to use the independent variables whose values are known to predict the value of the dependent value.

From this pioneering study, I discovered that hundreds of organizational behaviours could be distilled into 30 distinct behaviours (out of the 229 examined behaviour factors) that make up the blueprint of how people and organizations behave. These 30 behaviours drive a myriad of business outcomes – from outcomes that directly impact the bottom line (sales, performance, productivity) to outcomes that keep companies out of trouble (risk management, financial crime, safety compliance) and even outcomes that drive engagement and morale (wellbeing, trust, belonging, psychological safety).

Further, the research found that these 30 behavioural factors are arranged in 15 continuums, hence two dichotomous factors for each dimension, resulting in 15 dimensions. These 30 factors/15 dimensions are shown in Table 4.1.

TABLE 4.1 CultureScope behavioural dimensions

Collective: Emphasis is on working in partnership	VS	**Individual**: Emphasis is on individual success
Disenfranchise: Decisions escalated upwards	VS	**Empower**: Decisions delegated downwards
People Focus: Focus on people rather than outputs	VS	**Delivery Focus**: Outputs are the key focus
Neutral: Less likely to voice a thought or opinion	VS	**Expressive**: More likely to voice an opinion
Standardized: Focus on process and systems	VS	**Flexible**: Ability to work flexibly valued
Moderate: Consistency and stability valued	VS	**Radical**: New ideas and change valued
Team Focus: Reward recognizes team working	VS	**Self-Focus**: Reward emphasizes individualism
Tactical: Focus is on short-term results	VS	**Strategic**: Focus is on the longer-term
Active Learning: Structured development valued	VS	**Passive Learning**: Learning is laissez-faire
Innovate: Managed risk-taking and innovation valued	VS	**Consolidate**: Control and risk avoidance valued
Conformity: Acting in line with rules and values	VS	**Nonconformity**: Act in response to the situation
Transact: Getting it done more important	VS	**Relationship**: Getting along more important
Achievement: People valued for what they do	VS	**Status**: People valued for their position
Sequential: Order and scheduling emphasized	VS	**Synchronous**: Changing task priorities
Internal Focus: Focus on what happens internally	VS	**External Focus**: Focus on what happens externally

This research was instrumental in the development of the cloud-based SaaS product, CultureScope.

Behavioural measurement

Behavioural measurement, otherwise known as behavioural diagnostics, is all about 'how' we achieve the quantitative accurate measurement of the 30 behavioural factors. Behaviour measurement is achieved using two distinct psychometric type questionnaires, as follows:

- **Individual behaviour:** This pertains to how single members of the organization act and respond. It is driven by individual capability and the willingness to act in certain ways. For instance, an employee's dedication to continuous learning or their responsiveness to feedback.
- **Organizational behaviour:** This reflects the organizational environment. It's the behaviour that employees observe around them and is a powerful driver or inhibitor of individual behaviour. This pertains to organizational processes, systems and established ways of working. For example, the organization's informal reward systems that give accolades to employees who support their colleagues.

The above diagnostic method is already interesting in driving actionable insights. Remember how in previous chapters we discussed that culture change should be directed either at capability (the 'People') or the 'Place' for opportunity and motivation. Well, this measurement exactly corresponds to this methodology. The individual behaviour measurement corresponds to the 'People', and organizational behaviour measurement corresponds to the 'Place'.

To drive best diagnostic validity, the following question methods were examined:

- the normative method (Likert scale type questions)
- the ipsative method (non-leading, scenario based and forced choice)
- Item Response Theory (most and least type questions)

The above are psychometric diagnostic methods that I should define.

Normative diagnostic methods

A normative questionnaire asks a respondent to indicate how much they agree with a statement to which a Likert scale is attached. Normative items are used mainly in personality questionnaires, and are important in psychometric testing as they can delve into the personality traits of a respondent and compare them to others who have taken the test. This makes personality a measurable scale, which is easier to look at when having to go through the recruitment of many people.

An advantage of this method is that there is no way for individuals taking the test to deviate from what is being asked of them. It is therefore a straightforward way of assessing and comparing people's answers, ultimately making an index of 'normal' characteristics from which an employer could pick the most suited or desirable individuals.

The main fault with this type of approach is that it lends itself to problems such as the fatigue effect, meaning the respondent may become bored of the questionnaire and so just randomly tick boxes to get through the test quickly.[1]

Respondents can make a conscious effort to distort the results in, for example, a high-stakes selection situation (normally favourably). They also may semi-consciously be trying to create a favourable impression. This can be seen as individuals making the best of what they have rather than being highly critical (analogous in an application form to making the career highlights sound best and minimizing or omitting the negative outcomes, without committing the act of giving inaccurate facts).

Such impression management, conscious faking and social desirability are often difficult to differentiate in practice.[2, 3]

Ipsative diagnostic methods

Ipsative measurement involves the use of items for which the respondent is required to choose one of two options. These forced-choice formats (either rankings or ratings) and self-report questionnaires were introduced to reduce response biases.

A major benefit of the ipsative format is to reduce 'faking good' by forcing individuals to choose between options that are similar with respect to social desirability. Acquiescence responding, halo effects, impression management and social desirability bias are better controlled by means of ipsative methods than by normative methods.

The most frequently mentioned advantages of ipsative measures include the following:

- ipsative measures have higher discriminability value than normative tests[4, 5]
- they are said to be resistant to social desirability, and respondents can alter their results less as compared to normative tests[6]
- ipsative measures seem to be resistant to 'moderate responding'[7]

- ipsative measures might better reflect choices people make in real life, since they cannot choose all the possibilities, but are forced to choose only some[8]
- research proved that ipsativity can increase validity – if it reduces response bias[9]

ITEM RESPONSE THEORY

The Item Response Theory (IRT) model represents an important innovation in the field of psychometrics. The foundation of IRT is based on a mathematical model defined by item parameters mainly for dichotomous items.[10]

IRT was developed as an underlying response to forced-choice questionnaires. In fact, despite their advantages in reducing response biases, forced-choice-only questionnaires have been judged as limited because their traditional scoring methodology results in ipsative data, very special properties of which can pose threats to construct validity and score interpretation as well as other substantial psychometric challenges. These can be overcome with IRT.[11]

The basic assumption underlying the IRT model is that it tests behaviour not at the level of test scores, but at the item level.[12] These models have been developed to deal with responses to items that are scored dichotomously (i.e. only two possible scored responses exist, such as true-false, correct-incorrect, endorsed-not endorsed, etc.).

Advantages of IRT are:

- detailed descriptions of the performance of individual items
- indices of item and scale level precision that are free to vary across the full range of possible scores
- the score estimation process is more precise, allowing simultaneous consideration of both the number of right/endorsed items as well as the properties (e.g. discrimination, difficulty) of each item when estimating each person's score on the construct being assessed
- measures of response-profile quality
- computer-adaptive testing, which helps to reduce testing time

The key purpose of testing different diagnostic methods was to examine the best psychometric properties which are specifically required for CultureScope behavioural measurement: inter-organizational discrimination and consensual validity (homogeneity, stability, content and construct validity). These psychometric indices are generally not available with other culture measurements.

Finally, a combination of the ipsative method with IRT provides the best diagnostic validity. CultureScope goes further by making use of Adaptive Computer Testing (ACT) to drive enhanced validity and greatly reduce assessment time. ACT means that each respondent is connected in real time to the CultureScope diagnostic engine and accuracy as well as consistency are being measured in real time; hence the system can adapt by asking more and different types of questions to drive validity. Average completion time for each questionnaire is 12 minutes.

Mapping behaviours to organizational values/frameworks

Moving on from the science of behaviour measurement to focus on the adaptation for showing whether you are 'walking the talk' for your organizational values. As I already mentioned in prior chapters, there is no point in having organizational values if you are not going to live these values through behaviours. So, the fun part now is a mapping exercise using the above dimensions to map into the values.

For this demonstration, let's use the following three values:

- **Respect**: We value the rules and environment in which we operate safely. We fairly challenge poor performance through giving and receiving feedback respectfully. We appreciate value brought by different people and experiences.
- **Humility**: We empower people; the leader isn't in the best place to make each and every decision. We invite and value other people's input and points of view. We enable opportunities for ourselves and others and are dedicated to learning and development for career growth.
- **Positivity**: We maintain the highest level of quality, performance and timely delivery, but not at the expense of our people's wellbeing. Everyone's achievements are celebrated regardless of position. We engender an innovative and curious mindset in all employees and partners.

In order to map the behavioural factors to the values statements, you now need to refer to the full CultureScope factorial descriptors found in Table 4.2.

TABLE 4.2 Full behavioural factors descriptors

	CULTURESCOPE'S 30 BEHAVIOURS		
Goals are achieved through partnerships and alliances	Collective	Individual	Maintaining high individual performance and winning prevail over working relationships
The structure is hierarchical ensuring that leaders retain decision-making	Disenfranchise	Empower	Decisions are delegated to lower levels with supportive guidance
A working environment that focuses on people rather than purely on tasks and outputs	People Focus	Delivery Focus	There is a clear focus on results and task outputs; employees are accountable for their own actions
Employees show restraint when expressing thoughts and opinions	Neutral	Expressive	People do not hesitate to express their feelings and openness is valued
People value working within clear processes and systems	Standardized	Flexible	People value variability and deal with each situation afresh
Individuals value working steadily within assigned and streamlined processes favouring stability	Moderate	Radical	Continuous improvement and evolving ideas are valued; there is an emphasis on responding differently to different situations
Work is delivered through collaborating group efforts and team results are prioritized over individual results	Team Focus	Self-Focus	Individualism and independence are encouraged and rewarded
The emphasis is on short-term delivery and results	Tactical	Strategic	The emphasis is on long-term delivery, results; and focus is on the wider impact
Active steps are taken to improve employees' skill sets and careers; employee growth and development is considered an integral part of the job	Active Learning	Passive Learning	On-the-job experience is seen as the best approach for learning and skill development
New and creative ideas are pioneered. Intelligent risk taking is encouraged and praised	Innovate	Consolidate	Predictability and control are preferred. Risk taking is avoided until it is absolutely necessary. Tried and tested methods are encouraged
People place a high importance on laws, rules, values and obligations. They try to deal fairly with people based on these rules, but rules come before relationships	Conformity	Nonconformity	People believe that each circumstance, and each relationship, dictates the rules that they live by. Their response to a situation may change, based on what is happening in the moment, and who is involved
People believe that relationships don't have much of an impact on work objectives and, although they are important, people believe that they can work without having good relationships	Transact	Relationship	People believe that good relationships are vital to meeting business objectives, and that their relationships with others will be the same. People spend time building relationships with colleagues and clients
People believe that you are what you do, and they define your worth accordingly. These cultures value performance independent of status	Achievement	Status	People believe that you should be valued for your status. Power, title and position matter in these cultures, and these roles define behaviour
People like events to happen in order. They place a high value on punctuality, quality, planning and staying on schedule. In this culture, 'time is money', and people don't appreciate it when their schedule is thrown off	Sequential	Synchronous	People see the past, present and future as interwoven periods. They often work on several projects at once, in a fast-paced manner, and view plans and commitments as flexible
People believe that they can control nature or their environment to achieve goals. This includes how they work with teams and within organizations	Internal Focus	Outer Focus	People believe that their environment controls them; they want to work within their environment to achieve goals. At work or in relationships, they focus their actions on others

Your exercise is to read each organizational value and the call to action associated with each value, then choose which of the above behaviour factors map to each value. You could do this exercise with a team if you wish. The point of this exercise is to explain 'how' the organizational values should manifest in behaviours.

I suggest you break down each call-to-action statement as in Table 4.3.

Now do the same for the other two organizational values.

If you have involved a team, it would be interesting to see what different people have mapped and why. It's an illustration of how different people interpret the values and hence why a behavioural approach becomes important. Remember, you do not have to map all the behaviours; this is normal in organizational culture as you emphasize only the behaviours that are perhaps critical, otherwise it becomes rather robotic.

I hope you have enjoyed this exercise. See a full mapping in Table 4.4.

TABLE 4.3 Mapping example

Value	Text 'call to action'	Mapped behaviour
Respect	We value the rules and environment in which we operate safely.	Conformity
	We fairly challenge poor performance through giving and receiving feedback respectfully.	Expressive, Achievement, People Focus
	We appreciate value brought from different people and experiences.	Collective, People Focus

TABLE 4.4 Full mapping

Value	Text 'call to action'	Mapped behaviour
Respect	We value the rules and environment in which we operate safely.	Conformity
	We fairly challenge poor performance through giving and receiving feedback respectfully.	Expressive, Achievement, People Focus
	We appreciate value brought from different people and experiences.	Collective, People Focus
Humility	We empower people; the leader isn't in the best place for each and every decision.	Empower

(continued)

TABLE 4.4 (Continued)

Value	Text 'call to action'	Mapped behaviour
	We invite and value other people's input and points of view.	Expressive
	We enable opportunities for ourselves and others and are dedicated to learning and development for career growth.	Active Learning
Positivity	We maintain the highest level of quality, performance and timely delivery, but not at the expense of our people's wellbeing.	Sequential, People Focus
	Everyone's achievements are celebrated regardless of position.	Achievement
	We engender an innovative and curious mindset in all employees and partners.	Innovate

TABLE 4.5 Cluster values behavioural mapping

Respect	Humility	Positivity
Conformity		
Expressive	Expressive	
Achievement		Achievement
People Focus		People Focus
Collective		
	Empower	
	Active Learning	
		Sequential
		Innovate

I hope you have ended up with something like this yourself! Let's create a cluster map to check that we are not over-mapping, where the behaviours mapped are exactly the same for all the values (however, some overlapping is great as that will show that the values are connected and hence some behaviours are critical).

Another check would be the absence of competing behaviours, where you have the behaviour opposites mapped. This can happen, but is rather dangerous as the values are sending conflicting messages to employees. See Table 4.5.

The mapping works, the values are distinct by behaviours and there are no competing behaviours mapped. The behaviours of Expressive, Achievement and People Focus are mapped twice, which is a clear indication of the importance of these behaviours for this organization.

We now have behavioural clarity, hence launching behavioural measurement is possible as you know what you are measuring. Measurement as described before will articulate the following:

- Are our people living our values? If not, why not (which behaviours are absent)? Remember, this relates to capability.

- Does our workplace support and drive our values? If not, why not (which behaviours are absent)? Remember, this relates to opportunities and motivation.

In Chapter 5 you will learn about analytics and insights using the above example.

Notes

1. C-C Bowen, B A Martin and S T Hunt (2002) A comparison of ipsative and normative approaches for ability to control faking in personality questionnaires, *International Journal of Organizational Analysis*, **10** (3), pp. 240–59
2. Bowen, Martin and Hunt, ibid
3. Bowen, Martin and Hunt, ibid
4. H Baron (1996) Strengths and limitations of ipsative measurement, *Journal of Occupational and Organizational Psychology*, **69**, pp. 49–56
5. L E Hicks (1970) Some properties of ipsative, normative and forced-choice normative measures, *Psychological Bulletin*, **74**, pp. 167–84
6. Bowen, Martin and Hunt, ibid
7. H Baron, ibid
8. L V Gordon (1951) Validities of the forced-choice and questionnaire methods of personality measurement, *Journal of Applied Psychology*, **35**, pp. 407–12
9. Hicks, ibid
10. S E Embretson and S P Reise (2000) *Item Response Theory for Psychologists*, Lawrence Erlbaum Associates Publishers
11. Embretson and Reise, ibid
12. F B Baker and S-H Kim (2004) *Item Response Theory: Parameter estimation techniques* (2nd ed), CRC Press

5

Data analytics concepts for actionable insights

Are you walking the talk?

As this is a practical and evidence-based book for culture analytics, I might as well turn the three organizational values behavioural mapping completed in the previous chapter into insights to answer the often-lingering question, are you living your values? Or, as I often hear, are you walking the talk? And if you are not walking the talk, why?

Once you know the 'why', you will be able to design the behaviourally focused solution, thus turning behavioural insight into action. After all, and as we discussed before, actionable means working on the 'why', which provides the 'how' of culture change.

Table 5.1 illustrates the following insights:

- The value of Respect is behaviourally present at the Place and for the People, meaning that people tend to behave in that way and the organization tends to drive this. The presence for both people and place results in the full manifestation of the value of Respect.

TABLE 5.1 A values-based heatmap

	Respect	Humility	Positivity
The Place	Present	Absent	Absent
The People	Present	Very Absent	Somewhat Present

- The value of Humility is absent and very absent at the Place and for the People respectively.
- The value of Positivity is absent at the Place, and somewhat present (sometimes behave in that way) for the People. This will result in the value not being manifested fully, as you may remember we need it to be present for both the Place and the People.

The immediate question to follow the above insight is, why are you living your values (or not)? We can now take a detailed look at the behaviours, as illustrated in Table 5.2.

You can see that the absence of four behaviours is the answer to 'why', and can be summarized as follows:

1 **Expressive** (being open in expressing thoughts and opinions): The organization generally gives employees opportunities to be open in expressing thoughts and opinions; however, employees show restraint and tend to not be open with their ideas and concerns. How can we increase the capability and willingness of people to be more expressive?

TABLE 5.2 The presence or absence of the behaviour factors driving the three organizational values

Mapped Behavioural Dimensions	Respect		Humility		Positivity	
	People	Place	People	Place	People	Place
Conformity	Present	Present				
Expressive	Absent	Present	Absent	Present		
Achievement	Present	Present			Present	Present
People Focus	Present	Present			Present	Present
Collective	Very Present	Present				
Empower			Absent	Vey Absent		
Active Learning			Somewhat present	Somewhat present		
Sequential					Somewhat present	Absent
Innovate					Somewhat present	Very Absent

2. **Empower** (delegating decisions to lower levels with supportive guidance): The organization is encouraging hierarchical ways of working where leaders tend to retain decision-making power. How can we create more opportunities and motivation for better delegation and empowerment? How can we build the capability for empowerment?
3. **Sequential** (ordering and scheduling is emphasized): People like events to happen in order. The organization is not focused on punctuality, quality, planning and staying on schedule. Hence the Place is not providing that opportunity.
4. **Innovate** (encouraging new approaches and ideas rather than always leaning into predictability and control): The Place does not encourage acting on new ideas and approaches. How can we provide the opportunity and the motivation to be more innovative?

If you like your analytics and numbers, let me provide Table 5.3.

Table 5.3 represents a behavioural factor scale from 0 to 5. The scale interpretation is as per Figure 5.1.

TABLE 5.3 A numeric heatmap for the presence or absence of the behaviour factors driving the three organizational values

Mapped Behavioural Dimensions	Respect		Humility		Positivity	
	People	Place	People	Place	People	Place
Conformity	3.4	3.2				
Expressive	2.1	3.3	2.1	3.1		
Achievement	3.5	3.1			3.5	3.1
People Focus	3.4	3.2			3.4	3.2
Collective	4.1	3.6				
Empower			2.4	1.6		
Active Learning			2.5	2.7		
Sequential					2.6	2.1
Innovate					2.5	1.5

Since each behavioural factor has a dichotomous paired factor, a reminder that the absence in one direction will indicate a behaviour's presence in the other direction. This can be demonstrated using the radar graph in Figure 5.2. Notice the Expressive vs Neutral result.

Expanding on our previous chapters, we can now decide on what sort of interventions are needed – is it for the Place (opportunity and motivation) or the People (capability)? The same behavioural heatmap can be used to demonstrate this, as per Table 5.4.

From Table 5.4, it can be seen the two behaviours need a capability-type intervention (Expressive and Empower), and three behaviours need an opportunity and motivation-type intervention (Empower, Sequential and Innovate).

The insights shown in Table 5.3 are a behaviour-first approach to delivering insights. It means that we are opportunistically targeting the desired behaviours based on the mapping to values exercise I introduced. Hence you can use demographic data to analyse the presence or absence of these behaviours, providing the 'why' and the 'where' of behaviours. This is also known as opportunistic modelling.

This is a good time to further explain what behaviour-first or outcome-first analytics for insights really mean. Figure 5.3 shows this concept well: having measured the behaviours of the People and the Place, and defined the behaviour mapping to your organizational values (in the define and measure steps covered in Figure 2.2), you can now add and connect to demographics, such as function, division, tenure, seniority, gender, etc.

FIGURE 5.1 The behavioural factors scale interpretation

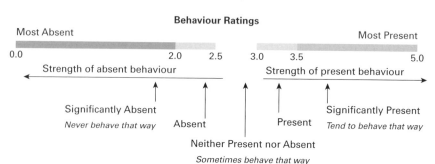

DATA ANALYTICS CONCEPTS FOR ACTIONABLE INSIGHTS 39

FIGURE 5.2 The dichotomous behavioural factor pairs and the scale

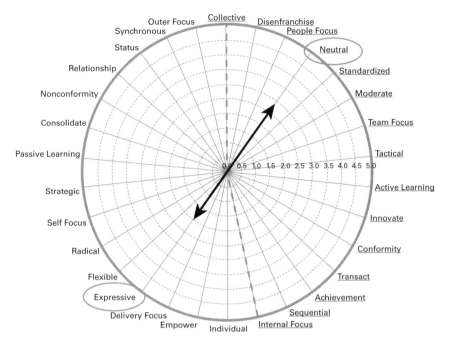

TABLE 5.4 The targeted behaviour factors and the type of intervention needed

Mapped Behavioural Dimensions	Respect		Humility		Positivity	
	People	Place	People	Place	People	Place
Conformity	3.4	3.2				
Expressive	2.1	3.3	Capability	3.1		
Achievement	3.5	3.1			3.5	3.1
People Focus	3.4	3.2			3.4	3.2
Collective	4.1	3.6				
Empower			Capability	Opportunity & Motivation		
Active Learning			2.5	2.7		
Sequential					2.6	Opportunity & Motivation
Innovate					2.5	Opportunity & Motivation

This will result in 'where' the targeted behaviours are present or absent, which can be presented in simple demographic behavioural heatmaps like Table 5.2.

However, when you have many demographics, is there an easier way of presenting the 'where' for specific and targeted behaviours on one page? The answer is yes! This is the quadrant distribution method demonstrated in Figure 5.4.

Figure 5.4 plots the Empower behaviour, with the X axis showing presence for the People, and the Y axis showing presence at the Place. This can then be populated with the applied demographics for the four resulting quadrants. Exploring each quadrant can prove the 'where' for Empower: for example, which of your organizational functions exists in each quadrant? Is there a difference by gender? By tenure or by seniority? A quick and easy way to examine one or more behaviours with length heatmaps.

As for the analysis, the demographics existing in the 'Strongly Aligned' zone have the Empower behaviour present for People and Place, and that is where you should go to learn from with a view to replicating it. The zone below marked 'Look at the Place' is where the capability for the Empower behaviour is present for the People, but absent at the Place – that is, the Place doesn't provide the opportunity nor the motivation, resulting in this behaviour not being fully manifested. (Remember what I explained before – both the People and Place are needed for a behaviour to fully manifest.) The People making up the demographics in this zone can be a quick win if you can fix the issues with opportunity and motivation. Hence, in future you would expect them to exist in the 'Strongly Aligned' zone.

FIGURE 5.3 A connected data approach to provide behaviour-first or outcome-first analytics for insights

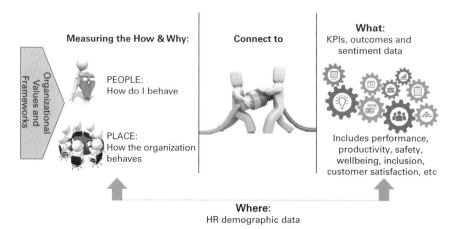

FIGURE 5.4 The 'where' of behaviour presence or absence using the quadrant dispersion method

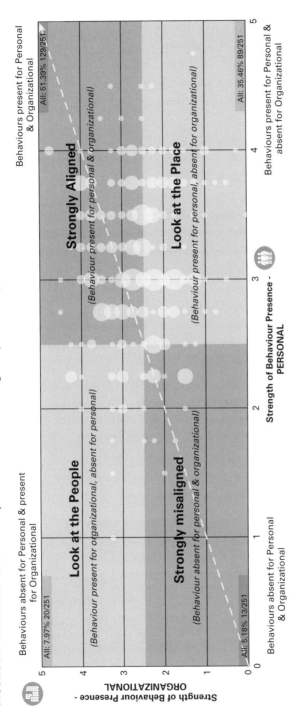

The bubbles represent size of the population as a proportion of the total population within each quadrant.

The zone marked 'Look at the People' shows you that the Empower behaviour is present at the Place as both opportunity and motivation are present, but absent by capability, which is what interventions should address. As an example, an organization is communicating to all leaders at all levels that empowerment is something they need to do in their daily work, and the organization is explaining the benefits of empowerment, but leaders in this zone indicate the absence of capability. This means that leaders are not sure how to empower their teams or the responsibilities, decisions and actions for empowerment.

That leaves us with that last zone. Essentially, the People making up these demographics indicate the absence of capability, opportunity and motivation for the Empower behaviour to manifest. Normally the People in this zone are the biggest drag when driving change and transformation.

The analytics for actionable insights process described in this chapter is framework-led; the process starts with frameworks that are available, followed by the behavioural mapping exercise to generate the behavioural clusters, to answer the key question of 'are we living our framework or our values?'. For clarity, a framework could include organizational values, risk and compliance, regulatory frameworks, etc.

If the specific question is about which behaviours drive or even predict a given outcome, the approach will be outcome-led analytics to drive actionable insights. This method will be covered in the next chapter.

6

The link between organizational culture and its impact on outcomes

Why did an incident happen? Which behaviours do we need to focus on to drive productivity and performance while maintaining psychological safety? How can we drive innovation?

These are all questions that need to be answered, and it may not surprise you to know that workplace culture plays a significant part in answering them. That is, behaviours become the actionable insight that you need to work on to affect the outcomes above.

Following on from the last chapter, in this chapter I will demonstrate the outcome-first approach. It is inevitable that I will have to visit some aspects of statistical maths to achieve the crown of all insights that is predictive analytics for actionable insights. So strap in while we visit some definitions first, to demystify predictive analytics.

Defining key statistical terms

The previous chapter metrics were all driven by what is known as 'descriptive statistics'. As the name suggests, this method helps articulate the current picture, giving you the ability to describe the trend using the following:[1]

- **Mean**: this is the average of the measured numbers, and is calculated by dividing the sum of measured numbers (say the measured behaviour factors) by the total number of numbers. Mean = (Sum of all the measured observations/Total number of observations, also known as sample size). This method was used in the behaviour heatmaps in the last chapter.
- **Median**: this is the middle number in a sorted ascending or descending list of numbers, and can be more descriptive of that data set than the

average. It is the point above and below which half (50 per cent) of the observed data falls, and so represents the midpoint of the data.
- **Standard deviation**: this is a measure of the amount of variation of a random variable expected about its mean. A low standard deviation indicates that the values tend to be close to the mean, while a high standard deviation indicates that the values are spread out over a wider range. This is very useful to describe the data in the distribution quadrant methodology I demonstrated in the last chapter.

Now let's move on from descriptive to predictive statistics. The term 'predictive statistics' (or analytics) refers to the use of statistics and modelling techniques to make predictions about future outcomes and performance. Predictive analytics looks at current and historical data patterns to determine if those patterns are likely to emerge again. Predictive analysis can also be used to improve operational efficiencies and reduce risk.

In behavioural science and specifically for culture metrics, you will get to accurately know 'why' it happened, 'how' to improve, change or sustain your outcomes, and, in our approach, your return on investment to drive behaviour change. The primary methodology to achieve predictive analytics is **multiple regression**, which needs some definition.

Multiple regression is a statistical technique that can be used to analyse the relationship between a single dependent variable and several independent variables.[2] The objective of multiple regression analysis is to use the independent variables whose values are known to predict the value of the dependent value. Multiple regression analysis allows researchers to assess the strength of the relationship between an outcome (the dependent variable) and several predictor variables, as well as the importance of each of the predictors to the relationship.

Multiple regression is used when we want to predict the value of a variable based on the value of two or more other variables. The variable we want to predict is called the dependent variable (or sometimes, the outcome, target or criterion variable). The variables we are using to predict the value of the dependent variable are called the independent variables (or sometimes, the predictor, explanatory or regressor variables).

For example, you could use multiple regression to understand whether exam performance can be predicted based on revision time, test anxiety, lecture attendance or gender. The output from this analysis will explain which of the four variables predict exam performance and how good this prediction is.

Multiple regression also allows you to determine the overall fit (variance explained) of the model and the relative contribution of each of the predictors to the total variance explained. For example, you might want to know how much of the variation in exam performance can be explained by revision time, test anxiety, lecture attendance or gender 'as a whole', but also the relative contribution of each independent variable in explaining the variance.

The *parsimonious model* is a model that accomplishes the desired level of explanation or prediction with as few predictor variables as possible. The *goodness of fit* of a statistical model describes how well it fits a set of observations. The *spurious model* occurs when two factors appear causally related to one another, but are not. The appearance of a causal relationship is often due to similar movement on a chart that turns out to be coincidental or caused by a third 'confounding' factor.[3]

The above will be sufficient to understand the methodology I am about to explain; however, if you'd like to know more about regression, I will provide you with a quick summary of how to read regression results.

Typically, a regression primary output summary will look like Table 6.1, and the parameters are defined as follows:

- **Multiple R** is the correlation coefficient that measures the strength of a linear relationship between two variables. The correlation coefficient can be any value between -1 and 1, and its absolute value indicates the relationship strength. The larger the absolute value, the stronger the relationship:
  - 1 means a strong positive relationship
  - -1 means a strong negative relationship
  - 0 means no relationship at all
- **R square** is the coefficient of determination, which is used as an indicator of the goodness of fit. It shows how many points fall on the regression line. The R^2 value is calculated from the total sum of squares; more precisely, it is the sum of the squared deviations of the original data from the mean.
- **Adjusted R square** is the R square adjusted for the number of independent variables in the model. You will want to use this value instead of R square for multiple regression analysis.
- **Standard error** is another goodness-of-fit measure that shows the precision of your regression analysis – the smaller the number, the more certain you can be about your regression equation. While R^2 represents

TABLE 6.1 Regression summary output

SUMMARY OUTPUT	
Regression Statistics	
Multiple R	0.491332608
R Square	0.241407732
Adjusted R Square	0.238887492
Standard Error	0.392270373
Observations	303

TABLE 6.2 Secondary regression output: Analysis of Variance (ANOVA)

ANOVA					
	df	SS	MS	F	Significance F
Regression	1	14.73941599	14.73941599	95.78759297	8.0871E-20
Residual	301	46.31668962	0.153876045		
Total	302	61.05610561			

the percentage of the dependent variables variance that is explained by the model, standard error is an absolute measure that shows the average distance that the data points fall from the regression line.

- **Observations** is simply the number of observations in your model, also known as sample size.

A secondary regression output will look like Table 6.2, and the parameters are defined as follows:

- **df** is the number of the degrees of freedom associated with the sources of variance.
- **SS** is the sum of squares. The smaller the residual SS compared with the total SS, the better your model fits the data.
- **MS** is the mean square.
- **F** is the F statistic, or F-test for the null hypothesis. It is used to test the overall significance of the model.
- **Significance F** is the P-value of F. The lower this value, the higher the significance of this model.

And the final part of a regression output is understanding the components of your analysis. As Table 6.3 shows, the most useful component in this section is **Coefficients** as it enables you to build a prediction; basically, how quickly the outcome will improve by changing the input, also known as the beta (β) coefficient. The beta describes the slope of the line for the outcome prediction.

As an example, see Figure 6.1. Notice how quickly the predicted outcome changes when the input changes. This slope is described by the β coefficient. Well, now that we've got the definitions out of the way, I hope I have demonstrated that interpreting predictive analytics results and turning them into actionable insights can be a complex business. This is exactly why I will be providing you with a vastly simpler way of representing the power of predictive analytics without compromising the methodology. This will be demonstrated in Chapter 11.

Let's turn our attention to the outcome-first method and how to use it.

As the name suggests, the method is about starting with the outcome, hence no behaviour mapping is assumed, as follows.

The first step is to obtain the data set containing behavioural data for the people and the place as per the diagnostic method outlined in Chapter 4. Obtain the outcome data at individual level as a preference, e.g. performance metrics or participants responding to outcome/sentiment questions.

FIGURE 6.1 A graph showing the β coefficient

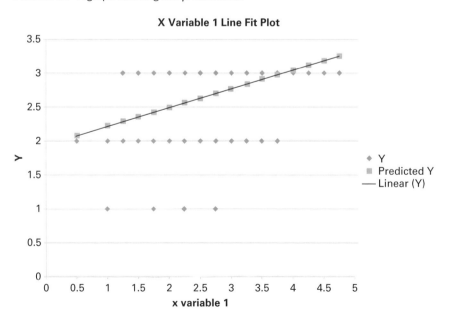

TABLE 6.3 Regression component analysis

	Coefficients	Standard Error	t Stat	P-value	Lower 95%	Upper 95%	Lower 95.0%	Upper 95.0%
Intercept	1.951043878	0.088186475	22.12407158	4.54599E-65	1.777503784	2.124583972	1.777503784	2.124583972
X Variable 1	0.274297483	0.028026392	9.787113618	8.0871E-20	0.219145004	0.329449962	0.219145004	0.329449962

Next, the multiple R coefficient value between each behaviour and the outcome should be obtained, using the multiple regression – this is the first-level modelling. There are 16 variations of regression analysis, e.g. linear, non-linear, polynomial, logistic, quantile, etc. The most relevant ones are linear regression for linear outcomes and logistic regression for binary outcomes. The behaviours with the best multiple R should be selected for each outcome.

Differences in regression models should be tested to identify the most parsimonious nested model – the best combination of CultureScope behaviours for predicting the outcome – this is second-level modelling. After years of research, I have always found that a nested behavioural model is a better predictor of outcomes than singular behaviours.

Never rely on just one thematic outcome to create the most parsimonious model. You should try to get as many outcome metrics as you can for a given theme, which could include sentiment, situational and measured data; this approach will act as a good validation method for your resulting model. To demonstrate, I will elaborate further in Chapter 9 on workplace culture outcome themes and how to leverage the behavioural data collected for multiple themes for connected analytics and actionable insights.

A key question I need to address is: for a given population size, what is the data collection completion rate needed to provide model statistical validity, and for analytics for insights validity? Let's define and answer each one as follows.

Statistical validity can be defined as the extent to which drawn conclusions of a research study can be considered accurate and reliable from a statistical test. To achieve statistical validity, it is essential for researchers to have sufficient data and to choose the right statistical approach to analyse that data. The statistical validity approach I took during my seven-year research, as outlined in Chapter 4, was derived from the effect size method, which tells you how meaningful the relationship between variables or the difference between groups is.[4] It indicates the practical significance of a research outcome; in most cases a minimum 30 per cent completion rate of a given population achieves statistical validity.

Analytics validity is defined by the number of criteria-based benchmarks one needs to generate to show demographic differences once a module has been developed. Essentially, the more the demographics you apply, a higher completion rate is needed. In my research outlined in Chapter 4, I found that ideally $n \geq 5$ (five participants or more are needed) for any generated criteria-based benchmark.

You may wonder: why five? This protects anonymity and, critically, will stop an outlier from totally deforming the model for a generated benchmark so as to render it unreliable.

Putting the above method into practice, let's go back to our example from Chapter 5, where the collected data was from 3,122 participants representing a 62 per cent completion rate. We now need to forget about the mapping exercise and assume nothing; that is, apply all 30 behavioural factors for the People and 30 for the Place as the independent variables, and the outcome as the dependent variable.

For this organization, the key question they wanted answering was: does our workplace culture support performance? If so, which behaviours do we need to focus on? I will now apply the performance scorecard data that this organization has been collecting as the dependent variable. The performance scale is as follows:

1 Does not meet performance expectations
2 Partially meets performance expectations
3 Consistently meets performance expectations
4 Often exceeds performance expectations
5 Consistently exceeds performance expectations

You can see from the above that the outcome is on a five-point scale, indicating that linear regression analysis is likely to be the best analysis method. Having applied this regression, the key component results are shown in Table 6.4 (focusing on a few important metrics only to simplify).

TABLE 6.4 Regression results key components

Behavioural Factors	Achievement, Empower, Radical, Consolidate, Team Focus
Multiple R	0.33
Standard Error	0.812
Number of observations	3,122
Significance F	3.30753663061259E-08
Beta Coefficient	0.55

FIGURE 6.2 Correlational effect size benchmarks

Effect Size Distribution Percentiles for Broad Relation Types

Relation type	k	N	20th	25th	33rd	40th	50th	60th	67th	75th	80th	Cutoffs[b]	Centroid[c]
						ES distribution percentile						Overlap with Cohen's medium ES range[a]	
(All effect sizes)	147,328	225	.05	.07	.09	.12	.16	.21	.26	.32	.36	0.00%	8.21%
Attitudes: attitudes	14,493	202	.10	.13	.18	.22	.28	.34	.39	.45	.50	40.26%	56.52%
Organization attitudes: job attitudes	1,263	240	.14	.16	.21	.25	.31	.36	.40	.45	.49	55.58%	61.96%
Organization attitudes: people attitudes	644	277	.15	.18	.24	.28	.34	.39	.43	.48	.51	70.45%	61.36%
Job attitudes: people attitudes	783	196	.10	.13	.18	.21	.26	.30	.35	.40	.43	25.82%	62.18%
Attitudes: intentions	1,717	237	.12	.15	.19	.23	.27	.33	.37	.42	.47	37.46%	66.61%
Attitudes: behaviours	7,958	220	.06	.07	.10	.12	.16	.20	.24	.29	.33	0.00%	0.00%
Intentions: behaviours	535	233	.07	.09	.11	.14	.19	.24	.27	.32	.33	0.00%	15.34%
Performance: attitudes	3,224	190	.07	.08	.11	.14	.17	.22	.26	.31	.36	0.00%	9.30%
Performance: organization attitudes	615	213	.07	.08	.10	.13	.16	.19	.22	.27	.30	0.00%	0.00%
Performance: job attitudes	1,271	188	.06	.08	.10	.13	.17	.22	.26	.32	.36	0.00%	9.85%
Performance: people attitudes	575	192	.08	.10	.13	.16	.22	.27	.32	.39	.43	6.77%	38.02%
Performance: knowledge, skills & abilities	1,385	202	.08	.10	.13	.16	.21	.26	.31	.36	.40	4.80%	32.99%
Performance: psychological characteristics	3,135	158	.06	.07	.10	.12	.16	.20	.23	.28	.31	0.00%	0.00%
Performance: objective person characteristics	1,395	200	.03	.04	.05	.07	.09	.11	.14	.17	.20	0.00%	0.00%
Movement: attitudes	866	309	.05	.07	.09	.11	.14	.18	.21	.25	.28	0.00%	0.00%
Movement: org. attitudes	200	309	.07	.08	.10	.13	.14	.19	.23	.27	.30	0.00%	0.00%
Movement: job attitudes	295	312	.06	.07	.09	.11	.13	.16	.18	.22	.25	0.00%	0.00%
Movement: people attitudes	44	266	.06	.06	.09	.09	.12	.21	.23	.31	.37	0.00%	0.00%
Movement: psychological characteristics	288	216	.04	.05	.07	.08	.11	.13	.17	.20	.23	0.00%	0.00%
Movement: objective person characteristics	461	293	.02	.03	.04	.05	.07	.09	.11	.14	.16	0.00%	0.00%

The regression showed that five People behaviours are the predictors for performance. The behavioural factors are:

- **Achievement**: People believe that you are what you do, and they define your worth accordingly. These cultures value performance independent of status.
- **Empower**: Decisions are delegated to lower levels with supportive guidance.
- **Radical**: Continuous improvement and evolving ideas are valued; there is an emphasis on responding differently to different situations.
- **Consolidate**: Predictability and control are preferred. Risk taking is avoided until it is absolutely necessary. Tried-and-tested methods are encouraged.
- **Team Focus**: Work is delivered through collaborative group efforts and team results are prioritized over individual results.

These behaviours yield a very good multiple R of 0.33, which ranks at the 80th predictive percentile of effect sizes observed as compared to the research I mentioned earlier.[5] For ease of reference, see Figure 6.2.

Analysing the other regression components, standard error is low and significance F is almost zero, which implies a highly significant model. A beta coefficient of 0.55 provides a good prediction model, as per Figure 6.3.

FIGURE 6.3 The predictive relationship between the nested five behaviours and performance rating

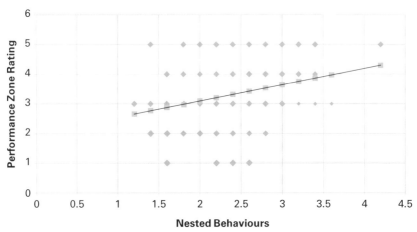

Now that we have developed the behavioural model for performance as a workplace culture theme, in the next chapter I will illustrate how we can apply the same analytics lens as in Chapter 5 to this model, to show to what degree these five behaviours are present or absent, and crucially where in the organization. Remember, if you want to drive performance, that's what you need to focus your interventions on.

Notes

1 P Saville and T Hopton (2014) *Psychometrics@work*, Saville Consulting
2 A W Moore, B Anderson, K Das and W-K Wong (2006) Combining Multiple Signals for Biosurveillance, *Handbook of Biosurveillance*, pp. 235–42
3 A Gupta. Model Selection Techniques – Parsimony & Goodness of Fit, *Medium*, 13 December 2020, https://medium.com/geekculture/model-selection-techniques-parsimony-goodness-of-fit-fc2f1863ccfd (archived at https://perma.cc/7TSG-9ZWL)
4 F A Bosco, H Aguinis, H, K Singh, J G Field and C A Pierce (2015) Correlational effect size benchmarks, *Journal of Applied Psychology*, **100**, pp. 431–49
5 Bosco et al, ibid

7

Applying predictive analytics to culture metrics

Having established from the previous chapter, through predictive analytics, the five behaviours that drive your workplace culture for performance, we can now establish a behavioural heatmap – firstly for the entire population, then looking at all benchmark demographics through that performance behavioural lens.

Figure 7.1 shows that for the cluster of all five behaviours for the entire measured population, the behaviours that drive performance are not all that present: the People yield a mean of 2.78 and the Place 2.67 (the scale is from 0 to 5). We really need to be aiming at a mean of 3.1 or more to truly drive performance, and as you can see, both the People and the Place need interventions to drive capability, opportunity and motivation.

To make the actionable insight more meaningful, we can use the quadrant method to examine where in the organization all five behaviours are present for the Place, or the People, or both. Further, I will set the quadrant threshold to 3 for both People and Place to drive meaningful insights (if you are wondering why 3, remember this is the presence threshold on the behaviour scale).

The result is shown in Figure 7.2, revealing that one team in the organization does have all five behaviours present for both People and Place, the Operations team. Furthermore, 63 per cent of the Marketing team have all five behaviours present, although they are absent at their Place. This is also encouraging, as fixing the Place for this team means that we move them to the greatness zone! Still, the team to learn from is Operations, and they can help by being the change champions.

(I just revealed another advantage to the quadrant distribution method; that is, to show you where your culture champions are.)

FIGURE 7.1 Heatmap results for the five behaviours that drive performance workplace culture

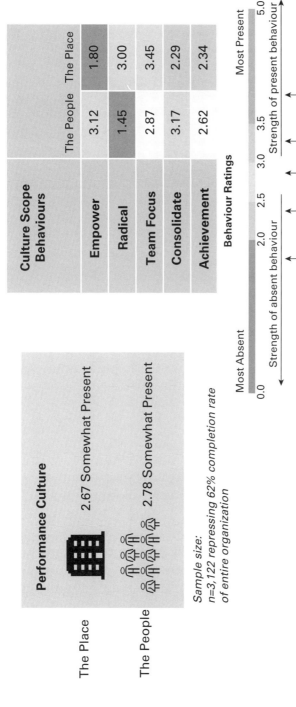

FIGURE 7.2 Quadrant distribution diagram showing where the five behaviours driving performance are present

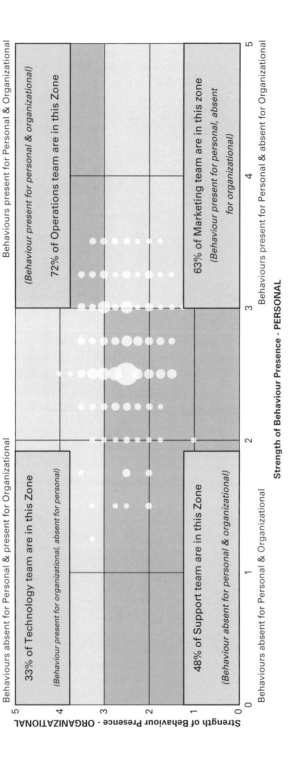

What about the two remaining zones in the quadrant? The top left zone indicates that Place is enabling the five behaviours; however, you will need to build capability for the People. One example here is the Technology team. For the final quadrant, in the bottom left, the five behaviours are absent for both Place and People. In this zone, you have the most 'drag' as you will need to design interventions that will build capability and provide opportunity and motivation to enact these behaviours. As you can see from Figure 7.2, the Support department requires these focused interventions.

You can also use this quadrant distribution method to examine singular behaviours, ending up with five diagrams giving further insight into each behaviour. This more detailed approach can be very useful if you want to find singular behaviour champions, especially in relatively large organizations, where a change programme may need many culture champions to maximize success.

I have mentioned workplace culture champions twice now, and you may be wondering: what does that really mean? Why call individuals in the top right corner of the quadrant 'champions'? The champions have all five targeted behaviours as present for them and their Place, hence they are walking the talk! That alignment results in highly engaged individuals, and this is meaningful engagement, as it drives the targeted performance culture outcome. Hence you will want them to actively inspire and energize the rest of the organization.

By contrast, the zone at the bottom left corner of the distribution quadrant will have individuals that are aligned to Place as all five behaviours are absent for them and their Place, hence behavioural alignment and possible engagement; however, for the wrong reasons, as this alignment works against the performance culture outcome. I will cover this critical topic further in the next chapter.

We can further validate this workplace culture for performance model by producing five benchmarks for the five-point performance scale; the scale banding is from 'consistently exceeds' to 'does not meet' performance criteria, as already shown in the previous chapter. This will illustrate how the presence or absence of the five predictive behaviours fares against the performance scale.

Figure 7.3 is a line graph showing and validating that the individuals awarded the best performance do indeed have the five behaviours present. You also see that the individuals with the lower performance grades exhibit lower presence of the five behaviours. In fact, 'does not meet performance criteria', which is the lowest performance grade, has all five behaviours absent.

Notice the difference between the People and the Place in Figure 7.3; in all the performance criteria, the People behaviours are more likely to be present. So the Place will impede performance, which is not what you want.

These results also beg a few questions: is the Place the key reason for the People's behaviours and hence performance? Should the five behaviours at the Place be somewhat consistent across all performance groups? So many questions to further investigate about performance culture, which should be a combination of quantitative and qualitative.

Having established a behavioural predictive model for performance culture, you can now compare the behaviours that drive your outcome with the behaviours mapped to your organizational values. The reason for comparing the mapping against the developed model for one or more outcomes is to answer a secondary question regarding your organizational values. Let me elaborate: you may remember we did a mapping exercise back in Chapter 4, in order to look at the behavioural results with that applied lens in Chapter 5, answering the primary question of: are we living our values? Ok, so what? If we are living our values, do we also achieve our desired outcomes? After all, that is what you want out of your values and workplace culture.

To answer this secondary, but very important question for organizational values, we need to make sure that some if not all the mapped behaviours are the same as per the outcome or even several outcomes in the developed model, and we also need to make sure that we do not have any competing behaviours, referring to the dichotomy construct of the behavioural pairs.

As an example, if one of your organization's values is Standardized behaviour, but the regression model for outcomes indicates the need for Flexible behaviour, being the dichotomous partner as illustrated in Figure 5.1 in Chapter 5, this will result in a conflict between living your organizational values and driving your desired outcomes.

The comparison between the organizational values behavioural mapping and predictive performance culture is illustrated in Table 7.1. It can be seen that we have a match with two of the behaviours, Achievement and Empower. A further two behaviours are not matched, but are simply additive as part of the performance culture model. That is fine – they could be unique to this culture theme, hence need focusing on just for that outcome.

If these two behaviours keep recurring while we develop more outcome culture themes, we can look to integrate them into your organizational values and perhaps adapt or evolve your values – an interesting idea and method in making your organizational values true to intended behaviours, and another example of linking outcomes to values.

FIGURE 7.3 Line graph showing performance grade against the five behaviours

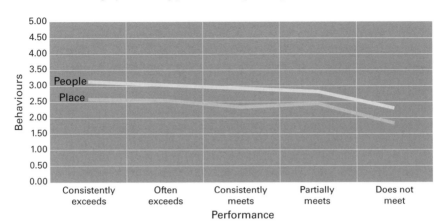

TABLE 7.1 Comparison between the organizational values behavioural mapping and predictive performance culture

Respect	Humility	Positivity	Performance Culture Model	
Conformity				
Expressive	Expressive			
Achievement		Achievement	Achievement	◉
People Focus		People Focus		
Collective				
	Empower		Empower	◉
	Active Learning			
		Sequential		
		Innovate	Consolidate	❗
			Radical	
			Team Focus	

What about the elephant in the room? I am referring to that fifth behaviour – yes, you may have noticed that Consolidate is the dichotomous partner of Innovate, which is mapped to your organizational values. Shock and horror! We don't need to be innovative to drive performance culture; this is a good example of 'never assume'. It's that old syndrome: 'if it works somewhere, it should work for us'. And this example shows how each organizational culture is unique and there is no one-size-fits-all; again, I will further elaborate in the next chapter.

For now, let me offer an interesting observation rather than a hypothesis based on the performance outcome; could this example simply be a case of wrongly mapped behaviour? Notice that Radical behaviour in Table 7.1 – perhaps that should be the mapped behaviour and we just need to fine-tune the organizational values behavioural mapping? It could be an easy mistake, and the difference in culture can be simply summarized as 'evolution rather than revolution'.

How do we adapt your organizational value 'Positivity' to reflect this change? Let us start by looking at the definitions of Innovate vs Radical:

- **Innovate**: New and creative ideas are pioneered. Intelligent risk taking is encouraged and praised.
- **Radical**: Continuous improvement and evolving ideas are valued; there is an emphasis on responding differently to different situations.

Now let's recall the mapping for 'Positivity' from Table 4.3 – this is shown in Table 7.2.

The words used in your organizational values, 'innovative and curious mindset', should now be changed, based on what we have learnt from the performance outcome. Perhaps that should read, 'As we evolve, we engender continuous improvement in all employees and partners'. The resulting mapping is demonstrated in Table 7.3.

Although this example of organizational values adaptation is based on just one outcome, and in practice we will need to validate against many outcomes to be absolutely sure, I hope that the process is now clear for how you can make your organizational values steeped in reality. Walking the talk drives your desired and intended outcomes.

TABLE 7.2 Behavioural mapping for Positivity

Positivity	We maintain the highest level of quality, performance and timely delivery, but not at the expense of our people's wellbeing.	Sequential, People Focus
	Everyone's achievements are celebrated regardless of position.	Achievement
	We engender an innovative and curious mindset in all employees and partners.	Innovate

TABLE 7.3 Changed values wording and relevant behavioural mapping

Positivity	We maintain the highest level of quality, performance and timely delivery, but not at the expense of our people's wellbeing.	Sequential, People Focus
	Everyone's achievements are celebrated regardless of position.	Achievement
	As we evolve, we engender continuous improvement in all employees and partners	Radical

The process in this chapter illustrates the linking that should happen between organizational values, workplace culture, behaviours and intended outcomes. Unfortunately, this process rarely happens in organizations, and if it does it's a disconnected, qualitative process at best, rendering organizational values 'just nice words'!

8

You have to know the 'why' before you get to the 'how' and 'where'

I hope you can see from the example in the previous chapter how analytics for behaviour-based actionable insights are a continuous loop of an outcome-first analytics approach leading to a behaviour-analytics-first approach.

Once a model has been developed with behavioural leading indicators, you need to perform further steps to deliver the full insights picture. The journey from Chapter 4 through Chapter 7, and assuming the behavioural measurement stage has been completed, I can summarize as follows:

1 **Define the outcomes**: you may have done so already as part of the 'Define' stage. Remember the five-step approach for measuring and driving workplace culture change that I shared with you in Chapter 2? Defining the outcomes was part of that; however, post behaviour diagnostics, you can still define further outcomes to help you validate or add to your insights.

2 **Gather outcome data**: that is, if you have not done so already. The process entails making sure that you have clean metric data, as per the example in Chapter 6. Check that you have up-to-date performance data – are there any gaps or even possible erroneous data, e.g. performance data reported that is outside the performance scale? If so, you can eliminate or correct it.

3 **Regression analysis**: for each outcome data, perform the regression analysis so you end up with the nested behaviours that predict your desired outcomes.

4 **Generate benchmarks using quadrant graphs and/or heatmaps**: based on the behaviour cluster, you can plot behavioural heatmaps and quadrant distribution graphs for People and Place to show exactly where the

behaviours are present or absent based on the demographics. You can also deliver remarkable insights by generating behavioural benchmarks for the outcome data, as I demonstrated using a line graph in the previous chapter (Figure 7.3). Remember you can also generate quadrant dispersion graphs for singular behaviours, giving a further deep layer of actionable insights. Depending on your audience, you may want to generate other infographics to illustrate the picture; again, the key is to tell the story of 'why' the outcomes happen, 'how', with examples of 'what' can we do to sustain or improve, and 'where' in the organization we need to focus on. In Chapter 11 you will try an easy method to show your audience 'so what?' – what do we get for it; what is the return on our investment?

The process just outlined follows the title of this chapter exactly: steps one, two and three together provide you with the 'why', answering the question, 'Why does an outcome happen (or not)?'.

Step three provides you with the 'how', answering the question, 'How can you improve, sustain or suppress an outcome?' – which behaviours, as the leading indicators, will maximize your chances for success. Step four will provide you with the 'where', answering the question, 'Where by demographics are the behaviour present or absent?', helping you know where in the organization to learn from, where to drive change and what type of intervention is needed, i.e. capability, opportunity, motivation or all three.

I am indeed hoping that the title of this chapter will stick, as it's far easier to remember than a detailed process.

This insight reporting mechanism is your best ally for helping you with the known unknowns, so they become known knowns. Let me explain. We know that workplace culture and behaviours impact outcomes – that's the known bit – but we don't know which behaviours and where – that's the unknown. The result of this process is turning the unknown to a known.

You may wonder why I am mentioning known unknowns. I am hoping that this will act as a reminder for you whenever you are examining outcomes, regardless of how good the outcome metrics are, to stop and think – are there any known unknowns? This is a critical question if you are to stop what I call 'false positives'.

I promised in the previous chapter to elaborate further on behavioural alignment vs engagement, and I am sure you would have often looked at employee engagement results and seen great results. However, you also know that other outcomes are not great. So what's happening?

The first thing to remember is that employee engagement is another outcome of workplace culture. Secondly, engagement survey data is naturally very transient, and can be sensitive to the current situation. In recent research that I have conducted, I have found that behavioural alignment between the People and the Place drives a positive engagement score.

As you may recall from Figure 7.2, the quadrant distribution graph example, there are two zones where there is behavioural alignment – the top right corner showing a behavioural presence for both People and Place, driving meaningful engagement, and the bottom left corner showing a behavioural absence for both People and Place, driving engagement, but for the wrong reasons.

To demonstrate the 'false positives' issue, I will share with you an example from some recent research I did. Figure 8.1 shows a quadrant distribution for large professional services organizations.

As before, the plot is for the targeted behaviours for both the People and the Place, however this time I have added their engagement index score to all four quadrants of the quadrant distribution graph. Notice the engagement score for the top right corner where the behaviours are present and aligned. Now look at the bottom left corner where the behaviours are absent but aligned. They have very similar engagement scores of 4.8 and 4.1 respectively. If we did not have the behavioural measurement, we would simply see both zones as showing positive employee engagement, masking issues and giving us a far rosier image as we would be reporting an excellent engagement score for 55 per cent of the organization.

FIGURE 8.1 Quadrant distribution graph showing behavioural alignment vs employee engagement scores

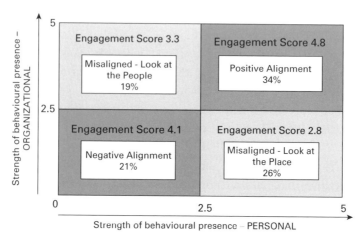

NOTE Sample size: n = 6,560, representing 54 per cent completion rate of the entire organization

In fact, knowing the leading indicators can now explain the 'why' for each zone, 'how' to improve and if we add demographics we will get to the 'where'.

Another important aspect of the known unknowns is that organizational culture is unique, and you cannot simply borrow models from other organizations and hope that all will be well. This uniqueness is driven by your organizational operating model, market conditions, processes and polices and organizational structure, just to name a few. Hence why I am normally very sceptical about off-the-shelf workplace culture models that can be adopted with no applied research of your own to explore how they will help, and critically what will be the outcomes. What I am really saying is that your known unknowns may not be the same as other organizations. I will demonstrate with a quick example, borrowing from Charles Dickens with a variation – 'a tale of two organizations'.

If you recall from the example in Chapter 6, the behaviours that will help you drive performance culture were Achievement, Empower, Consolidate, Radical and Team Focus.

For another organization in the same sector, and having applied the same performance culture behavioural research, I have found that the following behaviours drive their performance as follows: Collective, Relationship, People Focus and Achievement.

Comparing the two developed behavioural models yields only one common behaviour. Essentially, these two organizations are competitors, but their culture for performance is significantly different.

This demonstration is also the reason why people who have performed well in one organization may struggle in another. I have often come across this exact question relating to talent: why is this person struggling? They came to us as a top performer in their previous employment! To answer what is happening, I will have to take you back to the known unknowns, and there is no wrong or right answer. You will need to understand your organizational behavioural model as the leading indicator and how aligned or misaligned your talent is to the **targeted behaviours**. Remember that alignment does not have to be for all behaviours, just the critical few that drive your outcomes.

To further illustrate with another simple example, imagine you are a New Yorker, living and working in New York, and you are asked for the first time to travel and conduct detailed business transactions in Tokyo. As soon you arrive, it will all feel so different and most likely be very puzzling. You will need to work so hard to demystify and process what is happening, and although you are a top performer, suddenly in this very different environment you are not able to perform! Knowing 'why', then the 'how', is the only way forward to impact the future outcome of success.

In Part 2 of this book, I will provide further example case studies for workplace culture differences and driving similar outcomes between organizations, so the 'tale of two organizations' will continue.

The actionable insights process outlined so far is critical for any workplace culture initiative, management or change. These initiatives often target an outcome without knowing 'why' the outcomes really happen; so, at best, any success will be by chance.

Unfortunately, chance does not always work in your favour, and eventually your luck will run out! For so many organizations I have worked with, I often come across this syndrome known as 'get-me-there-itis' – just get me there now! We need to drive performance while we drive efficiency and drive retention, etc. My response is, no! What you need is to drive your workplace culture in a way that enables and predicts performance, efficacy and retention. You cannot take shortcuts or dangerously assume the 'why'. With digital quantitative tools available to us today like CultureScope, where behavioural science and people analytics work in harmony, it is far easier to deliver impactful and actionable insights in a matter of weeks for any size of organization.

The further good news with this onlined quantitative measurement approach is the ability to rate and validate. It's easy to redeploy to make sure that your behavioural action plan is working, and that the intended outcome is changing.

So, my last words of wisdom for this chapter are: do not leave workplace culture change to chance.

9

Leveraging leading indicators

How do you leverage one set of leading indicators to drive multiple outcomes? Is that really possible?

In today's fast-paced, competitive and demanding workplace environment, organizations are constantly seeking ways to optimize their operations and improve their overall performance. One effective strategy that has emerged in recent years is the use of leading indicators to drive multiple outcomes. As a reminder, leading indicators are defined as measurable factors that can be used to predict and influence future performance.

Traditionally, and as I have already demonstrated in previous chapters, organizations have relied on lagging indicators, which measure past performance to assess their success. While lagging indicators provide valuable insights into historical data, they do not provide proactive information that can drive future outcomes. Leading indicators, on the other hand, are forward-looking and can provide organizations with opportunities to improve performance before problems may occur.

The power of leading indicators lies in their ability to **affect multiple outcomes simultaneously**. By identifying and tracking a set of key leading indicators, organizations can proactively manage a range of objectives and drive superior results across various areas of operation. The different outcomes can be collected together thematically – for example, risk management, performance, efficiency, diversity, equity and inclusion, wellbeing, etc. Each theme can, and should, have multiple outcomes and metrics to manage the risk of overly depending on singular data points and enhancing validity or eliminating the inference without sufficient evidence.

Firstly, let us explore some example themes, but without the enrichment of behavioural data. My main reasoning behind doing so is to illustrate what adding behavioural data will actually provide.

This particular organization is a mid-sized nuclear energy generator, with a total sample size of 681.

Safety and accident prevention

One crucial aspect of many organizations is the safety of their workforce. By identifying indicators such as near-miss incidents, safety training completion rates or adherence to safety protocols, organizations can proactively address potential hazards and prevent accidents. This not only protects the wellbeing of employees, but also reduces costs associated with workers' compensation claims and lost productivity.

Quality and customer satisfaction

Another important outcome for organizations is the quality of their products or services and the level of customer satisfaction. Indicators such as customer feedback scores, product defect rates or employee training on quality standards can help organizations identify areas of improvement to enhance product quality and customer satisfaction. Addressing these indicators can help to increase customer loyalty, improve brand reputation and ultimately lead to higher revenue.

Employee retention

Organizations that prioritize employee retention enjoy numerous benefits, including lower turnover costs and less talent/knowledge drain. By tracking indicators like employee satisfaction surveys, training hours or employee turnover rates, organizations may identify potential issues or areas for improvement that directly impact employee retention.

Operational efficiency

Efficient operations are critical for organizations aiming to maximize profitability and minimize waste. Indicators such as production cycle times, equipment downtime or waste-reduction initiatives provide insights into the effectiveness and efficiency of operations. Analysing and actively managing these indicators can help organizations identify bottlenecks, streamline processes and optimize resource allocation, leading to increased productivity and reduced costs.

Financial performance

Financial success is a paramount objective for any organization. Indicators such as revenue growth rates, cost management metrics or investment return ratios

> can provide opportunities for improvement in financial performance. By proactively addressing these indicators, organizations can make data-driven decisions to optimize revenue generation, reduce costs and improve overall profitability.

I am sure the above cases all sound interesting and valid – but what is missing? Where is the role of workplace culture in these outlined metrics in each of the above cases? Armed with the knowledge that workplace culture translates into behaviours for Place and People, we simply cannot ignore such metrics for grassroots leading indicators.

As you have already learnt from the previous chapters, for each of the above illustrated themes you can run the behavioural diagnostic and regression analysis for the theme-relevant outcomes to add leading indicators and then, with the aid of multiple demographic data and benchmark generation, you can generate the quadrant distributions to articulate the 'where' – i.e., where we can learn from and where we need to improve.

But do you have to redeploy the behavioural diagnostic measurement for each theme? The (very) good news is that you don't! As long as the behavioural diagnostic includes all 15 dimensions (30 behavioural factors) outlined in Chapter 4, you can simply measure once and generate multiple and endless actionable insights. See Figure 9.1 as an example of one behavioural dataset driving multiple workplace culture themes.

Such a behavioural diagnostic approach to predicting multiple outcomes is a key differentiator between measuring behaviours and measuring sentiment, employee management or even theme-specific employee opinion surveys. Such methods will result in the need to deploy many different online questionnaires, driving employee questionnaire fatigue.

Using the above five thematic examples, let's explore how leveraging one set of leading indicators can positively impact multiple outcomes.

Theme 1: Safety and accident prevention

The outcomes that we have metrics for are:

- reported near-miss incidents
- safety training completion rates
- reported safety compliance incidents

FIGURE 9.1 Example of one set of behavioural data measurement, a leading indicator to many thematic outcomes

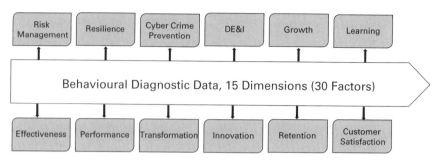

Differences in regression models for each of the above outcomes were tested to identify the most parsimonious model – i.e. the best number of behaviours required to predict the outcome. The regression model yielded 0.33 for reported near-miss incidents, and the predictive behaviours are Nonconformity, Flexible and Self-Focus. We know the opposite behaviours will suppress the number of near-miss incidents – they are Conformity, Standardized and Team Focus.

The regression model yielded 0.41 for the second outcome and predictive behaviours Active Learning, Standardized and Conformity.

Finally, the third outcome regression model yielded 0.38 and the predictive behaviours Neutral, Nonconformity, Synchronous and Self-Focus. To reduce the number of compliance incidents, you will need the oppositional behaviours, which are Expressive, Conformity, Sequential and Team Focus.

Already from the above you can see the advantages of the one set of leading indicators, i.e. the behaviours that drive more than one outcome. If you focus on Conformity, Standardized, Team Focus, Expressive and Sequential, you will gain all three outcomes.

Theme 2: Quality and customer satisfaction

For this theme, the outcomes that we had metrics for were quality related:

- improvement projects completion metrics
- team design quality metrics

Regression model analyses yielded 0.36 and 0.42, and shared similar behaviours – Sequential, Team Focus and Active Learning. Interestingly, we have seen all these behaviours in the first theme.

Theme 3: Employee retention

Apart from the regression analysis for the employee tenure outcome, we also looked at the alignment index between Place and People for the resulting behaviours. Regression model analysis yielded 0.32 for Collective, Conformity, Team Focus, Sequential and Active Learning. Apart from Collective, we have seen all these behaviours in the previous themes.

Looking at the above three examples, you can already see how a few behaviours are predicting multiple outcomes and multiple themes. In fact, for the last two themes, which are Operational efficiency and Financial performance, all the same behaviours already discovered are predictors with the addition of Achievement.

Table 9.1 demonstrates the eight predictive behaviours mapping against the five themes – notice how two critical behaviours (Team Focus and Sequential) are mapped to all themes. Sequential is a present behaviour; however, Team Focus is an absent behaviour, hence intervention design and implementation will be critical as this one behaviour will move the dial for all five themes.

So, how have we transformed the leading indicators story? We went from seemingly unconnected themes looking at outcomes only to finding out that the key leading indicators are eight behaviours. And for this organization the story gets better! Five of the behaviours are present (Sequential, Conformity, Collective, Active Learning, Standardized). So, they can now focus on improving the three remaining behaviours (Expressive, Achievement, Team Focus) for driving 16 outcomes across five themes.

TABLE 9.1 The eight behaviours mapped to all five themes

	Safety and Accident Prevention	Quality and Customer Satisfaction	Employee Retention	Operational Efficiency	Financial Performance
Sequential	✓	✓	✓		
Conformity	✓				
Standardized	✓		✓		
Active Learning		✓			
Collective			❗	❗	❗
Team Focus	❗	❗		❗	❗
Achievement				❗	
Expressive	❗				

The tick denotes the presence of a behaviour, while the exclamation mark denotes the absence of a behaviour

This demonstrates how managers and leaders don't have to be overwhelmed thinking about solutions for multiple outcomes across multiple themes and will only need to focus on driving interventions for a few behaviours. This is another demonstration of the power of organizational behavioural science as a leading indicator. In fact, if time and resources are an issue, then the absolute must-focus-on priority in this example is Team Focus, as this one behaviour will impact all five themes and will yield significant return on investment.

Apart from having robust and scientifically valid behaviour measurement, to effectively leverage a single set of leading indicators, organizations must also establish robust and relevant outcome measurement metrics. Regular monitoring, analysis and action planning based on these leading indicators are also essential to drive the desired outcomes.

In conclusion, leveraging one set of leading indicators can be a game-changer for organizations looking to drive multiple outcomes. By identifying key behavioural leading indicators and actively managing them, organizations can be very efficient at driving multiple outcomes with reduced effort.

Having demonstrated in this chapter how one set of behavioural data can drive multiple thematic outcomes, the question we have not answered is whether there is a sequence for the outcomes, as some outcomes will need to happen first to impact other desired outcomes. This is known as path analysis, and is the subject of my next chapter.

10

Understanding and applying path analysis as the roadmap for driving change

Unveiling the connections in complex systems

As I illustrated the power of behavioural leading indicators in Chapter 9, it's time to turn our attention to the relationships between the outcomes. As you will have seen in Chapter 3, some outcomes will sequentially predict other outcomes.

In this chapter, I will be getting into some deep maths. This chapter is not required for all readers as the topic of path analysis at a high level has been covered in Chapter 3, hence it is only for those readers who want to gain a deeper understanding of the maths behind path analysis.

As I explained in Chapter 3, path analysis uses a powerful statistical technique for investigating complex causal relationships among variables. It provides a comprehensive framework to test hypotheses, explore direct and indirect effects and refine models.

Path analysis is established using a technique called structural equation modelling (SEM). It is a statistical analytical approach that allows researchers to analyse complex causal relationships among multiple variables. Path analysis using SEM provides a rigorous framework for testing hypotheses and exploring the interplay between variables in a larger model.

SEM is a multivariate statistical technique that combines factor analysis and multiple regression analysis to examine the relationships between measured variables and behaviours. It enables researchers to investigate both direct and indirect relationships in a comprehensive way. However, path analysis goes further, as it helps you interpret the relationships between variables, providing valuable insights into causal pathways and mediating effects.

The advantages of path analysis using SEM are numerous, and can be summarized as follows:

- It allows researchers to examine complex relationships with multiple variables simultaneously, providing a more comprehensive understanding of the underlying mechanisms.
- It helps to identify direct and indirect effects, thereby allowing for a better understanding of the contribution of each variable to the overall outcome.
- It enables researchers to test competing hypotheses and compare alternative models, facilitating development and refinement.

Furthermore, path analysis using SEM can also control for measurement error, which enhances the accuracy of the estimates and reduces bias. It is particularly useful when dealing with latent constructs that are not directly observed and the measurement may not be error-free. By accounting for measurement error, path analysis using SEM provides more reliable and valid estimates of the relationships between variables.

SEM has also emerged as a powerful tool in uncovering the intricate relationships and connections even within complex systems. SEM goes beyond traditional linear regression techniques by considering both observed and unobserved variables simultaneously. SEM methodology combines elements of multivariate analysis, regression analysis and factor analysis. It enables researchers to examine the relationships between latent variables and observed variables within a framework.

For a definition of regression analysis, please refer back to Chapter 6. Here I will define multivariate and factor analysis. **Multivariate analysis** is a statistical technique that allows researchers to simultaneously analyse multiple variables to gain a deeper understanding of the data and extract meaningful insights. By considering the interconnections among variables, multivariate analysis enables us to uncover hidden patterns, identify correlations, make predictions and ultimately make more informed decisions.

One of the main advantages of multivariate analysis is its ability to handle complex data sets that involve several variables. Traditionally, univariate analysis focuses on one variable at a time, disregarding the potential interactions among other variables. By contrast, multivariate analysis considers the relationships among multiple variables simultaneously, providing a more comprehensive picture.

Multivariate analysis techniques can be broadly classified into two categories: exploratory analysis and confirmatory analysis. Exploratory multivariate analysis aims to uncover patterns and relationships in the dataset without any preconceived hypotheses. Techniques like principal component analysis (PCA), factor analysis and cluster analysis fall under this category. These methods help researchers explore the underlying structure of the data, reduce its dimensionality and identify groups or clusters.

Factor analysis is a statistical method used to identify underlying factors or dimensions in a set of observed variables. It is commonly used in psychology, sociology, marketing research and other fields where researchers aim to understand the latent structure or underlying concepts in a large set of data. Factor analysis offers several advantages over other data reduction techniques. It allows researchers to reduce the dimensionality of a large dataset, making it easier to analyse and interpret. It also provides insights into the interrelationships between variables, revealing underlying constructs that may not be apparent from the raw data.

In SEM, the underlying assumption is that variables can be decomposed into two main types: endogenous and exogenous variables. Endogenous variables are predicted by the other variables in the model, while exogenous variables are predictors in the model that are not predicted by other variables. SEM allows the researcher to estimate the strength and direction of relationships between endogenous and exogenous variables, ultimately providing a comprehensive understanding of the system under investigation.

SEM consists of three main components: the measurement model, the structural model and the identification strategy:

- The **measurement model** focuses on establishing the relationships between observed variables and their corresponding latent constructs. Latent constructs are often variables that affect the observed variables. Through the measurement model, researchers can assess how well the observed variables measure the latent constructs.
- The **structural model** explores the relationships between the latent constructs. It examines how the latent constructs influence each other directly or indirectly through observed variables. These relationships are represented by path coefficients, which indicate the magnitude and direction of the influence. By evaluating the strength of these paths, SEM allows researchers to understand the causal relationships and interactions between various constructs.

- The **identification strategy** ensures that the parameters estimated in the model possess a unique solution. Without identification, different model specifications could yield equivalent results, making it impossible to determine the true relationships between variables. Various identification strategies, such as setting anchor variables or using measurement model constraints, can be applied to achieve a unique solution.

SEM is widely used in behaviour and social sciences to study complex constructs such as behavioural traits. Researchers can evaluate the relationships between latent factors and observed variables to gain insights into the underlying dynamics of these constructs.

The advantages of using SEM are:

- **Simultaneous analysis**: One of the key advantages of SEM is its ability to analyse multiple relationships simultaneously. By considering multiple constructs and their interconnections, SEM offers a holistic understanding of complex systems.

- **Model fit assessment**: SEM provides explicit measures for evaluating the fit between the hypothesized model and the observed data. This allows researchers to determine the effectiveness of their models and make necessary adjustments, ensuring the validity and reliability of their findings.

- **Mediation and moderation analysis**: SEM allows researchers to evaluate mediation and moderation effects. Mediation analysis assesses the mechanisms through which one variable influences another, while moderation analysis examines how the relationship between two variables varies depending on a third variable. These analyses help unravel the underlying processes and provide a deeper understanding of complex systems.

One of the most significant issues with SEM is model misspecification. Hence the plethora of case studies in Part 2 of this book aiming at gaining experience in how to interpret it, particularly in the workplace culture context.

Steps for developing a path analysis using SEM modelling

To gain further practical understanding, let us explore a workplace culture example. This is a large financial institution interested in knowing how to drive proactive risk management and six key organizational culture outcomes, as follows:

- Living our Values
- Recognition
- Purpose
- Resilience
- Psychological Safety
- Development for the Future

The outcomes for proactive risk management were:

- Taking Ownership
- Collaboration
- Risk Anticipation
- Risk Avoidance
- Proactive Learning

The organization had a recent outcome metric measure for all the outcomes, and had launched behavioural measurement for circa 10,500 with a response rate of 4,622, representing a 44 per cent completion rate.

As described in Chapter 6, the methodology for predictive analytics was applied to each of the targeted themes using multiple regression analysis to find the most parsimonious model. Each theme ended up with a list of predictive behaviours. I will exhibit those behaviours later in this chapter; for now, let us focus on the new learning – that is, path analysis using SEM.

Step 1

Build a correlation coefficient table for all the thematic outcomes as per Table 10.1. This will show the relationship (if any) between all the outcomes. You will see the outcome titles and correlation value against other outcomes. The outcomes are not arranged in any order, and at this stage we are not building any hypothesis, we are just exploring the relationships between the outcomes (if any).

TABLE 10.1 Correlation analysis for all provided outcomes

	Collaboration	Management Role?	Living our Values	Recognition	Purpose	Resilience	Psychological Safety	Development	Risk Anticipation	Risk Avoidance	Proactive Learning	Taking Ownership
Collaboration	1	−0.036	0.177	0.232	0.189	0.186	0.225	0.14	0.343	0.339	0.325	0.409
Management Role?	−0.036	1	0.005	−0.011	0.137	0.104	0.041	0.095	0.003	0.029	−0.06	−0.021
Living our Values	0.177	0.005	1	0.317	0.145	0.256	0.325	0.126	0.204	0.181	0.152	0.175
Recognition	0.232	−0.011	0.317	1	0.167	0.319	0.419	0.193	0.211	0.236	0.232	0.244
Purpose	0.189	0.137	0.145	0.167	1	0.224	0.199	0.232	0.154	0.157	0.159	0.187
Resilience	0.186	0.104	0.256	0.319	0.224	1	0.407	0.156	0.159	0.195	0.199	0.17
Psychological Safety	0.225	0.041	0.325	0.419	0.199	0.407	1	0.164	0.213	0.236	0.228	0.227
Development	0.14	0.095	0.126	0.193	0.232	0.156	0.164	1	0.129	0.126	0.162	0.142
Risk Anticipation	0.343	0.003	0.204	0.211	0.154	0.159	0.213	0.129	1	0.436	0.249	0.455
Risk Avoidance	0.339	0.029	0.181	0.236	0.157	0.195	0.236	0.126	0.436	1	0.24	0.448
Proactive Learning	0.325	−0.06	0.152	0.232	0.159	0.199	0.228	0.162	0.249	0.24	1	0.308
Taking Ownership	0.409	−0.021	0.175	0.244	0.187	0.17	0.227	0.142	0.455	0.448	0.308	1

As a reminder, the correlation coefficient scale is from −1 to +1. A correlation coefficient greater than zero indicates a positive relationship, while a value less than zero signifies a negative relationship. A value close to zero indicates a weak relationship between the two variables being compared. A correlation coefficient of 0.2 and above will be interesting for our purposes.

From the generated table, we are interested in a correlation of 0.2 and above (refer back to Chapter 6 re correlational effect size). You will also notice that the second metric, Management Role?, is irrelevant as it has no correlation to any other outcome – the largest correlation is 0.137 to the Purpose outcome.

Step 2

Calculate the mean correlation for each outcome. Based on the mean correlation value, we can assign an impact rank value as shown in Table 10.2.

Step 3

Using the Table 10.2 correlation analysis, remove any correlation values below 0.2 and recalculate the mean as per Table 10.3. Essentially, this step will reduce the data noise and you can now start developing the real connections. The cell shading is applied to help you see the most and least correlations.

Step 4

In each column, we can remove all values that are less than the column's mean. For example, for the Collaboration column, we can see that the correlation of 0.232 with Recognition and 0.225 with Psychological Safety are both less than 0.312 (the average correlation for Collaboration). Then by removing these values we can see clearly which criteria are most correlated to Collaboration. We repeat this process for each column.

Consequently, we obtain Table 10.4. Calculate the resulting mean and rank for each column.

Step 5

To find our path starting point, we need to compute the average mean correlations and rankings from the three matrices of steps 2, 3 and 4 as per Table 10.5.

TABLE 10.2 Correlation analysis with the mean for each outcome calculated and ranked

	Collab-oration	Manage-ment Role?	Living our Values	Recog-nition	Purpose	Resilience	Psycho-logical Safety	Devel-opment	Risk Anticipa-tion	Risk Avoidance	Proactive Learning	Taking Ownership
Collaboration		-0.036	0.177	0.232	0.189	0.186	0.225	0.14	0.343	0.339	0.325	0.409
Management Role?	-0.036		0.005	-0.011	0.137	0.104	0.041	0.095	0.003	0.029	-0.06	-0.021
Living our Values	0.177	0.005		0.317	0.145	0.256	0.325	0.126	0.204	0.181	0.152	0.175
Recognition	0.232	-0.011	0.317		0.167	0.319	0.419	0.193	0.211	0.236	0.232	0.244
Purpose	0.189	0.137	0.145	0.167		0.224	0.199	0.232	0.154	0.157	0.159	0.187
Resilience	0.186	0.104	0.256	0.319	0.224		0.407	0.156	0.159	0.195	0.199	0.17
Psychological Safety	0.225	0.041	0.325	0.419	0.199	0.407		0.164	0.213	0.236	0.228	0.227
Development	0.14	0.095	0.126	0.193	0.232	0.156	0.164		0.129	0.126	0.162	0.142
Risk Anticipation	0.343	0.003	0.204	0.211	0.154	0.159	0.213	0.129		0.436	0.249	0.455
Risk Avoidance	0.339	0.029	0.181	0.236	0.157	0.195	0.236	0.126	0.436		0.24	0.448
Proactive Learning	0.325	-0.06	0.152	0.232	0.159	0.199	0.228	0.162	0.249	0.24		0.308
Taking Ownership	0.409	-0.021	0.175	0.244	0.187	0.17	0.227	0.142	0.455	0.448	0.308	
Mean	0.230	0.026	0.188	0.233	0.177	0.216	0.244	0.151	0.232	0.238	0.199	0.249
Rank	6	12	9	4	10	7	2	11	5	3	8	1

TABLE 10.3 Correlation analysis with all values less than 0.2 eliminated

	Collaboration	Management Role?	Living our Values	Recognition	Purpose	Resilience	Psychological Safety	Development	Risk Anticipation	Risk Avoidance	Proactive Learning	Taking Ownership
Collaboration				0.232			0.225		0.343	0.339	0.325	0.409
Management Role?												
Living our Values				0.317					0.204			
Recognition	0.232		0.317			0.319	0.419		0.211	0.236	0.232	0.244
Purpose						0.224		0.232				
Resilience			0.256	0.319	0.224		0.407					
Psychological Safety	0.225		0.325	0.419		0.407			0.213	0.236	0.228	0.227
Development					0.232							
Risk Anticipation	0.343		0.204	0.211			0.213			0.436	0.249	0.455
Risk Avoidance	0.339			0.236			0.236		0.436		0.24	0.448
Proactive Learning	0.325			0.232			0.228		0.249	0.24		0.308
Taking Ownership	0.409			0.244			0.227		0.455	0.448	0.308	
Mean	0.312		0.276	0.276	0.228	0.302	0.285	0.232	0.302	0.3230	0.264	0.349
Rank	3		8	7	11	5	6	10	4	2	9	1

TABLE 10.4 Correlation analysis with values less than the column mean removed

	Collaboration	Management Role?	Living our Values	Recognition	Purpose	Resilience	Psychological Safety	Development	Risk Anticipation	Risk Avoidance	Proactive Learning	Taking Ownership
Collaboration									0.343	0.339	0.325	0.409
Management Role?												
Living our Values				0.317			0.325					
Recognition			0.317			0.319	0.419					
Purpose								0.232				
Resilience				0.319			0.407					
Psychological Safety			0.325	0.419		0.407						
Development					0.232							
Risk Anticipation	0.343									0.436		0.455
Risk Avoidance	0.339								0.436			0.448
Proactive Learning	0.325											0.308
Taking Ownership	0.409								0.455	0.448	0.308	
Mean	0.354	0.321	0.352	0.232	0.363	0.384	0.232	0.411	0.408	0.317	0.405	
Rank	6	–	8	7	10.5	5	4	10.5	1	2	9	3

TABLE 10.5 The computed average mean correlations and rankings

		Collaboration	Management Role?	Living our Values	Recognition	Purpose	Resilience	Psychological Safety	Development	Risk Anticipation	Risk Avoidance	Proactive Learning	Taking Ownership
Step 2	Mean	0.230	0.026	0.188	0.233	0.177	0.216	0.244	0.151	0.232	0.238	0.199	0.249
	Rank	6	12	9	4	10	7	2	11	5	3	8	1
Step 3	Mean	0.312		0.276	0.276	0.228	0.302	0.285	0.232	0.302	0.323	0.264	0.349
	Rank	3		8	7	11	5	6	10	4	2	9	1
Step 4	Mean	0.354		0.321	0.352	0.232	0.363	0.384	0.232	0.411	0.408	0.317	0.405
	Rank	6	–	8	7	10.5	5	4	10.5	1	2	9	3
	Avg of mean correlations	0.299	0.026	0.261	0.287	0.212	0.293	0.304	0.205	0.315	0.323	0.260	0.334
	Avg rank	5.00	12.00	8.33	6.00	10.50	5.67	4.00	10.50	3.33	2.33	8.67	1.67

The column with the resulting highest mean correlation coefficient which will have also have the closest value to 1 in our resulting mean ranking will be the starting point. In this example it's the Taking Ownership outcome. Our first key practical outcome insight: we must get this outcome to manifest before we progress.

Step 6

We can now continue to build our path. To find the next outcome, we can use Table 10.4 from step 4 and look to see the highest corresponding correlation coefficient to another outcome. See the resulting Table 10.6 – the next outcome to manifest in our path is Risk Anticipation.

We can start drawing our resulting diagrammatic path – see Figure 10.1.

To continue with our path, we can remove what we have already used and look at the highest corresponding correlation coefficient to Risk Anticipation. See Table 10.7 showing that Risk Avoidance is our next outcome in the path analysis.

We can now also continue drawing the path – see Figure 10.2.

For our next outcome, we will need to look at the highest corresponding correlation coefficient to the Risk Avoidance outcome, and as before we can remove what we have already used. Table 10.8 shows that the next outcome is Collaboration.

The resulting diagrammatic path can be seen in Figure 10.3.

Let us look at the next outcome in our risk path. Having removed what we have already used in our path, let us examine the Collaboration column. The next outcome with highest correlation coefficient is Proactive Learning, as shown in Table 10.9.

FIGURE 10.1 The first two outcomes in the risk path analysis

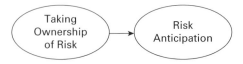

TABLE 10.6 The path starting point outcome that has the highest corresponding correlation coefficient to another outcome

	Collaboration	Management Role?	Living our Values	Recognition	Purpose	Resilience	Psychological Safety	Development	Risk Anticipation	Risk Avoidance	Proactive Learning	Taking Ownership
Collaboration									0.343	0.339	0.325	0.409
Management Role?												
Living our Values				0.317			0.325					
Recognition			0.317			0.319	0.419					
Purpose								0.232				
Resilience				0.319			0.407					
Psychological Safety			0.325	0.419		0.407						
Development					0.232							
Risk Anticipation	0.343									0.436		0.455
Risk Avoidance	0.339								0.436			0.448
Proactive Learning	0.325											0.308
Taking Ownership	0.409								0.455	0.448	0.308	

Highest outcome which corresponds to this correlation

TABLE 10.7 Risk Avoidance is our next outcome in the path analysis as it has the highest correlation coefficient with Risk Anticipation

	Collaboration	Management Role?	Living our Values	Recognition	Purpose	Resilience	Psychological Safety	Development	Risk Anticipation	Risk Avoidance	Proactive Learning	Taking Ownership
Collaboration									0.343	0.339	0.325	0.409
Management Role?												
Living our Values				0.317			0.325					
Recognition			0.317			0.319	0.419					
Purpose								0.232				
Resilience				0.319			0.407					
Psychological Safety			0.325	0.419		0.407						
Development					0.232							
Risk Anticipation	0.343									0.436		0.455
Risk Avoidance	0.339								0.436			0.448
Proactive Learning	0.325											0.308
Taking Ownership	0.409								0.455	0.448	0.308	

Highest outcome which corresponds to this correlation

TABLE 10.8 The highest corresponding correlation coefficient outcome to Risk Avoidance is Collaboration

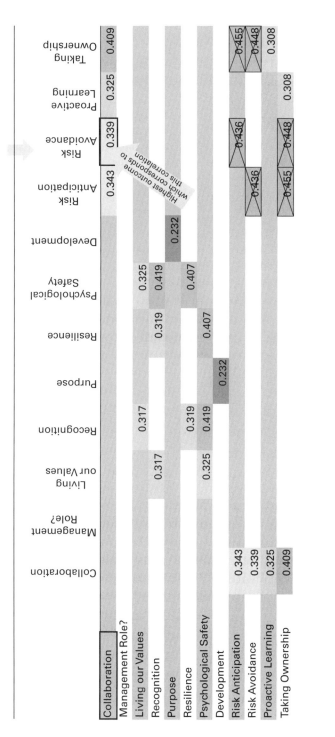

FIGURE 10.2 The sequence of how the three outcomes should manifest in the risk path analysis

FIGURE 10.3 The sequence of how the four outcomes should manifest in the risk path analysis

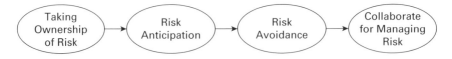

The resulting path analysis diagram can be seen in Figure 10.4.

All good so far – we can now once again remove what we have used so far and move to the Proactive Learning outcome column to see which is the corresponding outcome with the highest correlation coefficient. As you will see from Table 10.10, we have come to a dead end! But we do have more outcomes with a usable correlation coefficient. What is happening?

This means that our outcomes correlation matrix has more than one path. It is interesting to note that any outcomes regarding risk have all attributed to the risk management path, and we have come to this conclusion without any assumptions, illustrating the power of SEM for path analysis.

So, what have we learnt about our risk path for this institution? Examining Figure 10.4 tells us that the ability to take ownership is key as it's the starting point. The organization aces this outcome, which will positively impact their ability to anticipate risk issues before unforeseen events happen. They can now continue to improve as they drive down the path. This path is critical as each outcome metric will inform an organization where they are down the path, and of course which behaviours they need to focus on to improve.

Furthermore, and as an illustrative example of the power of path analysis insights, there is no point in focusing on the Proactive Learning for Risk outcome if they have not secured the Taking Ownership of Risk outcome.

TABLE 10.9 The highest corresponding correlation coefficient outcome to Collaboration is Proactive Learning

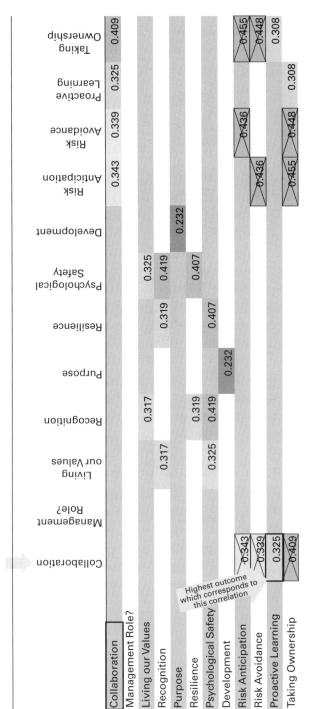

	Collaboration	Management Role?	Living our Values	Recognition	Purpose	Resilience	Psychological Safety	Development	Risk Anticipation	Risk Avoidance	Proactive Learning	Taking Ownership
Collaboration									0.343	0.339	0.325	0.409
Management Role?												
Living our Values				0.317			0.325					
Recognition			0.317			0.319	0.419					
Purpose								0.232				
Resilience				0.319			0.407					
Psychological Safety			0.325	0.419		0.407						
Development					0.232							
Risk Anticipation	0.343									0.436		0.455
Risk Avoidance	0.339								0.436			0.448
Proactive Learning	0.325											0.308
Taking Ownership	0.409								0.455	0.448	0.308	

Highest outcome which corresponds to this correlation

TABLE 10.10 Our first path has come to a dead end

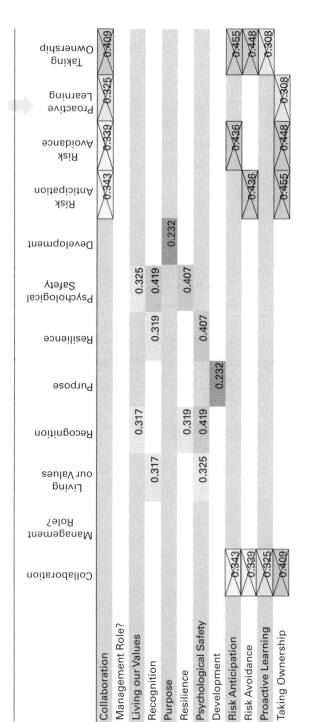

FIGURE 10.4 The sequence of how the five outcomes should manifest in the risk path analysis

As I mentioned earlier, I will come back to Figure 10.4 and add the behaviours. For now, let's develop our second path.

Step 7

To discover our second path, we will need to examine Table 10.5 from step 5 and remove the outcomes that formed our first path related to risk management. See resulting Table 10.11.

We will now need to find the highest remaining mean correlation coefficient (the result established from steps 2, 3 and 4); that should correspond to the average ranking nearest to 1 from the remaining outcomes. Your choice should fall on Psychological Safety as the starting point for the second path.

Back to the same process again. Look at the Psychological Safety outcome column and find out the corresponding outcome with the highest correlation coefficient, which is Recognition, as can be seen in Table 10.12.

We can also start drawing our second path, as seen in Figure 10.5.

Moving our focus to the Recognition outcome column, look at Table 10.13 and you will see that after removing what we have used already, the highest corresponding correlation coefficient outcome is Resilience.

So we can continue drawing our path – see Figure 10.6.

Next in line is the Resilience outcome column, and as you can see from Table 10.14, we have used both possible corresponding outcomes. However, step back to the Recognition outcome column and we will see that we still have one additional outcome with a very good corresponding correlation coefficient; that is the Living our Values outcome as circled in Table 10.14.

This means that Recognition drives two outcomes, as demonstrated in Figure 10.7.

If we remove Recognition and Living our Values, we have now reached a dead end, but we still have two outcomes with a good correlation coefficient. It seems we have a third path to develop.

TABLE 10.11 The computed average mean correlations and rankings, now with the first path outcomes removed

		Collaboration	Management Role?	Living our Values	Recognition	Purpose	Resilience	Psychological Safety	Development	Risk Anticipation	Risk Avoidance	Proactive Learning	Taking Ownership
Step 2	Mean	0.230	0.026	0.188	0.233	0.177	0.216	0.244	0.151	0.232	0.238	0.199	0.249
	Rank	6	12	9	4	10	7	2	11	5	3	8	1
Step 3	Mean	0.312		0.276	0.276	0.228	0.302	0.285	0.232	0.302	0.323	0.264	0.349
	Rank	3		8	7	11	5	6	10	4	2	9	1
Step 4	Mean	0.354		0.321	0.352	0.232	0.363	0.384	0.232	0.411	0.408	0.317	0.405
	Rank	6		8	7	10.5	5	4	10.5	1	2	9	3
	Avg of mean correlations	0.299	0.026	0.261	0.287	0.212	0.293	0.304	0.205	0.315	0.323	0.260	0.334
	Avg rank	5.00	12.00	8.33	6.00	10.50	5.67	4.00	10.50	3.33	2.33	8.67	1.67

TABLE 10.12 The highest corresponding correlation coefficient outcome to Psychological Safety is Recognition

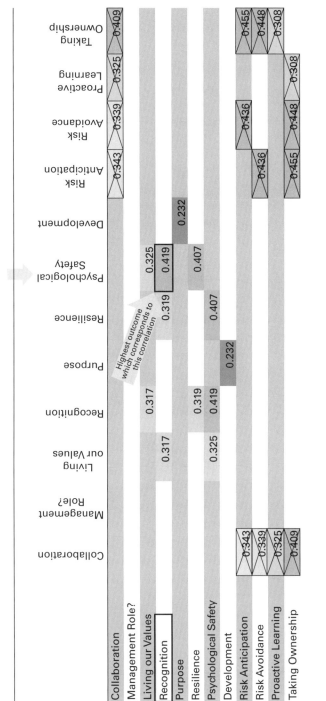

TABLE 10.13 The highest corresponding correlation coefficient outcome to Recognition is Resilience

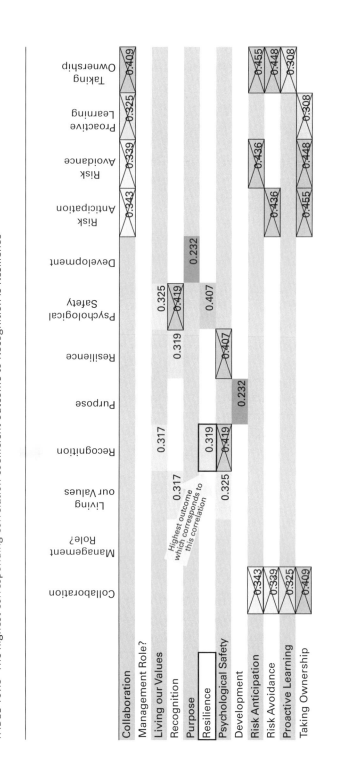

TABLE 10.14 The highest corresponding correlation coefficient outcomes have both been already used in the path

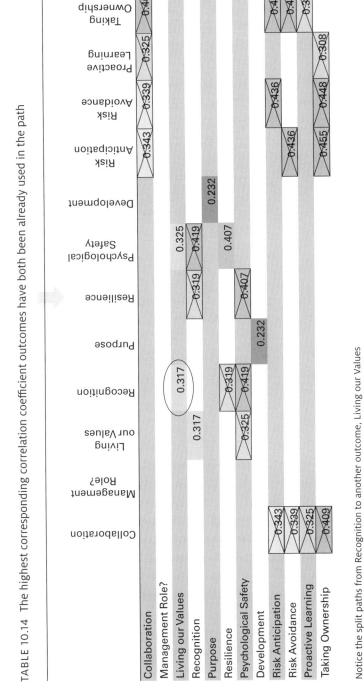

Notice the split paths from Recognition to another outcome, Living our Values

FIGURE 10.5 The outcome sequence for the second developing path

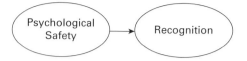

FIGURE 10.6 The sequence of the second developing path for the outcomes

FIGURE 10.7 The outcome sequence for the second full path

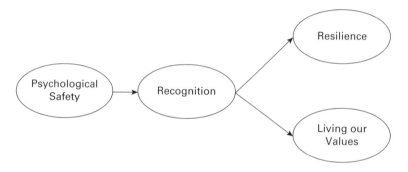

Step 8

I am sure by now you have got this process all sorted! So back to Table 10.5 from step 5 and remove the outcomes that formed our first and second paths. See resulting Table 10.15.

As before, we will now need to find the highest remaining mean correlation coefficient (the result established from steps 2, 3 and 4), which should correspond to the average ranking nearest to 1 from the remaining outcomes. Your choice should fall on Purpose as the starting point for the third path as the mean correlation coefficient is higher than for the Development outcome, although they both share a similar ranking.

Since we only have two outcomes, the third path is easy to draw without any further steps – see Figure 10.8.

TABLE 10.15 The computed average mean correlations and rankings, now with the first and second path outcomes removed

		Collaboration	Management Role?	Living our Values	Recognition	Purpose	Resilience	Psychological Safety	Development	Risk Anticipation	Risk Avoidance	Proactive Learning	Taking Ownership
Step 2	Mean	0.230	0.026	0.188	0.233	0.177	0.216	0.244	0.151	0.232	0.238	0.199	0.249
	Rank	6	12	9	4	10	7	2	11	5	3	8	1
Step 3	Mean	0.312		0.276	0.276	0.228	0.302	0.285	0.232	0.302	0.323	0.264	0.349
	Rank	3		8	7	11	5	6	10	4	2	9	1
Step 4	Mean	0.354		0.321	0.352	0.232	0.363	0.384	0.232	0.411	0.408	0.317	0.405
	Rank	6		8	7	10.5	5	4	10.5	1	2	9	3
	Avg of mean correlations	0.299	0.026	0.261	0.287	0.212	0.293	0.304	0.205	0.315	0.323	0.260	0.334
	Avg rank	5.00	12.00	8.33	6.00	10.50	5.67	4.00	10.50	3.33	2.33	8.67	1.67

FIGURE 10.8 The outcome sequence for the third path

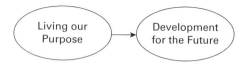

FIGURE 10.9 The first path with the behaviours now included

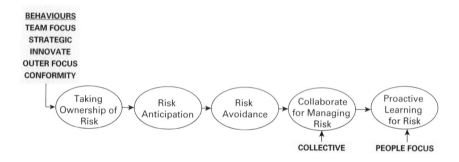

FIGURE 10.10 The second path with the behaviours now included

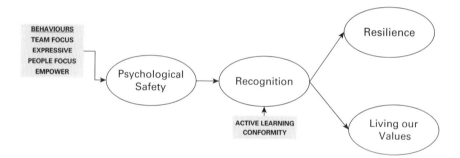

I am sure by now you may feel that we have been on a marathon with SEM and path analysis, but I hope you can see its importance. It can significantly inform which interventions to invest in as outcomes will drive other outcomes, and it should stop erratic organization interventions that will not yield any benefit and may even fail.

You may have also noticed from the developed paths that for this institution, their risk management and workplace culture are separate paths. This did myth-bust for them, as leaders assumed 'if we live our culture, we will manage our risk'. Hmm – no! These are separate paths you need to monitor and drive.

FIGURE 10.11 The third path with the behaviours now included

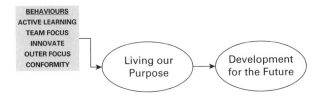

What about the behaviours that predict this path? As I did promise, I will now add behaviours to our three paths. Remember the behaviours were established using the same process outlined in Chapter 6.

Path one behaviours are Team Focus, Strategic, Innovate, Outer Focus and Conformity. These behaviours are critical for the starting point, and if absent for People or Place (or both), they must be the focus for intervention design and implementation. These behaviours will take you down the path to Collaborate for Risk, which will need another behaviour, Collective, and to achieve the final outcome, Proactive Learning for Risk, the behaviour People Focus needs to be present.

Figure 10.9 illustrates the first path with the behaviours now included.

Consider the first path, which is the risk management one. Here is a shock for you: Innovate is one of the predictor behaviours. You may have never thought so – again, the dangers of assumptions and hypotheses with no evidence. For this organization, Conformity, Strategic and Team Focus are present behaviours. Innovate is absent for People and Place, needing interventions to address capability, opportunity and motivation. Outer Focus is absent at the Place, needing opportunity and motivation-type interventions. Looking further into the path, Collective is present; however, People Focus is absent for the People, hence a capability-type intervention is required.

So, the message to this organization has great clarity and simplicity now. Don't chase or even invest in driving all your outcomes in Figure 10.9. You need to achieve your starting point first, as by improving the two behaviours, you gain and improve all your sequential outcomes till you arrive at the final outcome and another behaviour needs improvement. Before this actionable insight, the organization was simply trying to address each outcome on its own without the knowledge of the behavioural leading indicators.

FIGURE 10.12 The behavioural leading indicators and the outcomes they drive over the three paths

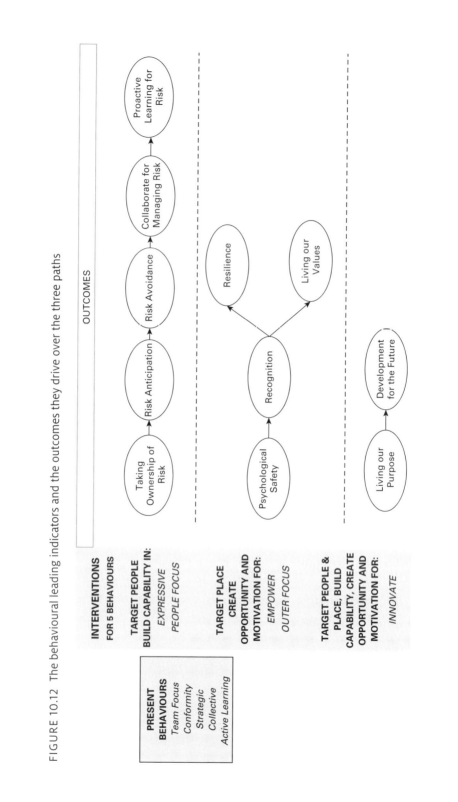

Let's look at the behaviours for the second path, Figure 10.10 reveals that four behaviours are driving the starting point. It shares one behaviour with the first path, that is Team Focus, which as you know already is a present behaviour; however, the other three behaviours all need attention. Empower is absent at the Place, and Expressive and People Focus are both absent for the People. Ace the starting point behaviours and you've got the entire path in sequence, as Active Learning and Conformity are both present.

It's fascinating to look closely at this path, to see how important Psychological Safety is as an outcome. Without achieving that goal, Recognition and Resilience will simply not happen and walking the talk by Living our Values will be impossible.

Interestingly, this organization thought that Living our Values would be the starting point – another reason not to assume, as workplace culture is so unique! Basically, if you don't have Psychological Safety and Recognition, you will not get to Living our Values.

The third path behaviours are illustrated in Figure 10.11. We have seen all these behaviours already as they are shared with the two previous paths. Innovate is absent for Place and People, and Outer Focus is absent at the Place. It's interesting to note that Innovate is part of living their purpose as an organization, and there is no point in future employee development if you do not live your purpose first!

For the final part of this chapter, we can now analyse how the behavioural leading indicators will help in shifting the dial for multiple outcomes. Ten behaviours in total drive the three paths; five are present and five need intervention design, planning and implementation. Figure 10.12 illustrates the return on investment for this organization as they focus on the five behaviours for improvement.

Although Figure 10.12 shows you the number of outcome gains by category, it does not show you by how much. Interesting questions for each outcome would be 'What is the likelihood for success?' and 'What is the likely return on investment?' – questions that will be answered in the next chapter for this exact example.

11

Simplifying the actionable insights and understanding ROI

In today's data-driven organizational environment, showcasing the return on investment (ROI) of a project or initiative has become essential. Executives and stakeholders need concrete evidence that their investment will yield positive outcomes. Statistics offer a reliable and tangible means of demonstrating ROI. In previous chapters I have already built the case for leading indicators and predictive analytics, but as you may remember from Chapter 6, reading and interpreting regression analysis can be complex and may take away from the insight's gravitas.

You will already know that to build predictive analytics, we need leading and lagging indicators. In the context of workplace culture, leading indicators are the valid and scientific behaviour measurement of the People and the Place. Lagging indicators include any outcome, sentiment or opinion data, and we also discussed that per workplace culture theme, it's important to examine multiple lagging indicators to validate the predictive analytics process.

Multiple regression analysis provides us with interesting and actionable insights as it produces a restricted set of nested behaviours that drive multiple outcomes across multiple themes. Understanding the regression analysis entails looking at multiple variables to articulate how good the resulting model is. As a reminder, that included the following:

- **Multiple R**: the correlation coefficient that measures the strength of a linear relationship between two variables. The correlation coefficient can be any value between −1 and 1, and its absolute value indicates the relationship strength. The larger the absolute value, the stronger the relationship:

    o 1 means a strong positive relationship.

- o −1 means a strong negative relationship.
- o 0 means no relationship at all.
- **Adjusted R square**: the R square adjusted for the number of independent variables in the model. You will want to use this value instead of R square for multiple regression analysis.
- **Standard error**: another goodness-of-fit measure that shows the precision of your regression analysis – the smaller the number, the more certain you can be about your regression equation. While R square represents the percentage of the dependent variables variance that is explained by the model, standard error is an absolute measure that shows the average distance that the data points fall from the regression line.
- **Significance F**: the P-value of F. The lower this value, the higher the significance of this model.
- **Assessing model fit (residual)**: residual plots help determine whether the linear regression model is an appropriate fit for the data. If the residuals are randomly scattered around the horizontal axis, it indicates that the model is a good fit.
- **Model coefficients**: these enable you to build a prediction; basically, how quickly the outcome will improve by changing the input, also known as the beta (β) coefficient. The beta describes the slope of the line for the outcome prediction.

As you can see, it can be a complex process to explain how good the prediction is and what is the likely ROI.

Since I have just mentioned the word 'likely' in the context of ROI, I had better explain! In regression analysis, we are trying to articulate the nature of the causative relationship between the leading and lagging indicators, if indeed the causative relationship exists; hence, what is the likely magnitude of gain from changing the leading indicator? In actual statistical terms we cannot surmise the exact gain, only the likelihood of increase or decrease in the lagging indicators.

So, is there a way to show the predictive power without having to explain to the audience all the regression analysis variables? Is there a way to bring the story to life in a simple diagram or plot? The good news is that you can, with something called the 'odds ratio'. This process follows regression analysis to produce the restricted nested behaviours.

Odds ratio

The odds ratio is a statistical measure used to determine the association between two events or variables. It is commonly used in medical and social sciences research to assess the strength and direction of an association between exposure to a risk factor and the likelihood of developing a disease or experiencing an outcome.

The odds ratio is calculated by comparing the odds of an event occurring in one group to the odds of the same event occurring in another group. It is commonly denoted as OR and is expressed as a ratio of two odds.

To illustrate how the odds ratio works, let's consider an example. Suppose a study aims to investigate the association between smoking and lung cancer. The researchers divide participants into two groups: smokers and non-smokers. They then calculate the odds of developing lung cancer in each group.

Let's say the odds of developing lung cancer in the smoker group are 0.3 (meaning that for every one case of lung cancer, there are three non-cases), and the odds in the non-smoker group are 0.1 (meaning for every one case of lung cancer, there are nine non-cases). The odds ratio would be $(0.3/0.1) = 3$.

The interpretation of the odds ratio depends on its value. If the odds ratio is 1, it suggests no association between the exposure and the outcome. If the odds ratio is greater than 1, it indicates a positive association, meaning the exposure increases the likelihood of the outcome. In our example, an odds ratio of 3 implies that smokers are three times more likely to develop lung cancer than non-smokers.

On the other hand, if the odds ratio is less than 1, it suggests a negative or protective association. For instance, an odds ratio of 0.5 would mean that the exposure decreases the likelihood of the outcome by half.

It is important to note that the odds ratio only provides information on the association between the exposure and outcome and does not establish causality. It's the regression analysis that provides the information that we need about which behaviours are the leading indicators and what are the outcomes that they influence. This is why the odds ratio in our context will be calculated after the regression analysis.

Specifically, for our purpose, odds ratio is an easy way to represent the likelihood of an outcome based on the absence and/or presence of a nested behaviour model to show how good the predictive model is.

To apply the odds ratio method, we will arrange the behaviours into four quartiles, and count the number of outcome occurrences per nested model quartile (remember, the nested behavioural model is the result from the regression analysis). On the behavioural scale of zero to five, the quartiles are defined as:

- 0 to 1.25 (less than or equal to)
- 1.25 to 2.5
- 2.5 to 3.75
- 3.75 to 5

Let us look at the step-by-step approach to developing an odds ratio for a specific outcome. In this illustrative example, the context is a small engineering organization with outcome data for classroom-type training and learning that includes simulation for incident management. Having deployed the CultureScope online diagnostic for the full saturated 30 factors (15 dimensions) behavioural measurement, and conducted the hierarchical regression analysis, a restricted behavioural nested model was developed that includes two behaviours, Active Learning and People Focus. The model yielded a regression value of $R=0.51$ and total sample size of $n=94$: nothing new here, just explaining the context.

To generate the odds ratio you will need to follow these steps.

Step 1

Develop a table with the number of occurrences per the nested behavioural quartile (i.e. how people achieving the desired outcome are in the 4th quartile, that is 3.75 to 5; how many in the 3rd quartile, 2.5 to 3.75, etc.). See resulting Table 11.1.

The table shows the behavioural quartiles, as well as the number of occurrences for each quartile vs the best and least desired outcome (this outcome can be a metric or even qualitative). You can then divide the number of occurrences of the highest number by the lowest number, providing you with the odds ratio per quartile. For the first behavioural quartile, the least outcome column occurrence is higher than the best outcome occurrence, hence the odds ratio will be 4 divided by 2 = 2.

TABLE 11.1 The number of best and least outcome vs behavioural quartiles

Quartiles		Occurrences		Totals	Odds for	Odds against
		Least Outcome	Best Outcome			
1st Quartile	0 – 1.25	4	2	6		–2
2nd Quartile	1.25 – 2.5	5	14	19	2.80	
3rd Quartile	2.5 – 3.75	2	29	31	14.50	
4th Quartile	3.75 – 5	2	36	38	18.00	
	Totals	13	81	94		

However, you should designate a minus to this number as the best outcome value is less than the least outcome. Insert the value in the 'Odds against' column.

You can now repeat for each behavioural quartile, applying the same logic. As another working example for the 2nd behavioural quartile, the best outcome has more occurrence than the least outcome, so divide 14 by 5 = 2.8. Since more occurrences are for the best outcome, insert the value in the 'Odds for' column.

Step 2

You are now ready to draw the diagram to reflect Table 11.1, as per Figure 11.1 (odds ratio figures have been rounded for simplicity). We can now shift the story away from describing the predictive analytics insights using six variables to one compelling simple story. Where the behaviours' presence is in the upper fourth quartile, you are **18 times more likely to get the desired outcome**, and where the behaviours' presence is in the first quartile you are **two times less likely to achieve the outcome**. Now, that is far simpler language to answer the question: 'Why should anyone invest in the two behaviours?'.

FIGURE 11.1 The odds ratio per behavioural quartile vs likelihood of outcome occurrence

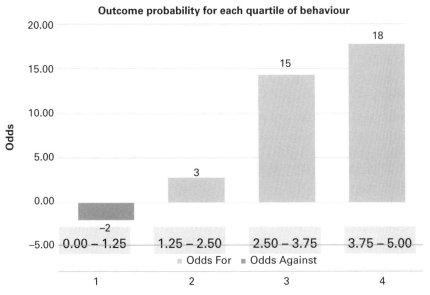

NOTE n=94, R=0.51. Behavioural factors are Active Learning and People Focus

To put this learning into practice, we can now apply an odds ratio to all the outcomes for the financial institution case study from the previous chapter. As a reminder, the behavioural measurement using CultureScope was deployed for around 10,500 employees, with a response rate of 4,622 representing a 44 per cent completion rate.

Let's now explore each outcomes odds ratio, and then we can look at the entire system.

> LIVING OUR VALUES
>
> Regression analysis for the saturated model led to the nested behaviours of Team Focus, People Focus, Conformity and Expressive with R=0.314 for this model. Figure 11.2 shows the odds ratio, and the interpretation is easy: this organization is almost 120 times more likely to live its values where these four behaviours are in the top quartile of their presence, and only twice as likely to live its values if these behaviours are in the first quartile of their presence.

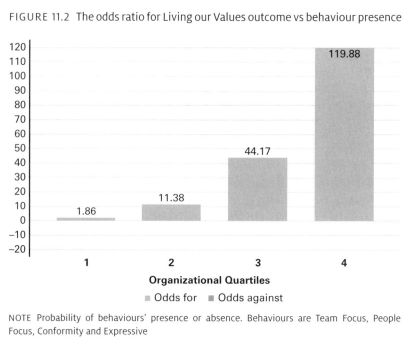

FIGURE 11.2 The odds ratio for Living our Values outcome vs behaviour presence

NOTE Probability of behaviours' presence or absence. Behaviours are Team Focus, People Focus, Conformity and Expressive

RECOGNITION

Regression analysis for the saturated model led to the nested behaviours of Team Focus, People Focus, Conformity and Active Learning with R=0.436 for this model. Figure 11.3 shows the odds ratio.

This organization is almost 190 times more likely to drive recognition where these four behaviours are in the top quartile of their presence, and three times less likely to drive recognition if these behaviours are in the first quartile of their presence.

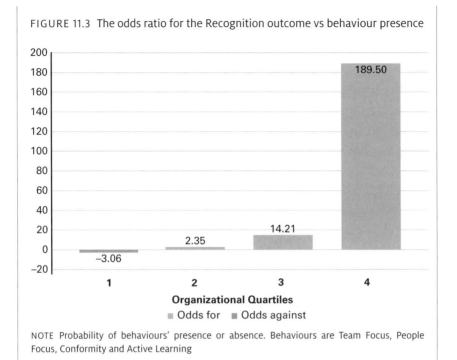

FIGURE 11.3 The odds ratio for the Recognition outcome vs behaviour presence

NOTE Probability of behaviours' presence or absence. Behaviours are Team Focus, People Focus, Conformity and Active Learning

PURPOSE

Regression analysis for the saturated model led to the nested behaviours of Team Focus, Outer Focus, Conformity, Innovate and Active Learning with R=0.302 for this model. Figure 11.4 displays the odds ratio.

This organization is almost 52 times more likely to live its purpose where these five behaviours are in the top quartile of their presence, and two times less likely to live its purpose if these behaviours are in the first quartile of their presence.

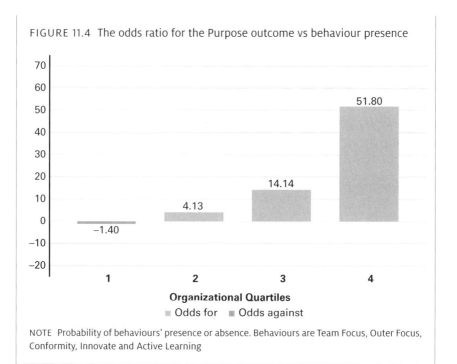

FIGURE 11.4 The odds ratio for the Purpose outcome vs behaviour presence

NOTE Probability of behaviours' presence or absence. Behaviours are Team Focus, Outer Focus, Conformity, Innovate and Active Learning

RESILIENCE

Regression analysis for the saturated model led to the nested behaviours of Team Focus, Empower, Conformity, People Focus and Active Learning with R=0.338 for this model. Figure 11.5 shows the odds ratio.

This organization is almost 53 times more likely to be resilient where these five behaviours are in the top quartile of their presence, and two times less likely to be resilient if these behaviours are in the first quartile of their presence.

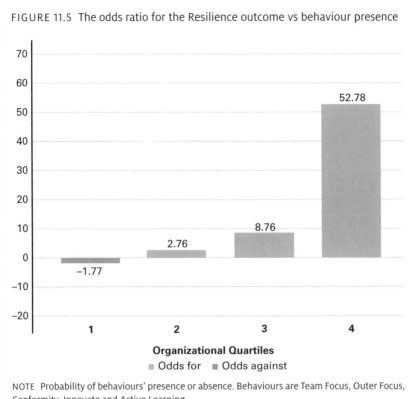

FIGURE 11.5 The odds ratio for the Resilience outcome vs behaviour presence

NOTE Probability of behaviours' presence or absence. Behaviours are Team Focus, Outer Focus, Conformity, Innovate and Active Learning

PSYCHOLOGICAL SAFETY

Regression analysis for the saturated model led to the nested behaviours of Team Focus, Empower, Expressive and People Focus with R=0.433 for this model. Figure 11.6 demonstrates the odds ratio.

This organization is almost 195 times more likely to drive psychological safety where these four behaviours are in the top quartile of their presence, and only one and a half times as likely to drive psychological safety if these behaviours are in the first quartile of their presence.

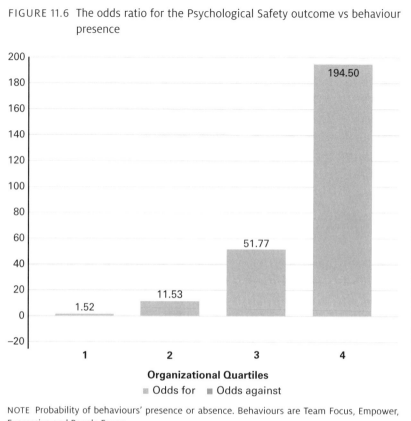

FIGURE 11.6 The odds ratio for the Psychological Safety outcome vs behaviour presence

NOTE Probability of behaviours' presence or absence. Behaviours are Team Focus, Empower, Expressive and People Focus

DEVELOPMENT FOR THE FUTURE

Regression analysis for the saturated model led to the nested behaviours of Active Learning and Team Focus with R=0.300 for this model. Figure 11.7 conveys the odds ratio.

This organization is 16 times more likely to drive talent development where these two behaviours are in the top quartile of their presence, and is only one time as likely to drive talent development if these behaviours are in the first quartile of their presence.

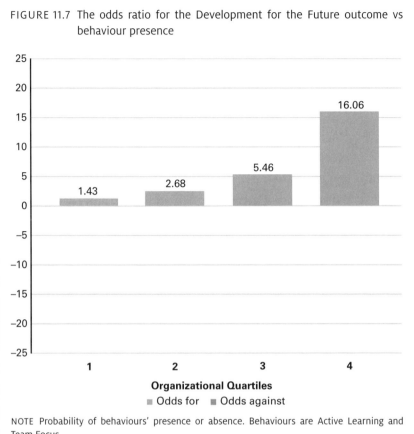

FIGURE 11.7 The odds ratio for the Development for the Future outcome vs behaviour presence

NOTE Probability of behaviours' presence or absence. Behaviours are Active Learning and Team Focus

TAKING OWNERSHIP OF RISK

Regression analysis for the saturated model led to the nested behaviours of Team Focus, Strategic, Outer Focus, Innovate and Conformity with R=0.371 for this model. Figure 11.8 shows the odds ratio.

This organization is almost 14 times more likely to drive taking ownership of risk where these five behaviours are in the top quartile of their presence, and two times less likely to drive taking ownership of risk if these behaviours are in the first quartile of their presence.

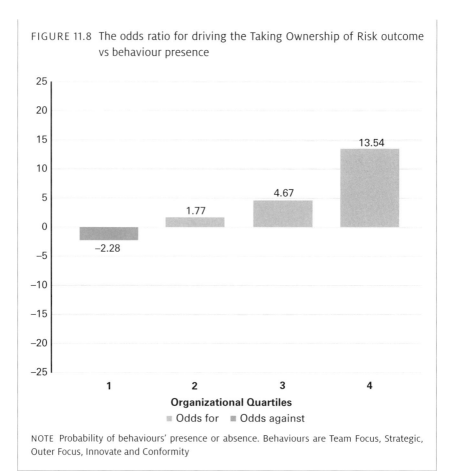

FIGURE 11.8 The odds ratio for driving the Taking Ownership of Risk outcome vs behaviour presence

NOTE Probability of behaviours' presence or absence. Behaviours are Team Focus, Strategic, Outer Focus, Innovate and Conformity

COLLABORATE FOR MANAGING RISK

Regression analysis for the saturated model led to the nested behaviours of Team Focus, Strategic, Outer Focus, Innovate and Collective with R=0.402 for this model. Figure 11.9 indicates the odds ratio.

This organization is almost nine times more likely to drive collaborative risk management where these five behaviours are in the top quartile of their presence, and three times less likely to drive collaborative risk management if these behaviours are in the first quartile of their presence.

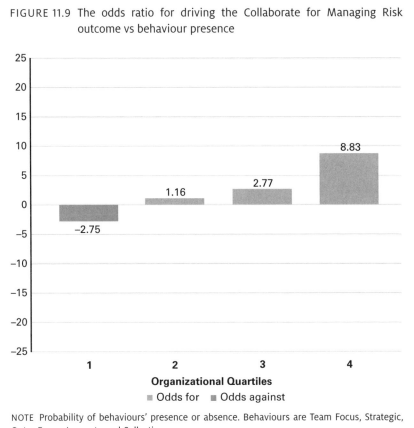

FIGURE 11.9 The odds ratio for driving the Collaborate for Managing Risk outcome vs behaviour presence

NOTE Probability of behaviours' presence or absence. Behaviours are Team Focus, Strategic, Outer Focus, Innovate and Collective

RISK ANTICIPATION

Regression analysis for the saturated model led to the nested behaviours of Team Focus, Strategic, Outer Focus, Innovate and Conformity with R=0.347 for this model. Figure 11.10 shows the odds ratio.

This organization is almost 18 times more likely to drive the anticipation of risk where these five behaviours are in the top quartile of their presence, and two times less likely to drive the anticipation of risk if these behaviours are in the first quartile of their presence.

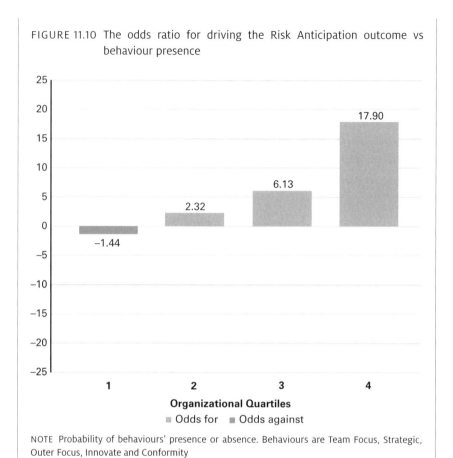

FIGURE 11.10 The odds ratio for driving the Risk Anticipation outcome vs behaviour presence

NOTE Probability of behaviours' presence or absence. Behaviours are Team Focus, Strategic, Outer Focus, Innovate and Conformity

RISK AVOIDANCE

Regression analysis for the saturated model led to the nested behaviours of Team Focus, Strategic, Outer Focus, Innovate and Conformity with R=0.331 for this model. Figure 11.11 displays the odds ratio.

This organization is 131 times more likely to drive risk avoidance where these five behaviours are in the top quartile of their presence, and two times less likely to drive risk avoidance if these behaviours are in the first quartile of their presence.

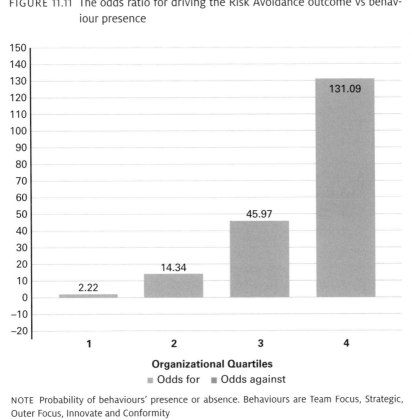

FIGURE 11.11 The odds ratio for driving the Risk Avoidance outcome vs behaviour presence

NOTE Probability of behaviours' presence or absence. Behaviours are Team Focus, Strategic, Outer Focus, Innovate and Conformity

PROACTIVE LEARNING FOR RISK

Regression analysis for the saturated model led to the nested behaviours of Team Focus, Strategic, People Focus, Innovate and Collective with R=0.414 for this model. Figure 11.12 shows the odds ratio.

This organization is almost four times more likely to drive proactive learning for risk where these five behaviours are in the top quartile of their presence, and almost five times less likely to drive proactive learning for risk if these behaviours are in the first quartile of their presence.

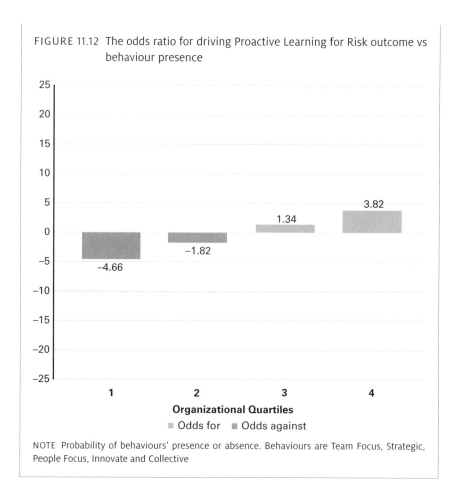

FIGURE 11.12 The odds ratio for driving Proactive Learning for Risk outcome vs behaviour presence

NOTE Probability of behaviours' presence or absence. Behaviours are Team Focus, Strategic, People Focus, Innovate and Collective

We have just been on a small marathon translating all the outcome predictive models into easier language using the odds ratio method. That is all well and good for each individual outcome, but can we show that insight as a whole system? Yes, we can; and as I have already illustrated in Figure 10.12, we can simply add the odds ratio to create Figure 11.13.

The detailed workings in this and Chapter 10 are so well summarized by Figure 11.13, and the key message is that you will get all your desired outcomes if you focus interventions on the five absent behaviours and look at that likelihood of success!

Demonstrating possible ROI using odds ratio statistics is crucial for stakeholders to assess the success and value of their investment. With the outlined method, you can effectively communicate the impact.

FIGURE 11.13 The behavioural leading indicators and the outcomes they drive as well as the likelihood of outcome manifesting over the three paths

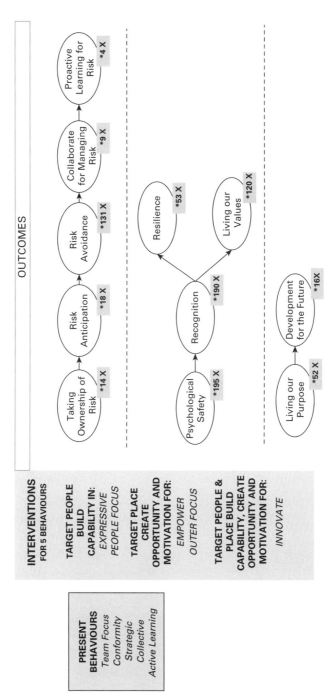

*Likelihood of this outcome manifesting from a behavioural intervention (i.e. 23 × more likely to manifest if you have the presence of behaviours and other outcomes)

Additionally, using comparative analysis and addressing limitations and risks enhances credibility when you present the likelihood of ROI, by showing: What will happen if we do nothing? How absent are these behaviours currently? And so on.

12

Cultural types

Difficult as it may be, we often find people trying to put labels on organizations. The label acts as a description of that culture; essentially it is typifying or characterizing the organization. Why would anyone find it useful to do that? Does it connect to the organization's aspired-to values? Does it help to communicate change from one workplace culture type to another?

Indeed, these are all valid questions and useful to answer, particularly after having gone through the process of predictive behaviour analytics. Workplace culture types will simply be an additional lens.

As I have already discussed in Chapter 4, the seven-year extensive research study I conducted provided the evidence and clarity that the 15 behavioural dimensions (30 behavioural factors in dichotomy – as outlined in Table 4.2) are mutually exclusive and collectively exhaustive, in a behavioural approach for measuring organizational culture. However, I have illustrated in previous chapters that we can create behavioural nested clusters as a behavioural map for organizational values, or how these clusters are developed as a result of predictive analytics.

Therefore, can we now create clusters of behaviours to represent workplace culture types? Yes, we can! And once we have done so, you can map the actual diagnostic results to the culture type clusters to typify your current versus target culture.

There are two layers to the culture types: primary and secondary.

Culture type – primary behavioural clusters

Figure 12.1 shows the behavioural clusters, five behaviours to a cluster, and the culture type is tagged for each generated cluster. The behaviours are organized in the outermost layer; the first inner layer has the culture type label.

FIGURE 12.1 The behaviours and related culture type for a behavioural cluster

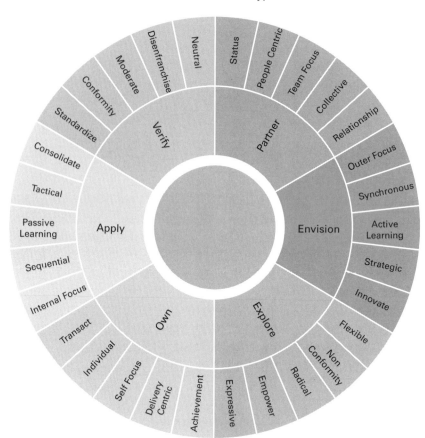

In the primary culture types, we have generated six clusters as follows:

1 **Partner type**: in this culture it's all about the people, the teams, relationships and external alliances.

2 **Envision type**: in this culture, it's all about driving innovation, being pioneering and working at a fast pace with competing properties and some errors along the way.

3 **Explore type**: in this culture, it's about providing empowerment and flexibility so the environment can drive exploration without boundaries.

4 **Own type**: in this culture, it's about owning it and making it happen. The focus is individual accountability and performance.

5 **Apply type**: in this culture, it's about applying what we have and know with no space or time for errors.

6 **Verify type**: in this culture, it's about command and control, following the rules, standards and processes and getting on with minimum noise.

CULTURAL TYPES

Organizations are very rarely one culture type, so the exercise here is to circle the present behaviours for Place and People. You will get two or more relevant clusters showing that workplace culture is type 'X' as the dominant type, with some aspects of type 'Y'. To demonstrate this concept, I will apply the present and the target behaviours for the financial institution results from the previous chapter to the culture cluster types:

- The present behaviours are Team Focus, Conformity, Strategic, Collective and Active Learning.
- The targeted behaviours are Expressive, People Focus, Empower, Outer Focus and Innovate.

The results are shown in Figure 12.2 and the present behaviours are circled indicating that the current culture types are Partner and Envision. The target culture type is a lot more focused on Envision, along with Partner and some Explore.

FIGURE 12.2 The culture types with the present and targeted behaviours marked

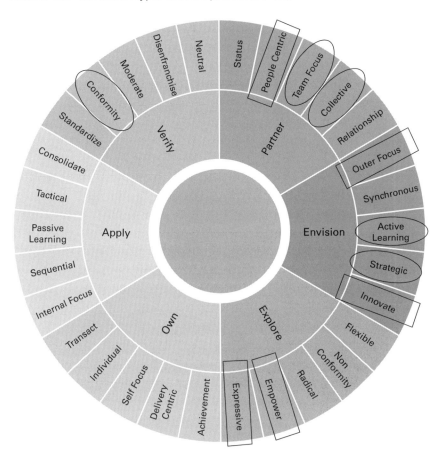

SOURCE Present behaviours are circled and targeted behaviours are squared

Culture type – secondary behavioural clusters

The secondary clusters are generated at the innermost circle, as demonstrated in the combined Figures 12.3, 12.4 and 12.5. This is another useful lens and can in fact show you how drastic the workplace culture type change is that is targeted.

The definitions for these dichotomies are as follows:

- **Consider First**: Taking time to think and learn, partnering to make it happen and ensure compliance; vs **Act First**: Explore and test on the go, own and deliver as we don't have time to consider, it's all about the here and now, we don't need to worry about compliance.

FIGURE 12.3 Consider First vs Act First culture types

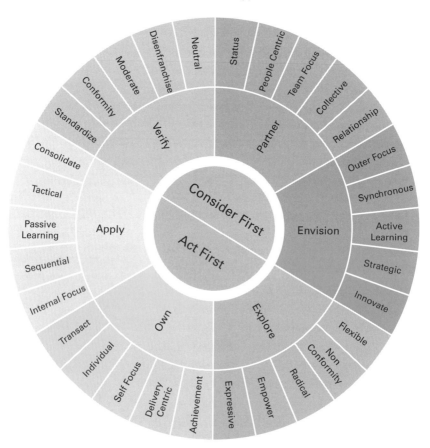

CULTURAL TYPES 125

FIGURE 12.4 Question and Listen vs Define the Answer culture types

- **Questions and Listen**: People and partner opinions are important; openness and collaboration are the best route for exploring, learning and pioneering for long-term success; vs **Define the Answer**: We know what needs to happen and no one needs to question it, it's down to us to make it happen now as time is of the essence, and as long as we are compliant, we will follow the tried-and-tested.

- **Navigate Possibility**: We are pioneers at what we do, and regardless of the market condition and competition, we will revolutionize regardless of market needs; we should not worry about compliance, it's all about being highly competitive and being first in the market; vs **Ensure Safety**: Tried-and-tested is the best way forward, being compliant, on time and to budget are critical factors, we don't need to invent it, let's seek alliances to deliver.

FIGURE 12.5 Ensure Safety vs Navigate Possibility culture types

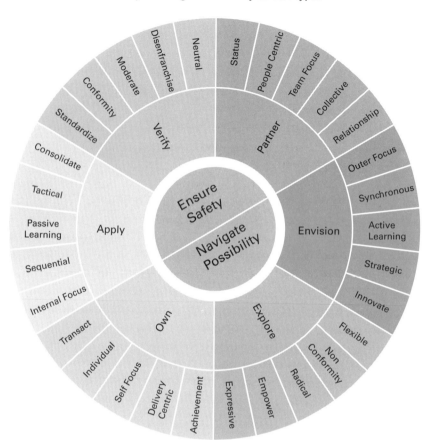

As you may have noticed, the secondary inner clusters are constructed from three primary clusters and 15 behavioural dimensions.

Using the same working example from the previous chapter, let's mark and then analyse the present behaviours and targeted behaviours for the inner secondary clusters. See Figures 12.6, 12.7 and 12.8.

In Figure 12.6 present behaviours indicates that the culture type is 'Consider First'. When taking the targeted behaviours into consideration, that still seems to be the dominant type.

Let us now examine the next secondary cluster in Figure 12.7. The target seems to be more of 'Question and Listen', so no change in culture type there.

CULTURAL TYPES   127

FIGURE 12.6 The Consider First vs Act First secondary culture types

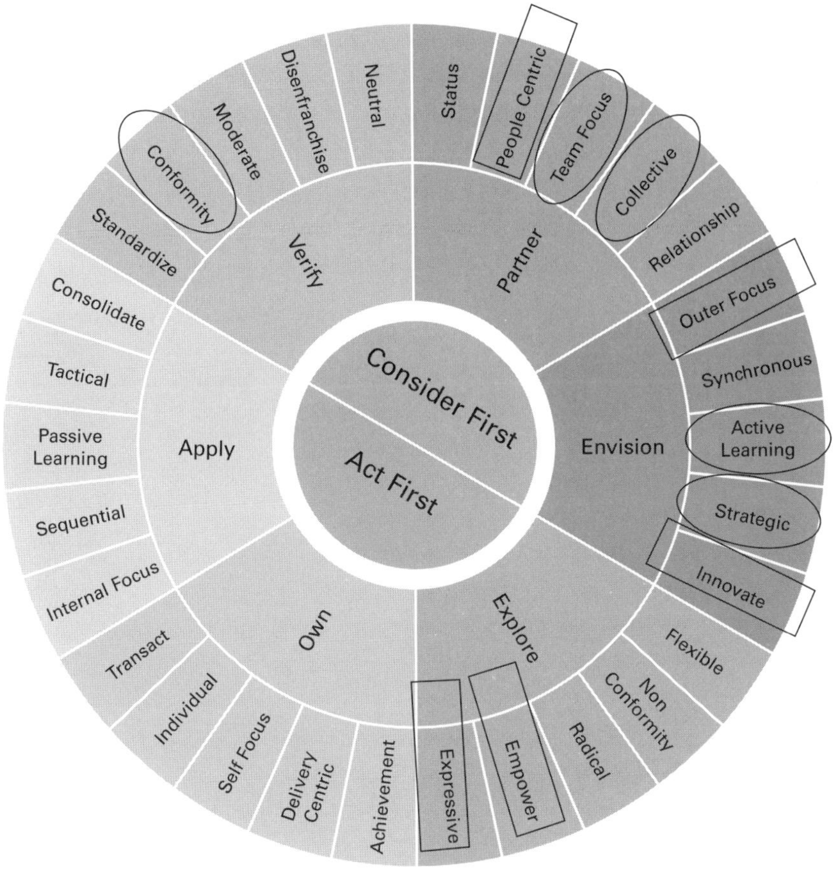

SOURCE Present behaviours are circled and targeted behaviours are squared

Moving on to the final secondary cluster in Figure 12.8, this does indeed show a culture type change, targeting 'Navigate Possibility' as the dominant culture type while maintaining some 'Ensure Safety'.

So, with the culture types approach, we know now that this organization is targeting a culture for 'Navigate Possibilities', which means a drive towards Envision and Explore. The behaviours core to this change are: Outer Focus, Innovate, Empower and Expressive.

FIGURE 12.7 The Question and Listen vs Define the Answer secondary culture types

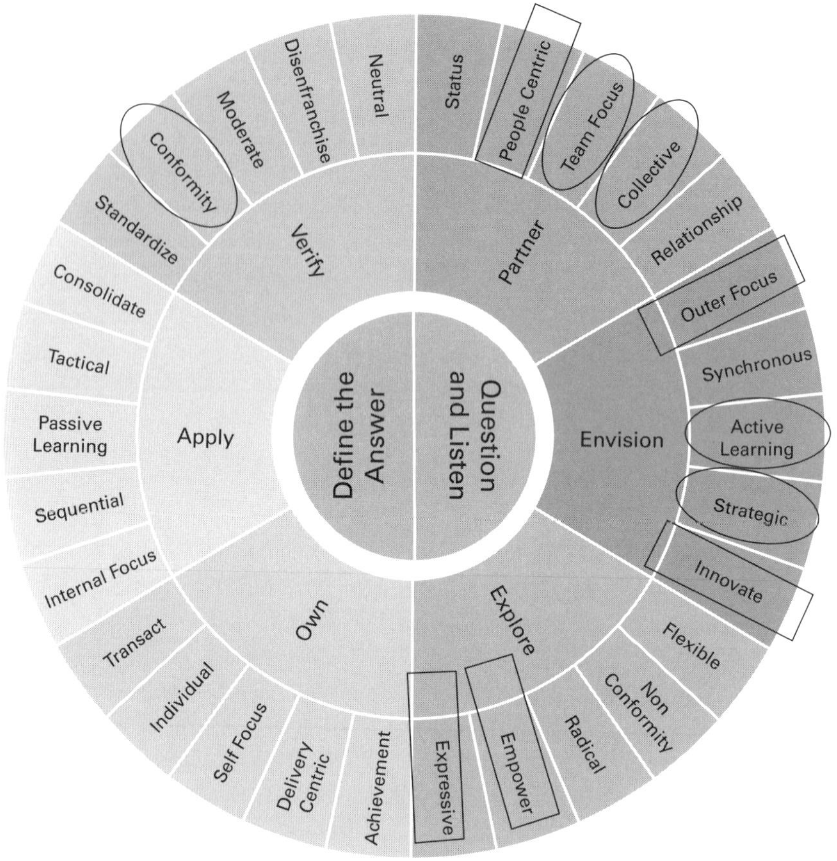

SOURCE Present behaviours are circled and targeted behaviours are squared

I hope this illustrates how culture types can be useful to communicate and explain a targeted culture change.

Another good use for the culture types is in generating or changing organizational values. With the diagnostic approach measuring the ground-up behaviours of an organization, followed by the predictive analytics process and then applying the culture types lens, you will be able to create the values based on the targeted culture rather than a 'gut feel' approach that is not steeped in reality and evidence.

Using the example above, perhaps one of the organizational values for this financial institution should be 'pioneering for a better future'.

CULTURAL TYPES   129

FIGURE 12.8 The Navigate Possibility vs Ensure Safety secondary culture types

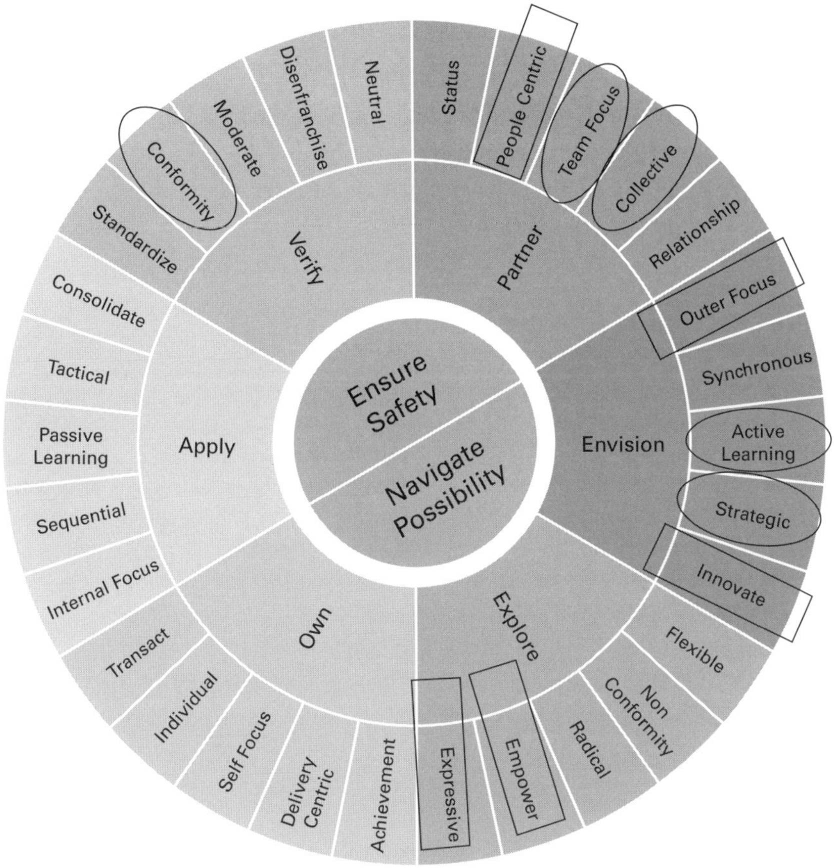

SOURCE Present behaviours are circled and targeted behaviours are squared

Workplace culture tensions

The culture types methodology also shines a light on the idea that your organizational culture can't be all things to all people, and you will need to make choices. Essentially there are three workplace culture tensions you will need to make a choice on as to where you lean towards:

- The **risk tension:** As the name may suggest, this is about how you manage risk. It's the culture types dichotomy between Explore and Verify. For ease of reference, Table 12.1 shows the behaviours and definition reminders.

- The **progressive tension:** This is about how progressive the organization wants to be. It's the culture types dichotomy between Apply and Envision. For ease of reference, Table 12.2 shows the behaviours and definition reminders.
- The **independence tension:** This is about how partnership-, alliance- and team-oriented the organization wants to be. It's the culture types dichotomy between Own and Partner. For ease of reference, Table 12.3 shows the behaviours and definition reminders.

TABLE 12.1 Culture types and behaviours for the Risk Tension

Verify	Explore
Neutral Feelings and opinions are expressed delicately and with concern for how they will be received; there is a focus on being audience aware and frankness is seen as blunt and inconsiderate.	Expressive Feelings and opinions are expressed openly whether they are comfortable or not; there is a focus on people calling it like they see it and frankness is seen as honest and helpful.
Disenfranchise Hierarchical, command-and-control work styles dominate, and senior leaders are held directly responsible; there is a clear focus on keeping decision-making at the top and directing.	Empower Enabling, non-hierarchical work styles dominate where senior leaders trust others. Decisions are delegated to lower levels with supportive guidance.
Moderate Stability and working in steady, known ways are admired and actively encouraged; there is a clear focus on following process and trusting what has worked in the past.	Radical Continuous improvement and originality are admired and actively encouraged; there is a clear focus on needing to try new things and push boundaries.
Conformity High emphasis and regular attention are given to formal laws, rules, standards and obligations; there is a clear focus on trusting in the rules and sticking tightly to them.	Nonconformity Rules are seen as a starting point which should guide, but not overly constrain, judgement; there is a clear focus on interpretation and doing what feels right in the moment.
Standardized Those who eliminate ambiguity and establish efficient operating templates are admired; there is a clear focus on getting consistency and uniformity in how things are done.	Flexible Those who appreciate ambiguity and build flexible, easily varied ways of working are admired; there is a clear focus on giving license to work in different ways and be adaptable.

TABLE 12.2 Culture types and behaviours for the Progressive Tension

Apply	Envision
Consolidate 'Risk' is seen primarily as a negative threat to be minimized; there is a clear focus on reinforcing existing, known value and steering clear of what could go wrong is seen as praiseworthy.	**Innovate** 'Risk' is seen primarily in terms of opportunity, and a degree of failure is accepted as inevitable; there is a clear focus on seeking new value and being creative is seen as praiseworthy.
Tactical 'Getting things done' is a driving mantra and this is seen in terms of imminent delivery; there is a clear focus on execution and meeting pressing, immediate business needs.	**Strategic** 'What we are trying to achieve' is a driving mantra and is seen in terms of broader direction; there is a clear focus on looking past delivery to overarching purpose and longer-term needs.
Passive Learning Development is seen in terms of know-how picked up as a byproduct of on-the-job experience; learning is prioritized when there is a clear practical need for specific skills or knowledge.	**Active Learning** Development is seen as ongoing personal and professional growth; learning is seen as inherently valuable and ongoing and is treated as a valuable outcome in of itself.
Sequential Perspectives are grounded in the here-and-now and those who work in an ordered, applied way are admired; there is a clear focus on not getting distracted and keeping it simple.	**Synchronous** Those who explore differing perspectives and see issues within a wider context are admired; there is a clear focus on the 'why' and treating issues and decision making as interconnected.
Internal Focus Bringing the environment and those around us into line with the 'right' way of doing things is valued; there is a clear focus on asserting what we know is important and what works for us.	**Outer Focus** Looking outside and being influenced by other environments, people and perspectives are valued; there is a clear focus on questioning assumptions and actively checking how what we do affects others.

TABLE 12.3 Culture types and behaviours for the Independence Tension

Own	Partner
Transact Relationships are valued for their usefulness and are seen as a means to an end; there is a clear focus on prioritizing your immediate, practical stakeholders and then moving on.	**Relationship** Fostering longer-term relationships is seen as important and admirable; there is a clear focus on deepening and sustaining connections over time beyond key stakeholders.
Individual Goals are formulated and achieved based on individual responsibilities; across the business there is a clear focus on individual competition and outperforming others.	**Collective** Goals are formulated and achieved through groups and partnerships; across the business there is a clear focus on succeeding (and failing) together.
Self Focus Personal competence is actively prized, and independence is admired; within teams there is a clear focus on ensuring people meet their own obligations before helping others.	**Team Focus** Team capability is actively prized, and collaboration is admired; within teams there is a clear focus on prioritizing what will help the group the most before personal interests.
Delivery Centric Getting things done is more highly prized than the manner in which they are achieved; there is a clear focus on tangible outcomes and organizational effectiveness.	**People Centric** How things got done and the impact on people is as important as whether they got done; there is a clear focus on creating a sense of community where everyone is encouraged.
Achievement Status is downplayed and the best contributions and inputs are recognized no matter where they come from; what needs to be said is more important than who is saying it or who is listening.	**Status** Status is highly prized and 'who thinks what' can be a bigger focus than what makes sense; there is a clear focus on what important people want and being loyal to one's seniors.

FIGURE 12.9 The percentage behavioural tension as alignment or misalignment between Place and People

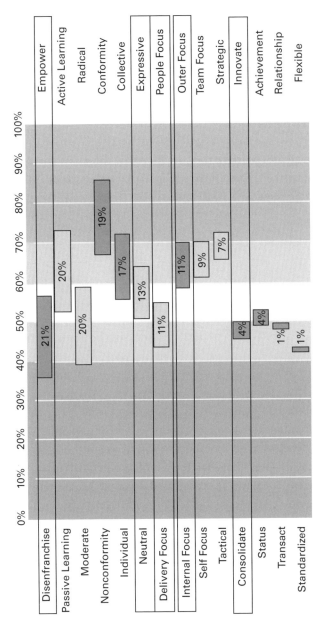

To showcase these tensions, I will apply the financial institution results for present and targeted behaviours to the three tensions:

- The **risk tension**: they are targeting two behaviours from Explore and one behaviour from Verify, hence they are slightly leaning towards risk-taking, but not massively as it's only two behaviours.
- The **progressive tension**: they are targeting four behaviours from Envision and none from Apply, hence heavily leaning towards being more progressive.
- The **independence tension**: they are targeting three behaviours from Partner and none from Own, hence reasonably leaning towards more partnership and alliances.

These tensions are yet another lens to help you articulate your current culture and what you are aiming to be.

That chapter should also help you turn quantitative into qualitative, to tell culture stories and illustrations. It helps you simplify the message, having explained the potential ROI as per the previous chapter.

Talking about tensions, there is another tension type to consider: the tension between the People and the Place, showing how aligned or misaligned the behaviours are. This is useful as we do want both aligned against the target for the behaviours to fully manifest. Figure 12.9 illustrates the alignment or tension between Place and People. The diagram shows the behavioural dimensions tension in percentage terms for the dichotomous factors for each dimension, and it also indicates for each targeted behaviour how aligned or misaligned it is and to what degree is this alignment against the targeted behaviour. Consider the Empower behaviour: it has the most tension between Place and People, and the People are more aligned to the targeted behaviour; hence the Place is the inhibitor of that behaviour manifesting.

Figure 12.9 is not showing you new data; it is, however, showing the behavioural tensions between Place and People and their alignment with the targeted behaviours. Again, it could be useful to demonstrate the behaviours most in tension.

13

Applying behavioural interventions

As I have already shown in Chapter 2, it's important to take action on behavioural insights. I have already outlined the details behind the Culture by Design approach using capability, opportunity and motivation, so to remain practical let us now apply this approach to this chapter.

Culture by Design has five stages, summarized as follows:

- **Stage 1: Behavioural selection and context**: Understanding how the target behaviours manifest in your organization and using a model of behavioural change to understand exactly what needs to change and where. This involves workshops with selected teams based on 'where' the targeted behaviours are absent or present. This information can be found using the quadrant distribution graphs showing functional/geographical areas to understand localized context.

- **Stage 2: Design the intervention**: Using the outputs from Stage 1, this will lead you through the process of designing impactful behavioural interventions and the most appropriate methods to bring about the desired change at the targeted level. The proposed interventions should be assessed according to the APEASE criteria – Affordability, Practicability, Effectiveness, Acceptability, Side effects and Equity.

- **Stage 3: Plan the intervention**: Establishing a clear plan for the specific intervention content, sequence the interventions and provide an implementation roadmap ready for implementation.

- **Stage 4: Implement**: Implement according to the action plan, keeping track of who is doing what, where and by when. Progress should be reviewed regularly – I suggest weekly – to make sure that you stay on track and apply corrections to the master plan.

- **Stage 5: Validate**: This is a remeasure stage, measuring the behaviours and targeted outcomes to check progress. This should be done between six and nine months from implementation. Compare before and after to validate that what you have implemented is working – you should expect behaviour and outcome changes. This stage will provide with the evidence needed to keep going or make adjustments. If any adjustments are needed, you will need to go back to Stage 2.

Let's get into the details for each stage.

Stage 1: Behavioural selection and context

The first action to take is to articulate the shift from current to future for the targeted behaviours, which is another team exercise that you can do.

To do this classroom-based exercise, you will need to select teams from each of the quadrants of the quadrant dispersion graph. This process was outlined in Figure 5.3. What you are seeking to know is 'what happens' for each targeted behaviour for the teams in the top right corner of the quadrant (as a reminder; the targeted behaviour is present for Place and People) versus 'what happens' for the teams in the other three quadrants.

To achieve this, you should provide breakout rooms for the teams as per the quadrant information, and for each targeted behaviour they should complete Table 13.1. Before the start you should explain to them what the behaviour means, and that you are asking them to explain the context for this behaviour in their own world. The teams in the top right corner of the quadrant will most likely elaborate well on 'where are we now' and will struggle with 'where we need to be'. That's OK, as for this team, you are really interested in the 'where are we' as that will be the target for other quadrants.

Notice that Table 13.1 includes People and Place (Place is labelled 'Organization'). You can get more specific if the target behaviour is only a Place or a People issue, which is in line with the COM-B model as outlined in Chapter 2.

The number of workshops will be in line with the number of targeted behaviours; as an example, if you are targeting three behaviours then you should plan for three workshops, and the participants for each workshop should be selected to represent all four quadrants.

To provide you with an example, see Table 13.2. The targeting behaviour is Empower and the example is an output from one of my many workshops.

TABLE 13.1 Template to be completed as a team exercise to show the current and future shift for each targeted behaviour

Where Are We?	Where Do We Need to Be?
Organization	Organization
Behaviour – What happens here Belief – Why it happens	Behaviour – What should happen Belief – Beliefs we will embrace
People	People
Behaviour – What I do Belief – Why I do it	Behaviour – What I will do Belief – Beliefs I will own

TABLE 13.2 Exercise showing the current and future shift for the Empower behaviour

Where Are We?	Where Do We Need to Be?
Organization	Organization
Behaviour – Decisions are escalated up to our managers most of the time – A lot of managers talk about needing to know what is happening in their area – Those who act without direct and formal approval are frowned upon – Managers delegate responsibility only once they are sure there is no risk – The vast majority of meetings concentrate on what the most senior people think – Communication happens through senior managers	Behaviour – Taking and escalating decisions are both common – A lot of managers talk about trusting their people to know when to involve them – Those who act without formal approval are often spoken about as having shown initiative – Responsibility is delegated to the people who are best placed to manage the risks – Meetings concentrate on relevance of views and who is doing the work – Communication happens through key project drivers

(continued)

TABLE 13.2 (Continued)

Where Are We?	Where Do We Need to Be?
Belief – The default assumption is: 'check in with the boss' – The status of the person speaking is more important than insight – It is a manager's job to ensure everyone is doing what they ought to be doing – It is not junior people's place to speak for the team	Belief – The default assumption is: 'I am trusted to know what to own and what to escalate' – The substance is more important than the speaker – It is a manager's job to create an environment to allow their team to do their jobs well – Everyone in the team should have a voice in the business
People	People
Behaviour – I look to my manager to tell me what I should and should not be doing – I make sure I am only doing what I am confident I have been told to do – I give feedback to peers who try and have a voice which may differ from that of their boss – I share stories of those who got into trouble by not working within the system – I wait to be told where the team is prioritizing Belief – My manager knows better than me, their manager knows better than them, and so on – It is safer to do as you are told – It is not my place to lead – If I try to lead, my manager will be upset – I will be better off if we stick to clear lines of authority	Behaviour – I reach out to my manager to figure out together what I should be doing – I do what I feel supports the goals of the team and my manager – I counsel others to be willing to lead discussions – I give feedback to people who just wait to be told – I call out others for telling cautionary tales about people failing to fall into line – I set to play an active part in where the team should be going Belief – My manager and I know different things – My manager needs my help to lead the team well – It is often my place to lead – If I help lead, my manager will appreciate the support – Rigid hierarchy can sometimes hold us back

If during the workshop you find the teams are struggling to complete Table 13.1, you can further facilitate by asking direct questions about capability, opportunity and motivation. Example questions for capability might be:

- How aware are they of the behaviour and precisely what it entails?

- How well do they know how to do it?
- How well do they understand the benefits of doing it? Or not doing it?

For opportunity, example questions might be:

- How far is it considered 'normal' within their environment?
- How much support do they get to do it?
- Do they have time to do it?

For motivation, example questions might be:

- How worthwhile is it to do it?
- Will doing it service a need?
- Will people be recognized for it?

Post-workshop, you will need to assess the responses by quadrant and create a table for each target behaviour summarizing the findings in terms of the 'what' and the 'where'. This will help you crystallize all your findings in one simple table before the design stage. See Table 13.3. Note that you can have more than one entry per behaviour, i.e. more than one row.

TABLE 13.3 Example extract for Empower behaviour analysis post-workshop

EMPOWER (targeted behaviour) – Some people are able to empower others; however, the place generally doesn't provide the opportunity to delegate decisions nor provide supportive guidance. What changes can we make at the place to provide this opportunity? vs DISENFRANCHISE – The structure is hierarchical, ensuring that leaders retain decision-making.			
Behavioural Dimension	Behaviour manifests (reason it happens)	Where does this happen/not happen	Who is involved
Empower vs Disenfranchise Need to increase empowerment and reduce disenfranchise throughout the organization	Some people are able to empower others; however, the place generally doesn't provide the opportunity to delegate decisions nor provide supportive guidance. What changes can	Throughout the company with the exception of the Operations team (that's the place to learn from).	Everyone starting from executive leadership team down is suffering from this. Even executive leaders suffer from a lack of empowerment from the board of directors.

(continued)

TABLE 13.3 (Continued)

EMPOWER (targeted behaviour) – Some people are able to empower others; however, the place generally doesn't provide the opportunity to delegate decisions nor provide supportive guidance. What changes can we make at the place to provide this opportunity?
vs
DISENFRANCHISE – The structure is hierarchical, ensuring that leaders retain decision-making.

Behavioural Dimension	Behaviour manifests (reason it happens)	Where does this happen/not happen	Who is involved
	we make at the place to provide this opportunity?		
Empower vs Disenfranchise	Too many team leaders, at all levels, turn up to every meeting.	All organization, slightly less prominent in Operations team.	As above
Empower vs Disenfranchise	Everyday decisions have to be checked by many leaders and committees.	All organization, better in Operations team.	As above

Stage 2: Design the intervention

Once you have completed this exercise for each of the targeted behaviours, and have generated the summarized analysis for the context, you can now move to designing the intervention.

Before we start the intervention design, it is important to remind you of the COM-B process for driving behaviour change. I introduced this concept in Chapter 2.

Figure 2.1 should now start featuring in Table 13.3 as we identify for each row whether it's a physical capability, psychological capability, physical opportunity, social opportunity, reflective motivation or automatic motivation. You can also tag each entry as an inhibitor or enabler. See Table 13.4.

Table 13.4 provides clarity for the type of intervention needed. The intervention must turn the inhibitor into an enabler, and it must function as a psychological capability, physical and social opportunity enabler and provide reflective motivation. Some interventions can target multiple behaviours.

TABLE 13.4 The COM-B function labelled with the behavioural inhibitors for Empower

		COM-B Functions		
Behavioural Dimension	Behaviour manifests (reason it happens)	physical capability psychological capability physical opportunity social opportunity, reflective motivation automatic motivation	Inhibitor	Enabler

EMPOWER (targeted behaviour) – Some people are able to empower others; however, the place generally doesn't provide the opportunity to delegate decisions nor provide supportive guidance. What changes can we make at the place to provide this opportunity?
vs
Disenfranchise – The structure is hierarchical ensuring that leaders retain decision-making.

Behavioural Dimension	Behaviour manifests	COM-B Functions	Inhibitor	Enabler
Empower vs Disenfranchise	Too many team leaders, at all levels, turn up to every meeting.	psychological capability physical opportunity social opportunity reflective motivation	x	
Empower vs Disenfranchise	Everyday decisions have to be checked by many leaders and committees.	psychological capability physical opportunity social opportunity	x	

As an example, to use a psychological capability to enable Empower, training must be provided to show them how to delegate effectively, and how to communicate the outcomes they require from their teams with clear parameters and supportive (explanatory, not directive) guidance. Empowered teams can design and decide as to 'how' they can achieve these outcomes.

As another example, using a physical opportunity to enable Empower, the board and leadership team will need to define the role and position within the 'delegation chain' and communicate that to all relevant teams and functions. This intervention will also cascade into 'who' should be attending 'which' meeting and 'why'.

For each intervention the following validity criteria must be considered:

- The intervention must be context-applicable – can we do this at our organization?
- Is the intervention focused on unlocking the target behaviour?
- Is it a sustainable intervention, or temporary?
- Is it measurable in terms of behaviour and outcome?
- Can it be applied company-wide, or for the entire targeted team? You certainly don't want it to work against inclusion!

Eventually you should summarize all interventions in one table. As examples, please see Table 13.5 for an executive committee, and Table 13.6 for team leaders addressing more than one behaviour.

Stages 3 and 4: Plan the interventions and implement

You can have a high-level time plan for ease of reference and presentation, but you should also have an Excel-type time plan for tracking progress and resources. See Figure 13.1 for an summary time plan.

It is critical to review progress on the above events weekly. You should have an Excel-style sheet to track the implementation. As an example

TABLE 13.5 Intervention design for an executive committee

Intervention & Aim	Training	Process	Technology	Internal / Partner	Behaviours
To review role and position within the 'delegation chain'. Need to pull back from the line and empower subordinates and be properly empowered by the Board. Outcomes must be communicated.	–	X	–	Internal	Empower

(continued)

TABLE 13.5 (Continued)

Intervention & Aim	Training	Process	Technology	Internal / Partner	Behaviours
Team dynamics training. Provide Executive team with improved team dynamics moving forward, the ability to understand how event-driven behaviours manifest in teams; to improve situational awareness, managing complexity, resolving conflict and thereby enhancing teamwork for minimizing risks and driving performance.	X	–	–	Partner	Empower Team Focus

TABLE 13.6 Intervention design for leadership team

Intervention & Aim	Training	Process	Technology	Internal / Partner	Behaviours
Leadership delegation training. This training focuses on leaders being able to effectively delegate – being able to communicate the OUTCOMES they require from their team with clear parameters and supportive (not directive) guidance. Colleagues are then empowered as to HOW they achieve these outcomes.	X	–	–	Partner	Empower People Focus

(continued)

TABLE 13.5 (Continued)

Intervention & Aim	Training	Process	Technology	Internal / Partner	Behaviours
360 leader reviews. 360 leader reviews should be conducted focused on Empowerment and People Focus. Specific questions on HOW things are achieved as well as WHAT, and also on the ability of a leader to delegate effectively.	–	X	X	Internal / Partner	Empower People Focus
Review and allocate mandates for leadership group. Each leadership level should have clear and empowering parameters in terms of their mandate, to include things such as budget, paper sign-off/review/recruitment and regulatory impact. This will detail when they are expected to be the sign-off and when it should be delegated or promoted up the line.	X	X	–	Internal	People Focus Empower

detailed time and resource implementation plan, see Figure 13.2 covering interventions for Expressive behaviour only.

Additionally, you should consider how applying behavioural nudges might help. Nudges have emerged as a powerful tool for influencing indi-

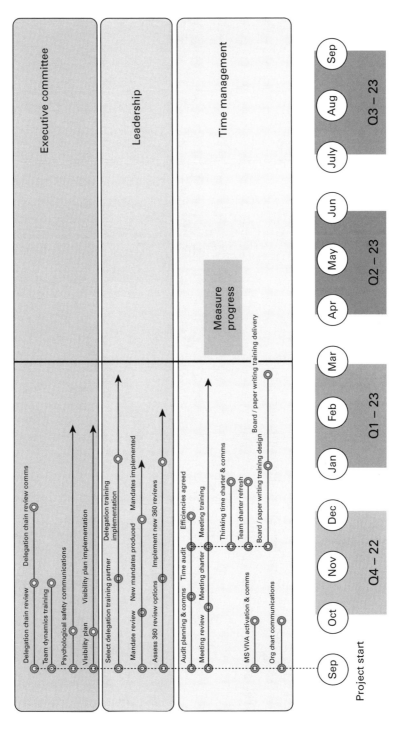

FIGURE 13.1 Intervention time plan implementation

FIGURE 13.2 Example behavioural interventions time and resource plan

Target Behaviour: **EXPRESSIVE**

Company Name: XXXXX
Lead(s): ...

Implementation Start: Mon, 2/19/2024
Display Week: 1

TASK	ASSIGNED TO	PROGRESS	START	END
Employee Continuous Improvement (CI) Tool				
Assess if an internal solution exists	Name	20%	2/19/24	2/22/24
Investigate external partners & availability in Arabic language		60%	2/22/24	2/24/24
Follow procurement process		0%	2/24/24	2/28/24
Define the tool tech roll-out plan		10%	2/28/24	3/4/24
Define the tool communication plan		20%	2/23/24	2/25/24

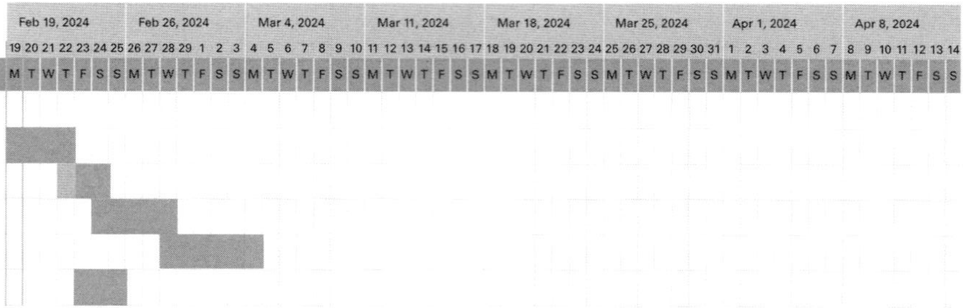

vidual choices and fostering positive behavioural change. In both personal and organizational contexts, applying behavioural nudges strategically can lead to the improved adoption of desirable behaviours.

Behavioural nudges involve subtle interventions designed to guide individuals towards making better choices without restricting their freedom. These aim to influence behaviour by leveraging cognitive biases that often drive decision-making.

For completeness, I would like to share the core principles of effective nudging as follows:

- **Defaults and opt-out mechanisms**: Nudges often leverage the power of defaults. By setting a particular option as the default (which individuals can opt-out of if desired), decision-makers are more likely to stick with the default choice.
- **Social norms**: People are influenced by what they perceive as normal behaviour within their social context. Nudges can tap into this by providing information about what others are doing.
- **Simplicity and clarity**: Nudges should be simple and easy to understand. Complex messages can lead to decision paralysis. Clarity in communication is key to ensuring that the nudge is effective in guiding behaviour.
- **Immediate feedback**: Providing immediate feedback on behaviour can reinforce positive actions.
- **Application timing**: The timing for applying the nudges would be important – i.e. when you start, and for how long.

Back to our context, this will be an interesting and fun exercise to do with your team. Divide the team by four and take each of the above principles and design a nudge.

For this example, the organization provided digital nudges in the form of emails and group Teams messages across the entire year. The nudge message was clear, and consisted of the following:

- Do you need to attend all the meeting in your calendar for this week? Will you make a difference?
- By empowering your team, you can, on average, gain 32 per cent effective time back in your calendar.
- Have you blocked some think time in your calendar today?

In fact, if you have deployed an organizational network and calendar analysis system, you will be able to customize feedback messages weekly showing progress. And I mean customized for each individual; an excellent method for a customized nudge!

Stage 5: Validate

This is a remeasure stage, measuring the behaviours and targeted outcomes to check progress. Compare before and after to validate that what you have implemented is working – you should expect behaviour and outcome changes.

As an example, having targeted Empower for seven months as per the intervention design and implementation outlined in this chapter, an organization redeployed the behavioural measurement and remeasured the targeted outcomes.

Empowerment increased by 18 per cent from absent to present at the Place. The outcomes related to Empowerment improved by 48 per cent, which is a significant shift; these outcomes included speed of decision-making, improvement in leadership time management and process-related performance efficiencies, to name a few.

This is an excellent result and will help the organization stay focused on their implementation plan to yield more outcome benefits.

If any adjustments are needed, you will need to go back to Stage 2 – design the intervention.

14

The impact of growth on organizational culture

Navigating the dynamics of change

Growth is a natural and often sought-after aspect of an organization's journey towards success. However, as organizations expand and evolve, they must confront the profound impact that growth can have on their workplace culture.

I will now remind you of the thought-provoking idea I shared at the end of Chapter 1, that growth can be the enemy of organizational culture. Hence, growth must be treated as a workplace culture change, and as I have already covered throughout this book so far, one must not leave workplace culture to chance! This concept is even more critical if any change is happening or about to happen.

Many organizations of all shapes and sizes also battle with answering a significant question as part of their journey – do we drive growth organically, or through a merger or acquisition? Both paths can present significant opportunities and risks; however, leaders often forget to think about the significant role that culture will play. For organizations that are on a significant organic growth path and have a great current culture, the oddity is that such growth could risk partial or total destruction by culture!

We have seen this before – remember the Boeing story I shared with you in Chapter 1? And this is the key reason why one must not gamble with workplace culture. The key is validated measurement and management. In fact, culture is key in driving 'how' growth can be sustained.

As you grow and add people or even suppliers to your team, your culture is at risk. After all, the more people involved, the greater the opportunity for dilution. To help curb this effect, recruit with your target culture in mind and hire people whose values and behaviours are compatible with your organization. Before I hear the shout 'What about diversity?', I am not suggesting you only hire people from a certain background, ethnicity, gender, etc… not at all. I am suggesting that you must know which few behaviours are critical for your workplace culture, as they drive and predict many of your desired outcomes, and hire in line with the those behaviours.

I must also remind you that I am not talking about personality measurement as part of the recruitment strategy – that may be hazardous for diversity. I am merely referring to the few behaviours that are critical for you.

Effective communication is also key to manage the growth effect on organizational culture. As organizations grow, communication channels may become more complex and fragmented. This can lead to misunderstandings, reduced transparency and an overall breakdown in the flow of information. Leaders must invest in robust communication strategies, leveraging technology and fostering open lines of dialogue to maintain a cohesive and inclusive culture throughout periods of growth.

Growth often necessitates changes in leadership styles and organizational structures. The leadership that successfully guided a small start-up may not be equipped to manage a larger, more complex organization; hence, as the organization grows, leaders must adapt their styles, delegate effectively and foster a workplace culture of empowerment. This adaptability is crucial for maintaining a positive and cohesive organizational culture. Again, the only way leaders will be well informed and prepared is by articulating the behaviours that got us here so far and the behaviours that they need in their workplace culture for their next destination.

The role of workplace culture in mergers and acquisitions as a strategy for growth

Having already stated that growth can be driven by mergers and acquisitions (M&A), why is it that the results of mergers and acquisitions don't always live up to expectations?

M&A growth strategies promise a plethora of strategic opportunities; from rapid growth, to eliminating competition, to access to new markets. And many organizations are currently embarking on, or have embarked on, merger and acquisition growth strategies to varying effect.

When asked about the primary causes of these mixed results, most leaders cite a misalignment between the two organizations' cultures. This friction can wreak havoc as the members of different groups integrate to drive the performance gains that M&A strategies forecast.

Companies of all shapes and sizes are actively engaged in M&A growth strategies to help position themselves to compete. And organizations of all sizes must be mindful of how company culture plays a role in M&A success.

Typically, M&A activities are conducted with a focus on the external impact. How are we going to gain access to new opportunities? How will this position us better to gain market share? How will this afford us economies of scale to keep ahead of our competitors? Post-M&A, the focus shifts to systems – how do we integrate our human resource, financial and customer management systems? How will we ensure that our operations can integrate as quickly as possible?

The risk here is two-fold. First, if the transaction was initiated for externally focused reasons, becoming hyper-focused on internal integration can distract people from why the deal happened in the first place. Second, and perhaps more problematic, is that the promises of financial gain can be seductive, leading the organization to find data and examples to support the notion that the organizations are ideally suited to integrate, rather than looking at data objectively.

It's not uncommon to hear executives talk about how the cultures of the organizations are well-aligned, and how this will facilitate an easier integration. We've seen it play out time and time again as leaders convince themselves that the integration is a 'marriage made in heaven' when, in fact, they have no real understanding or data on which to base that claim. It seems ludicrous that companies would roll the dice with something so critical without understanding the magnitude of organizational culture and its impact on the M&A outcomes.

A culture-first approach to mergers and acquisitions

With significant advancement in behavioural diagnostics and people analytics, it is now possible to approach post-M&A integration with a scientific focus to measure organizational culture and effect on key performance indicators and outcomes.

Take the opportunity to really understand the culture of each organization. You can achieve this using behaviour diagnostics (the leading indicator) for each company to examine 'how' each company lives its culture and, very importantly, the impact on each organization's outcomes (the lagging indicator).

FIGURE 14.1 Steps involved in the workplace cultural integration of two independent companies

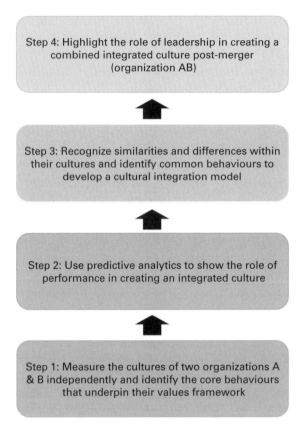

Having looked at each organization's own culture, you can now start building the 'third' resulting target culture by knowing what behaviours you want to sustain, change or eliminate. Where are the culture misalignments that will cause pressure points? Most importantly, you can build a predictive model for how the 'third' resulting culture will be our hero in making the M&A a great success, rather than the villain that will destroy it, Figure 14.1 summarizes this approach and sequence of actions.

Using this approach will also allow you to shed a critical light on what each organization 'says' and how it relates to what they actually 'do'. To demonstrate, two organizations may use the term 'customer-centric'; however, their approach to this word is very different and drives very different behaviours. The risk in this situation is that both organizations define customer success differently, and how they deliver success looks so different that it can create frustration or even confusion as employees struggle to figure out what the new 'right way' looks like across the new integrated organization.

Guiding a successful 'culture first' integration is a tricky transition and needs focus and intention, as most leaders want to complete the integration process as quickly as possible in order to reap the financial benefits of the transaction, but this can come back to bite them.

Using behaviour analytics to find out which behaviours are the key drivers for the manifestation of organizational culture will allow you to dig deep into 'what right looks like' in each organization, to ensure you don't jump onto a directionless culture bandwagon and drive yourself into the first ditch.

In today's environment, you'd be hard-pressed to find a business executive who has not lived through (some may say survived) a merger or acquisition in their careers. Why is it, then, that we continue to try to convince ourselves that culture is not going to present a significant risk to our future transactions and their ability to drive the returns that we hope for? Whatever expansion strategy you embark on, organic or through M&A, organizational culture is 'valued currency' in driving sustainable growth.

Whatever your approach for growth and even if you seek to modify your organizational culture as you grow, behavioural diagnostics and analytics should be your guiding ally for success.

Growth is an exciting and challenging phase in any organization's journey. Recognizing the impact of growth on workplace culture and proactively addressing the associated challenges, by taking an active approach through measuring, adapting and validating to better navigate the dynamics of growth, will help you preserve the intended aspects of your unique workplace cultural identity while driving your objectives and projected outcomes.

15

Cultural navigation in the digital age

As we find ourselves firmly entrenched in the digital age, organizations are facing unprecedented challenges and opportunities. The rapid evolution of technology has not only transformed institutional operations, but has also significantly influenced workplace culture.

The digital age brings with it a wave of technological advancements that can reshape the way organizations operate, from cloud computing and artificial intelligence (AI) to remote collaboration tools. Embracing so-called 'digital transformation' is essential as the way we work is rapidly changing. Organizations must navigate this shift with a keen understanding of how these technologies impact their workplace culture, and what opportunities this brings for culture and people analytics.

In this chapter, I want to address three aspects: the impact of the digital age on workplace culture, the opportunity for connected data to provide actionable workplace culture analytics, and finally the ethical use of data for workplace culture analytics.

The impact of the digital age on workplace culture

I am sure you will immediately connect with this, as the emergence of virtual work environments and remote working has become a defining feature of the modern workplace. Suddenly workplace culture has no walled confines – but I would argue that workplace culture had no walled confines in many industries already. To explain this concept and as an example, think about the transport industry. The airline or train operators rarely have their core workforce in a single office building, or even in one geographical location, yet organizational culture travels so well and you can observe how the majority of employees enact their respective workplace cultures. Additionally, that applies to managing risk and operational performance. Having myself lived on a flight deck for part of my career, I am still fascinated by how behaviour risk travels remarkably well from head office to every airliner cockpit and cabin literally thousands of miles away.

This concept is also no different with big brands that have cross-border satellite offices. It is also remarkable to study how such workplace cultures manifest alongside the geographical culture (known as ethnography).

So, the elephant in the room is: how do you manage this level of complexity for organizational culture? The good news is that the approach outlined in this book will be exactly the same for all types of employees: remote, part-time, interns, casual, full-time… you name it! Hence it is an inclusive approach and a good demonstration of how a valid, evidence- and data-based approach is imperative in managing complexity.

The key approach remains the same – valid, easy-to-deploy behavioural diagnostics, the availability of multiple relevant thematic outcomes to drive actionable insights, and the work on the leading indicators. Remember it is an iterative cycle so keep measuring, adapting and validating.

Additionally, managing workplace culture in the digital age demands a unique set of leadership skills: the ability to lead remotely, communicating effectively through digital channels and leveraging data-driven insights are all crucial skills. Progressive organizations in the digital age go beyond traditional hierarchies and leaders should create the environment that emphasizes collaboration, empowerment and inclusivity.

The digital age should not mean that we must all have a knee-jerk reaction and become 'off the scale' innovative. You should specifically assess what it means for your organization, as I have already made the case for in Chapter 1. A copy-and-paste approach will not work, and it cannot replace the evidence-based process outlined.

The opportunity for connected data to provide actionable workplace culture analytics

To drive effective and actionable analytics and insights, I have already outlined the importance of connecting the lagging and leading indicators. Actually I went a lot further towards building the full analytics picture and I have already covered how you can bring in quantitative and qualitative outcomes, as well as any organizational values into the mix. Therefore, I

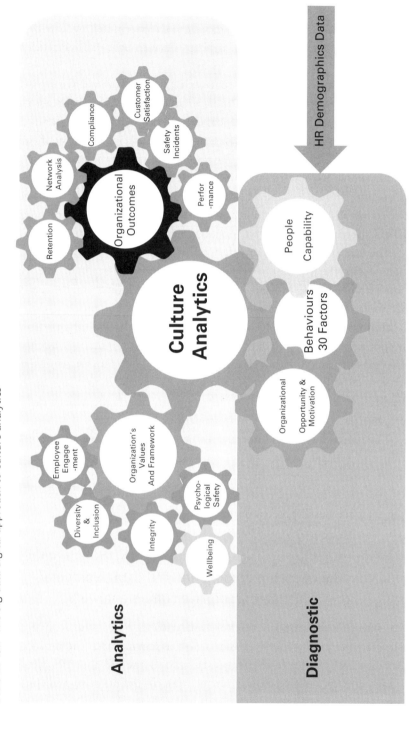

FIGURE 15.1 The big data digital approach to culture analytics

would like to argue the need for a big data approach. Even if you have not set up the technology to connect all the needed data through application programming interfaces (APIs), no problem. I am sure most platforms have an export function so you can test what connected analytics would do for your organization.

Figure 15.1 helps you visualize everything I have already covered in previous chapters in one image, and as you look at this image, do allow your thoughts to go wild! You should be inquisitive as to what your workplace culture is driving without you even knowing.

Let's analyse Figure 15.1 as to the different layers and elements:

- The **diagnostics layer** includes any leading indicators measurement. In the context of workplace culture, it is the behavioural measurement for People and Place. You will also notice that I am suggesting the injection of HR demographics data at that layer. It may seem odd that I am suggesting so many pre-analytics; however, HR demographics will play a role in two ways. Firstly, it will help you decide if you have achieved statistical and analytics validity – the so-called 'effect size'. I have already explained what that is in Chapter 6. Secondly, HR demographics will provide you the 'where' in your analytics for actionable insights.

- The **analytics layer** includes organization thematic quantitative outcomes. As is shown in Figure 15.1, that can include performance data, compliance incidents, organizational network analysis data, talent retention data, etc. This data can be 'line by line' or at team level for each outcome, and remember you can have more than one outcome per theme. This layer will also include qualitative data and organizational values or any frameworks-type mapping. Qualitative data can include employee engagement, wellbeing, psychological safety and any other outcomes. This data is generally collected through quick Likert scale-type sentiment surveys, but other means of data collection can be added – perhaps a combination of qualitative and quantitative data feeds can be added for some themes.

- The **culture analytics function** in the middle is where all the model development happens (regression analysis, path analysis, distribution analysis and odds ratio calculations). The functionality will also include all the graphics to show the insights, as described in previous chapters.

Ethical considerations for using employee data for workplace culture analytics

As we are in an era where data is fast becoming a cornerstone of organizational decision-making, measuring and analysing organizational culture through data is gaining prominence. While data-driven insights offer valuable perspectives on organizational dynamics, it is crucial to address the ethical considerations surrounding the use of data in this context, with the emphasis on the importance of responsible practices to ensure integrity and fairness.

The first notion to consider here is that the type of behavioural diagnostics and analytics data will be analysed at team, division or organizational level, and not intended for individual reporting. Also, this solves an immediate critical issue around data privacy as you will not need to process personal identifier-type data, e.g. name, email address or employee ID number. All you really need to examine the data and produce a model for predictive analytics is a pseudo-randomized ID that will be used to connect the diagnostics with the corresponding demographics and outcome metrics.

A word of warning about the HR demographics, as these should not include any criteria that can only be attributed to one employee. I have already explained in Chapter 6 why generated benchmarks for analytics should use five or more employees.

You will still need to obtain informed consent from employees, and individuals should be made aware of the data collection methods, the purpose of gathering data and how the insights will be utilized. The best approach is to prepare a culture metrics and data analytics privacy notice, which should include:

- what data are you collecting
- why you need this data
- where the data is stored
- conditions for data processing
- how the data will be used
- who can access the data and any access restrictions
- data retention

This transparency builds trust and ensures that employees feel comfortable contributing to the data collection process without concerns about privacy violations.

Bias mitigation in data collection

Ethical concerns arise when data collection methods introduce biases that may skew the interpretation of organizational culture. However, the CultureScope behavioural diagnostic mitigates this risk through the questionnaire methods and approach to drive validity, as described in Chapter 4.

It is also essential to use inclusive and diverse sampling methods to ensure that data accurately reflects the entire workforce. Additionally, you should regularly review and update your data collection sampling processes to identify and rectify any unintentional biases.

Fair and objective analysis

When analysing data to measure organizational culture, it is crucial to maintain objectivity and fairness. Avoiding preconceived notions and letting the data speak for itself ensures that interpretations are unbiased. Ethical considerations should guide the interpretation of data insights to avoid reinforcing stereotypes or discriminatory practices.

As a final word on navigating organizational culture in the digital age, it is a multifaceted challenge that requires strategic thinking, adaptability and a commitment to providing the best actionable insight based on multiple data sources.

Embracing the possibilities of connected multiple data sources will provide you with the best approach for analytics validity, resulting in actionable insights focused on the leading indicators and vastly improving the organization's odds of yielding their targeted outcomes and return on their culture investment, making organizational culture the hero it should be!

PART TWO

16

Gaining predictive insight into employee sentiment through behavioural science and analytics

Why four parts Place and one part People matters in whether employees share their voice at work

Welcome to Part 2! Having established in Part 1 of this book all the principles and methodologies for driving culture analytics using leading and lagging indicators, and having provided practical exercises and working examples, it's time to examine thematic case studies. Each chapter from this one onwards will be dedicated to a single case study.

To satisfy as many readers as possible, I will follow two methods for presenting the case studies. Chapters 16 to 19 will be 'white paper' style – this approach will remind you of the entire culture analytics process. Chapters 20 onwards will be purely focused on analytics for actionable insights.

Although the case studies are anonymized, all the analytics and insights are 'real world'. Also, in some case studies, where the remeasure has been deployed post-culture intervention design, planning and implementation, the progress in behaviour and outcome results will be included.

Whether it is the sharing of information between co-workers to get ahead of problems, refine and improve working practices and diffuse better practices throughout the organization, or whether it is the upward communication that helps organizational leaders keep abreast of what is happening in their organization, most recognize that encouraging employee voice is an essential factor in the success of organizations.

Background

Research published by the McKinsey Institute, 'Why agility pays', shows that involving employees in shaping an organization's vision is one of four critical management practices that drive the agility of organizations in adapting to and successfully introducing change.[1]

At the level of the individual employee, research supports the link between employee voice and William Kahn's original conception of employee engagement, and voice or lack of it has been shown to relate to staff turnover, higher employee commitment and higher satisfaction with both work and employer.[2]

Before we go further, I should define what I mean by employee voice, which refers to the communication of ideas, suggestions, opinions and concerns about work-related issues with the intention of improving the functioning of the organization. It includes the constructive challenge of the current status quo in the organization or work unit about the way in which tasks are assigned and executed. It does not include criticism for the sake of criticism. The key attributes of effective employee voice are that it is constructive and focused on improvement.

In contrast, employee silence represents the withholding of valuable input and often reflects a feeling of futility (voice will be ignored or dismissed), fear about negative consequences from sharing a point of view or a desire to protect co-workers.

The connection between employee voice and employee engagement is easily understood when you consider that sharing information is key to employee learning, and that the notion of talent in many organizations is predicated on the employee being an active contributor as recognized in many performance appraisal and reward systems used by organizations.

Yet, while evidence supports the individual and organizational benefits of encouraging employee voice, research also shows that employees are often reluctant to speak up. That reluctance has remained stubbornly at around 50 per cent of employees feeling uncomfortable at expressing voice at work for nigh-on the last three decades.[3]

What does that mean? Essentially, it means that speaking up and voicing a view or an opinion is not the natural default behaviour in the workplace. It means that expressing a voice or remaining silent is a choice, and that choosing to remain silent is not necessarily a passive act.

Whether it is out of fear of negative consequences or a sense of futility ('they won't listen anyway'), employee silence may actually represent a conscious choice reflecting the belief that speaking up is too risky in terms of the impact that may have on their relationships with co-workers, with their line management, on their employment prospects and on their own wellbeing at work.[4]

If the assumption that employees will naturally share their voice is misplaced, then that has serious implications and potential consequences for organizational leaders. For one, that misplaced assumption may lead to complacency and the belief that 'no news is good news' when in fact organizational leaders may have a much more limited view of what is happening in their organization than they credit themselves with. Silence may not be quite as 'golden' as leaders might assume. More about this in Chapter 19.

That blindness to what is happening in the organization may also have serious and very tangible consequences for the organization. Regulators now recognize the importance of employee voice and employee silence as factors related to the potential for organizational misconduct and even illegal practices. Indeed, regulators in the banking and finance sectors now look at employee voice or its absence as signalling what they are calling 'broken cultures'. To quote one UK regulator, 'Employee voice is critical – are people able to contribute and challenge, be listened to, and therefore be treated fairly?'[5]

So, how do organizations promote effective employee voice? The prevailing wisdom seems to be that if organizations put the right structures and processes in place, then employee voice will follow. Examples include manager training schemes, town hall forums and employee suggestion processes as well as whistleblowing systems adopted in many banking and other companies.

These efforts are based on at least two assumptions. The first is that employees have the talents required to constructively raise a suggestion or voice a concern. The natural extension of that assumption is that if we, the organization, recruit and train the right people then they will speak up.

The second assumption is that processes, systems and manager and executive training will naturally create the right context to encourage employee voice. Research on psychological safety and employee voice suggests that these may be further examples of unwarranted assumptions.[6]

To borrow from the field of architecture, these assumptions represent a misconception that form will follow function.[7] That is, by creating the right organizational 'forms' (structure and processes), employee voice will naturally function.

This misconception fails to recognize that form and function will only work to support employee voice if the culture of the organization promotes the behaviours needed for those forms to function. And the proof that those forms are functioning lies in whether those structures and processes are promoting behaviours that support effective voice.

Context

Here is where our story begins. A large global financial institution had invested in a variety of initiatives to promote employee voice over several years, with mixed success by their own judgement. Conscious of the active interest of regulators in whether financial organizations understand the mechanisms through which employee voice is supported, we were engaged by a global retail and investment bank to help them identify the key factors in their organization that acted for and against employees speaking up.

To help this organization gain insight into what drove or suppressed employee voice in their organization, we deployed the CultureScope behavioural analytics platform. This approach takes a very tangible approach to understanding culture by focusing on behaviour in the workplace and applies two lenses to those behaviours by combining data on the People, individual employees, and the Place, the workplace at the level of the organization through to the work unit or work team.

How People or individuals behave is likely to make intuitive sense to you, but you might be curious about the idea of how the Place behaves. Research in the field of social psychology has long shown that the social context in which we find ourselves can have a substantial, even overriding effect on how we behave. Whether it is people acting against their conscience, conforming to opinions shown objectively to be clearly erroneous or the condition of learned helplessness, the Place sets a powerful frame for how the People behave at work.[8]

You might ask: 'Isn't how the Place behaves somehow the sum of the behaviour of individual employees?' How the Place behaves reflects strongly embedded and often obscure beliefs and feelings that develop into norms for behaviour. Those behavioural norms may have developed historically, reflecting an inheritance from previously significant figures in an organization's development, or may be a factor of the impact of significant figures, leaders and influential employees.

They may also be a factor of the geographical region in which the organization is located. Our data across many organizations shows that the Place can behave in very different ways depending on where you look, so organizations can be made up of a number of distinct 'Places' reflecting very different expectations of employees.

What we have often seen in our data is a conflict between how the Place behaves and how People typically behave. That conflict creates opportunities for misbehaviour in the workplace and frequently derails efforts to achieve work goals and the strategic aims of organizations.

So, why not explore the beliefs, feelings and attitudes of employees to understand those norms? We believe that exploring these influences on employee behaviour does offer value, but we also believe that exploring the Place in terms of how the People and the Place behave provides a much more direct and tangible approach to understanding organizational culture by focusing on observable actions and outcomes.

Like many similar establishments, this organization regularly surveys employees to gauge employee attitudes and sentiment. Survey questions are deployed on a quarterly or annual basis and include questions regarding whether the employee feels able to share opinions and to speak up without negative consequences (we will refer to these questions as Speak Up) and believes that there is mutual trust between employees and leaders (Mutual Trust), and whether line managers take into account the wellbeing of employees (Wellbeing).[9]

We tracked the pattern of results from employee surveys for three quarters after the deployment of CultureScope to develop a predictive model through two waves of analysis. The first explored the relationship between the three sets of survey questions to understand the functional relationships between them. Through testing the fit of various models to the survey data, we arrived at a model in which Mutual Trust and Wellbeing acted as key drivers of whether employees reported comfort in speaking up.

Our next step was to develop and evaluate a model that linked the behaviour of the People and the Place to trust and wellbeing at work, and to use that model to understand the direct and indirect impacts of the behaviour of the People and the Place on employee voice.

What we found surprised us and the organization. Finding a relationship between culture, trust, wellbeing and speaking up was not where the surprise lay. That surprise was in the strength of the predictive relationships we found and how that relationship helped to unpack the behavioural drivers behind employee attitudes in the workplace.

The various waves of this organization's surveys showed that those employee attitudes were fairly stable and, on the surface, potentially reassuring for the organization. As we have already seen, various surveys and research studies over the past three decades have shown the odds of an employee speaking up at work have sat stubbornly at around 50:50.

This organization's surveys showed that, overall, 60 per cent of employees reported high or very high comfort in speaking up, ten percentage points above the baseline set by those three decades of wider research. Yet, there was also a persistent percentage of 16 per cent or around one in six employees who reported low or very low comfort in speaking up and sharing their opinions at work and a further 24 per cent, or around one in four employees, who reported uncertainty about the value of stating their opinions at work.

This is where using behavioural analytics helped us and the organization get under the skin of these survey statistics. Here is a summary of what we found:

- That below the surface of those employee survey results lay a very strong relationship with the behavioural profiles of the People and the Place, and that relationship was only apparent once the connections between behavioural diagnostics and employee attitudes had been surfaced.
- That the relationship remained strong up to nine months after the behavioural analytics had been deployed and explained why employee sentiment remained so consistent over the time period we explored with this organization. In short, if the behaviours do not change, then employee attitudes, including the likelihood of speaking up, are unlikely to change.
- That the relationship was driven by a specific set of common or complementary behaviours, and that this finding in itself offered the organization value in narrowing down what they needed to focus on.
- That the Place has an overriding impact specifically on levels of mutual trust, and this is where we found the impact of behaviour to be around four parts Place to one part People.

Our model showed that the People and the Place operate as drivers of employee voice both directly and indirectly through mutual trust and employee wellbeing.

The path model we landed on has been illustrated in Figure 16.1. As you can see, the Place acts both as a direct driver of employee voice and as an indirect driver through employee wellbeing and mutual trust.

FIGURE 16.1 Path model for employee voice for this organization

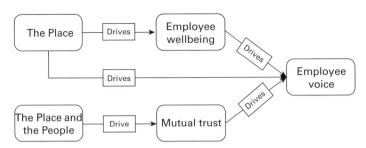

When it comes to mutual trust – do I trust my leaders, and do I believe they trust me? – both the People and the Place have an impact roughly in the ratio of four parts Place to one part People. Why that ratio? We think that this is confirmation of the overriding impact that the Place has when it comes to behaviour in context. This is not about whether People, employees, naturally trust others, but about whether they trust and feel trusted by their leaders where they work.

Figures 16.2, 16.3 and 16.4 show the level of the direct impact that the People and the Place have on wellbeing, mutual trust and employee voice respectively. What these quadrant figures show are the odds of employees positively endorsing their wellbeing at work, their sense of mutual trust and their comfort in speaking up at work. These figures show how the odds vary for employees reporting high levels of trust (though we refined that by focusing on one specific trust question as explained below), high levels of wellbeing at work and high comfort in sharing their voice at work (again we focused on a specific aspect of employee voice).

For trust and speaking up, the results we shared focus on two specific questions. Regarding trust, employees reported lower trust in leaders than the trust they experienced from leaders. As such, it seems that the dynamic of trust amongst these employees is asymmetric and may reflect differences in trust with immediate leaders and the broader leadership in the organization. To boost trust as a driver of employee voice, it seems that trust in leaders was the key aspect of trust to focus on.

For employee voice, the surveys captured both promotive voice (sharing ideas and opinions aimed at improving team and organizational performance) and prohibitive voice (speaking up to stop harm to others and the organization). The data showed lower endorsement rates among employees for promotive voice, which was of concern to the organization at a time

FIGURE 16.2 Direct impact of the Place on employee wellbeing

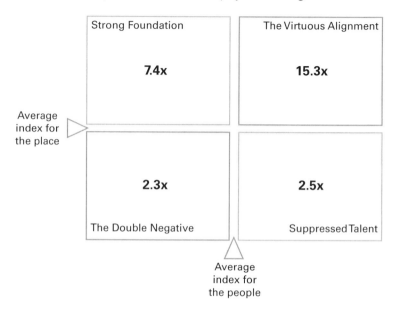

FIGURE 16.3 Direct impact of the People and the Place on trust

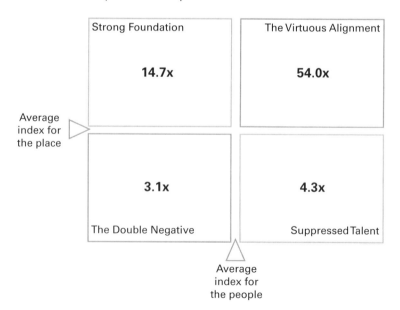

FIGURE 16.4 Direct impact of the Place on employee voice

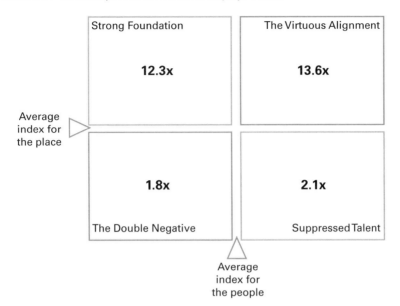

when competition in their industry had increased, with the arrival of challenger banks leveraging new customer service models and applications of customer service technologies.

While we focus on these specific aspects of trust and employee voice, we checked our analyses to see whether this focus gave a biased view of the functioning of our model. It does not, so we feel comfortable sharing the view of our findings based on these specific questions.

We developed two indices to capture the relative strength of the behavioural profiles of the People and the Place. In Figure 16.4, employees have been segmented by broad levels of those indices to create four quadrants. Essentially, and for the purposes of this case study, we have split our People and Place indices at the 50th percentile to create a lower and a higher banding of employees on each index.

The multiplier you see in each of the four quadrants created by splitting our indices in this way is the ratio of positive endorsements (high or very high responses to a survey question) to the ratio of negative endorsements (low or very low responses to a survey question). Those ratios give the odds of an employee in any quadrant reporting higher trust, higher wellbeing or higher comfort in speaking up. The higher the multiplier in a quadrant, the higher the odds of an employee reporting higher trust, higher wellbeing and higher comfort in sharing their opinions at work.

Our analysis shows that comfort among employees in sharing voice in the workplace is 7.5 times higher when the Place is stronger and aligned. While the data shows that there is some comfort in sharing voice even when the Place is weaker in its support for employee voice, the strength of that endorsement is exponentially higher when the Place is stronger in those critical behaviours that drive employee voice.

For the quadrant we have called Virtuous Alignment (we will look at these more fully in Chapter 18), employees were 13.6 times more likely to report comfort in sharing opinions. In contrast, the odds for that comfort were 1.8 times for the quadrant we have called the Double Negative, and the ratio of those two numbers is how we arrive at the 7.5 times higher comfort for when the Place is stronger and aligned.

Note that the multipliers for employee voice by quadrant are substantially higher when our index for the Place is stronger (upper two quadrants), emphasizing the stronger direct impact of the Place on employee voice. Also note that these multipliers represent the direct impact of the Place on employee voice and that the Place also has an indirect impact on voice through employee wellbeing and trust, which we will explore next.

When we look at wellbeing, we see a similar pattern in the impact of the Place. Employees in our Virtuous Alignment quadrant are more likely to report higher wellbeing than those in the Double Negative quadrant by 6.7 times.

For wellbeing, the difference between employees in the quadrant we have called Strong Foundation and the Virtuous Alignment quadrant suggests an opportunity to develop employees in the behaviours they can utilize to support their own wellbeing at work.

In other words, rather than look to the Place and specifically the line manager as the sole driver of employee wellbeing, there is an opportunity for this organization to explore how employees in the Strong Foundation quadrant can become more active agents in supporting their own wellbeing at work. This is a good example of how combining behavioural analytics and employee survey data helped the organization to understand levers in the organization for promoting employee wellbeing and, through wellbeing, the sharing of employee opinion.

Another lever from our model is trust in leadership and here we see a direct impact of both the People and the Place to the extent that employees in the Virtuous Alignment quadrant are 17.2 times more likely to report high comfort in speaking up than employees in the Double Negative quadrant.

The synergistic impact on trust of both the People and Place can been seen by another comparison among our four quadrants. In contrast to the quadrant we have called Suppressed Talent, where the odds for reporting trust in leaders are 4.3 to 1, the odds for employees reporting high trust in leadership in the Strong Foundation quadrant are 14.7 to 1 – over three times higher.

The finding for trust clearly shows how the Place can modify and even suppress the behaviour of employees even when those behaviours strengthen the opportunity for employees to build trust between themselves and leaders in the organization.

Is this simply the effect of better leaders demonstrating the behaviours needed to build trust? In part, the answer to that question is yes. The impact of good leadership is irrefutable. That said, good leadership needs good followership to be effective and that is shown by comparing the odds of reporting higher trust in our quadrants for Virtuous Alignment and Strong Foundation – the odds of reporting high trust in leadership are almost four times higher for the Virtuous Alignment quadrant where the Place and the People are stronger.

So, what were the behaviours that we found underpinned trust, wellbeing and employee voice and that make up our indices for the People and the Place? Figure 16.5 summarizes the six behaviours from the CultureScope framework that, between the People and the Place, we found drive higher employee trust in leaders, higher employee wellbeing and substantially higher levels of comfort in speaking up and sharing opinions and ideas at work.

Two of the behaviours are common and one, Expressive, will seem immediately intuitive since the willingness among employees to share opinions and the encouragement of the workplace to do so is an obvious element in supporting the sharing of employee voice.

The other common behaviour, Active Learning, may seem a little less intuitive but a reading of the research literature shows that obtaining value from encouraging employee voice does depend to a large extent on whether that voice leads to more effective ways to deal with issues and problems, better ways of working and meeting stakeholder needs, and diffusion of effective working practices across the organization. Those benefits point to learning and a key question for any organization wanting to build and sustain effective employee voice is whether the people they recruit and promote are active learners, and whether the workplace encourages active learning through experimentation and managed risk.

FIGURE 16.5 The six behaviours that drive trust, wellbeing and employee voice

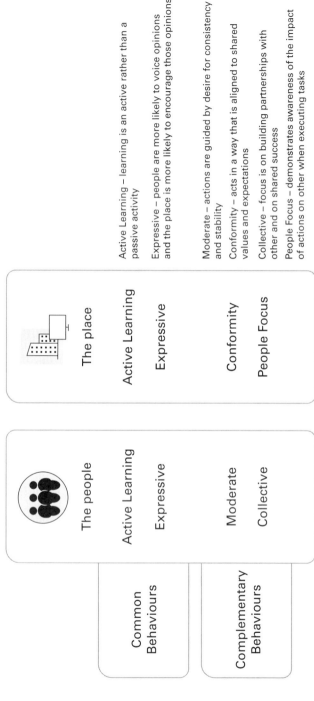

Active Learning – learning is an active rather than a passive activity

Expressive – people are more likely to voice opinions and the place is more likely to encourage those opinions

Moderate – actions are guided by desire for consistency and stability

Conformity – acts in a way that is aligned to shared values and expectations

Collective – focus is on building partnerships with other and on shared success

People Focus – demonstrates awareness of the impact of actions on other when executing tasks

Four of our six behaviours operate as complementary pairs; again, one pair is highly intuitive in that voice is more likely to be received positively when it is shared in a way that is seen to be focused on building and strengthening partnerships within the workplace rather than just for the benefit of the individual sharing their voice.

This is how we see Collective operating in our predictive model and how it plays through the actions of leaders to build trust among employees. That behaviour from the perspective of the People is complemented and strengthened in workplaces by demonstrating an awareness of the impact of actions on others when executing tasks and achieving objectives, which the CultureScope framework captures through People Focus.

Our other complementary pair can be understood if we turn to trust in the workplace where we found the behaviour of both the People and the Place had a synergistic impact. Trust depends on expectations of others and whether others can be expected to act in ways that are predictable. That view of trust in part explains the contribution of Moderate from the perspective of the People – how employees behave through their expression of voice – and Conformity from the perspective of the Place.

Conformity in the CultureScope framework does not just talk to playing by the rules, though that is important in employees having faith that there is justice in the workplace.[10] It also speaks to the manner in which leaders receive employee voice, and we believe that goes some way to explaining the higher levels of trust in leaders that we saw in this organization's data where Conformity in the Place was higher.

So, where is this organization on their journey to strengthen employee voice and to make that voice more effective in driving organizational transformation and change? Armed with a clear and manageable focus on six behaviours, they have started a series of cascading conversations through their organization framed by those six behaviours. Those conversations are not just about how to have better conversations in the workplace. They include HR processes such as performance appraisals to ensure that those key behaviours are being reinforced through one of the key forums through which the People and the Place interact.

Those conversations also include organizational structures and workflows to examine where the form of the organization is getting in the way of the function of employee voice.

Through further segmentation of the data and using the six behavioural clusters as shown in Figure 16.5, we used the quadrant analysis method to know 'where' in the organization these behaviours are present and where absent. Teams within the Virtuous Alignment quadrant have these key behaviours embedded and the outcome has manifested. Hence they can learn from teams in the other three remaining quadrants where their investment needs to happen, and by virtue of the different quadrants they will know if the interventions should be focused on the People (capability-type intervention) or the Place (opportunity- and motivation-type interventions), or both.

How we crunched the numbers

Our data sets were taken from a CultureScope behavioural diagnostic deployment in the last calendar quarter of 2020 and four waves of client employee surveys that occurred quarterly from the end of 2019 through to the end of 2020. While a large portion of survey questions appeared in all four surveys, some appeared only annually. Our sample sizes were 9,121 for CultureScope measures and 6,912 for employee surveys across all four quarters.

Quarterly employee attitude surveys were based on stratified random sampling across the organization by level (status), geography and business function. Employees responding to each quarterly attitude survey varied quarter on quarter, with only a small percentage of employees completing the survey more than once.

To manage this, we conducted a series of analyses within each quarter as well as with data aggregated across all calendar quarters for which data were available. For those employees sampled more than once, we used the average of their survey responses to each question.

At the aggregated data level, maximum likelihood factor analysis with oblique rotation of the five survey questions – two for trust, two for speaking up and one for wellbeing – yielded two factors that offered a good fit to the data. Those factors were defined by the trust questions and the wellbeing question with cross-loadings for the two speak up questions.

This suggested to us a model in which speaking up (employee voice) was the dependent or outcome variable while trust and wellbeing operated as causal factors or independent variables influencing whether employees felt comfortable in sharing opinions or speaking up when they saw something wrong.

We tested this through a series of path models, rotating each of the attitudinal variables – trust, wellbeing and speak up – as dependent variables. The model in which speaking up served as the dependent variable offered a stronger fit than when wellbeing served as the dependent variable, and equivalent fit when trust served as the dependent variable.

We then used a series of hierarchical regressions to explore the relationships between CultureScope behavioural measures for the People and the Place and trust, wellbeing and speaking up. Again, we explored these models within each calendar quarter and for the data aggregated across calendar quarters. We used a fully saturated model with all 15 CultureScope dimensions as our baseline to test more restricted and nested models with fewer CultureScope dimensions to arrive at our final predictor set of six CultureScope behaviours.

The path model presented was also tested using path models analysis and yielded the equivalent to a Multiple R of 0.50 (accounting for 25 per cent of the variance in the data) in predicting employee voice.

The effect size obtained from our model in predicting employee attitudes for nine months outranks at the 80th percentile of effect sizes observed in research on employee attitudes.[11]

Notes

1 M Bazigos, A De Smet and C Gagnon, Why agility pays, *McKinsey*, 1 December 2015, www.mckinsey.com/capabilities/people-and-organizational-performance/our-insights/why-agility-pays (archived at https://perma.cc/GV4F-A4GB). This research was based on 1,000 companies and explored the relationship between 37 management practices and organizational agility, defined as the ability of an organization to adjust to changes and new ways of doing things. Associated research had shown that organizational agility is related to the share value and EBITDA of for-profit organizations. The other three management practices identified alongside the involvement of employees in shaping organizational vision were financial management, financial incentives and capturing external ideas.

2 W A Kahn (1990) Psychological conditions of personal engagement and disengagement at work, *Academy of Management Journal*, 33, pp. 692–724

3 This statistic was drawn from a number of sources, including:

   o Ipsos (2012) Mental well-being in the workplace. Cited by M L Frazier, S Fainshmidt, R L Klinger, A Pezeshkan and V Vracheva (2017) Psychological safety: A meta-analytic review and extension, *Personnel Psychology*, 70, pp. 113–65

- M Kirrane, D O'Shea, F Buckley, A Grazi and J Prout (2017) Investigating the role of discrete emotions in silence versus speaking up, *Journal of Occupational and Organizational Psychology*, **90**, pp. 354–78
- F J Milliken, E W Morrison and P F Hewlin (2003) An exploratory study of employee silence: Issues that employees don't communicate upwards and why, *Journal of Managerial Studies*, **40**, pp. 1453–76
- K D Ryan and D K Oestreich (1991) *Driving Fear Out of the Workplace: How to overcome the invisible barriers to quality, productivity and innovation*, Jossey-Bass, San Francisco
- Towers Watson (2014) *Employee Voice: Releasing voice for sustainable business success*, Towers Watson, London

4 The distinction between employee voice and employee silence is a topic of debate amongst academics in this area. Some such as Morrison see voice and silence as opposites on a continuum. Others such as Van Dyne see voice and silence as distinct behaviours driven by similar but distinct employee motivations. For more on this debate, see:

- E W Morrison (2011). Employee voice behaviour: Integration and directions for future research, *The Academy of Management Annals*, **5**, pp. 373–412
- E W Morrison (2014). Employee voice and silence, *Annual Review of Organizational Psychology and Organizational Behavior*, **1**, pp. 173–97
- L Van Dyne, S Ang and I C Botero (2003). Conceptualizing employee silence and employee voice as multidimensional constructs, *Journal of Management Studies*, **40**, 1359–1392

5 Financial Conduct Authority. Transforming culture in financial services, March 2018, www.fca.org.uk/publication/discussion/dp18-02.pdf (archived at https://perma.cc/2TSQ-6CS8)

6 For examples of research on the antecedents of employee voice, see:

- M A Chamberlain, D W Netwon and J A LePine (2017) A meta-analysis of voice and its promotive and prohibitive forms: Identification of key associations, distinctions, and future research directions, *Personnel Psychology*, **70**, pp. 11–71
- M L Frazier, S Fainshmidt, R L Klinger, A Pezeshkan and V Vracheva (2017) Psychological safety: A meta-analytic review and extension, *Personnel Psychology*, **70**, pp. 113–65
- J A LePine and L V Van Dyne (1998) Predicting voice behaviour in work groups, *Journal of Applied Psychology*, 83, pp. 853–68

7   'Form follows function' is an axiom attributed to the architect Louis Sullivan and states that the purpose of a building should be the starting point for its design. We borrow from this axiom to emphasize that the purpose of any processes and structures implemented by an organization to encourage employee voice should focus on the behaviours that support effective employee voice and should be evaluated in terms of whether a process or a structure is encouraging those behaviours.

8   Key researchers and research in this area include:

   o   S E Asch (1956) Studies of independence and conformity: A minority of one against a unanimous majority, *Psychological Monographs*, **70**, pp. 1–70

   o   S Milgram (1963) Behavioral study of obedience, *Journal of Abnormal and Social Psychology*, **67**, pp. 371–78

   o   M E P Seligman (2006) *Learned Optimism: How to change your mind and your life*, Vintage Books, New York

9   One limitation of this project was the framing of the survey question asked of employees about their wellbeing at work. The specific question used asks whether the manager is invested in the employee's wellbeing rather than the wellbeing the employee generally experiences at work. However, we feel that it is a reasonable inference that employee wellbeing is correlated with the extent to which an organization, through its managers, is concerned about and invested in employee wellbeing.

10   Models of organizational justice show that perceptions of justice in the workplace depends on whether employees see that process by which decisions are reached are fair (procedural justice), whether the distribution of rewards is fair (distributive justice), whether the involvement of people is fair (relationship justice) and whether the sharing of information is fair and reasonable (informational justice).

11   Many researchers use Jacob Cohen's correlations effect size benchmarks to gauge the strength of relationships. Those benchmarks are 0.2 for a small effect, 0.3 for moderate effect and 0.5 for a large effect. The results of our model for predicting employee voice would benchmark as a large effect size (R=0.496). More recent research suggests that the size of an effect varies depending on what is being studied and that different benchmarks reflecting different fields of study are required. We obtained our 80th percentile benchmark for research on employee attitudes from F A Bosco, H Aguinis, H, K Singh, J G Field and C A Pierce (2015) Correlational effect size benchmarks, *Journal of Applied Psychology*, **100**, pp. 431–49

17

Driving organizational change through workplace culture and behavioural analytics

Addressing the root causes of why change programmes fail

Transformation has become the new buzzword, replacing the perhaps less dramatic word 'change'. Organizations use the two terms interchangeably, but are they really the same? When it comes to change versus transformation, what are the differences? I am sure to spark a big debate here, but I will simply offer my opinion: change can be seen as incremental, perhaps driven by a response to a situational event or events. However, transformation implies a drastic shift from one state to another. Naturally, transformation could include multiple and significant changes. It could be the difference between evolution and revolution.

This case study will be in three parts as it will address the most common reasons why organizational change programmes, often associated with transformation, fail.

The first reason is simply not knowing which behaviours are required as an ally to achieve desired outcomes. Most organizations have no problem defining their destination, but few have the tools to identify and implement the corresponding behaviours required to attain their desired destination.

Indeed, identifying your destination is the first step. However, you will need to identify and focus on the workplace culture journey and lead drives to ignite change.

The second reason is failing to tailor the change approach. As we have already shown in Part 1 of this book, each organizational culture is unique; going even further with this thought, different people perceive and react to change in different ways and the change you are implementing is going to mean different things to different people and teams. Many organizations cascade one-size-fits-all approaches that some buy into, but many resist.

The third reason is relying on assumptions, rather than a data-driven approach. Often, we see transformation strategies based on abstract theories rather than data-driven interventions.

So, before you embark on your transformation journey, gather precise data to ensure that any culture and behavioural intervention is tailored to the unique context and capability needs of your organization. If not, you might be aiming at outcomes that are irrelevant, distracting or even harmful to your organization.

In this three-part case, I will focus on the behavioural aspects of why culture change fails and how to increase your chances for success.

Part 1: Do your change champions have what it really takes to effect change?

The statistics have remained stubbornly negative for decades. Whether it is the bleaker 70 per cent of change programmes failing to achieve their objectives[1] or the more benign statistic of 50 per cent success for Forbes 1,000 companies[2], at best that gives change programmes a one in two chance of succeeding.

Change has become the new normal, alongside increased economic and social uncertainty as well as the growing impact of technology. Yet, the question that continues to plague leaders, managers and those that support organizations through change is 'Why are the odds stacked so heavily against change programmes succeeding?'

More specifically, and given that the problem is not that organizations are incapable of launching change programmes, why is it that change programmes so often fail to land effectively and deliver the outcomes they were launched to deliver?

The prevailing wisdom is that change programmes must have a compelling purpose for change, must be supported by effective processes for managing the programmes and must have clear commitment and support from organizational leaders.[3] But we have known all of these must-haves for decades, and yet those damning statistics on the failure of change programmes remain negative or 50:50 at best.

What is new is the growing interest in exploring the application of behavioural psychology to improve the success of change programmes.[4] This is the focus of this section. Though the application of behavioural psychology to change programmes is still at a relatively early stage, we explore how behavioural psychology allied with data analytics addresses three of the root causes for why many change programmes fail.

Why workplace culture change programmes fail

In essence, change programmes are about changing behaviour, whether that is how an organization functions once new structures and processes have been introduced or how individuals and teams interact among themselves and with those outside the organization. It is about changing how the workplace behaves and how employees behave.

With behavioural change in mind, our experience shows that there are three behaviourally related reasons for why change programmes fail. We do not claim that these are the only reasons, but they do point to common blind spots that all too often undo the well-intentioned and significant efforts devoted to change programmes. Those three reasons stem from a lack of knowledge about the organization's people and how the workplace influences employee behaviour.

When we talk in this chapter about the People, we mean the deep-seated behavioural profiles of employees at any level and in any location, and those behavioural profiles include their appetite for personal change. Yet, few organizations have detailed insight and data on the behavioural profiles of their employees, and this includes the ones they nominate or who offer themselves to be champions for a change programme.

So, the first reason that we see for culture change programmes failing is that organizations either do not know or lack insight into whether their change champions have what it takes to be effective in delivering change programme objectives. While it seems an obvious factor to consider, it remains a significant blind spot for most organizations.

The second reason that our experience has shown for why programmes fail is a lack of insight into the size of the change task – the 'ask' – that those programmes demand. From a behavioural perspective, improving the odds of achieving a goal depends partly on how difficult challenging that goal is, and partly on the context in which that goal is set.

This is where insight on the Place (our shorthand for the workplace) or, to be more accurate, the Places that make up the organization becomes important. The question here is not the natural behavioural profiles of the People that occupy those Places, but how those Places act to frame and influence employee behaviour. As research in social psychology has shown, the Place exerts a strong influence on how we behave, so strong that the Place can override how a person would naturally behave outside that work context.[5]

One way in which a lack of data and insight into the Place undermines the success of change programmes is in the setting of common change objectives for the entire organization. That supposes that every business function, location, team and individual employee is facing the same challenge in achieving those change goals, whether that is the specifics of what needs to change, or the size of the change needed to achieve the goal of the change programmes. Yet, we understand that organizations are not that homogenous, just as their target clients or customers and the markets that different parts of the organization serve are also rarely homogenous.

This mistake of adopting a one-size-fits-all approach plays out in at least two ways. It may be that change targets are imposed on parts of the organization where the gap between where the organization wants to go behaviourally and where it is today is either small or non-existent. These are parts of the organization that are already where the change programme wants to get to. These are also potential hubs of good practice that may be hidden from those designing change programmes and that offer resources that could support learning elsewhere in the organization. But that potential is all too frequently squandered through a one-size-fits-all approach to change.

Conversely, there may be parts of the organization where there is a substantial behavioural gap between how the Place behaves today and where the organization wants to be tomorrow. Closing that behavioural gap at the same pace as other parts of the organization may well be, and in our experience often is, too much of an ask.

The third reason we see for behavioural programmes failing is a lack of a behavioural roadmap and, specifically, a data-driven behavioural roadmap. We are not saying that the judgement and intuitions of leaders, managers and employees do not count, but we are saying that those judgements and intuitions are best supported by valid and objective data ahead of launching a change programme.

So, what is our notion of a behavioural roadmap? Essentially, that roadmap combines data of the People and the Place to identify where in the organization the People are more likely to embrace change and deliver the goals of the organization with data on the Place in terms of how big an ask is being made and where specifically different parts of the organization should focus. It also serves to identify where in the organization the desired behavioural profile may already exist, and how the resources for learning can be marshalled to support the odds of change programmes succeeding.

We will tackle each of these three reasons that we see for change programmes failing in this chapter. We will come back to how to size the behavioural ask of employees and how to construct a behavioural roadmap in the second and third parts. For the remainder of this first part, we will address the question: 'Do your change champions have what it really takes to deliver change effectively?'

A metric for whether employees are really up for change

Just how willing are employees to change their behaviours? That was the question that emerged from discussions with this large organization in the financial sector preparing to launch a major change programme. The CultureScope behavioural diagnostic was deployed, and the organization agreed that we add a simple sentiment type question to the diagnostics and asked respondents to tell us how willing they were to change how they as individuals behaved.

Only 20.3 per cent, or around one in five, employees across the organization responded positively. With 79.7 per cent saying no to the question, that suggested that the starting odds in terms of employee buy-in to changing their own behaviours were a resounding 4:1 against. That also suggested that the change programme the organization was about to embark on was a poor bet in terms of success.

The question that we posed was that, given that the disposition to change of individuals is more of a continuum than a binary change vs no-change condition, could we identify the behavioural profiles of those more open to personal change and develop a metric to help this organization understand what to look for in those who were more vs less likely to commit to change?

To develop that metric, we used the data on the People (those deeply ingrained behaviours we all have as individuals) provided by CultureScope. We will come to the specific behaviours that drove that metric and what that metric offered the organization a little later in this chapter.

Figure 17.1 shows how that metric differentiated the disposition to personal change in significantly more detail than the binary yes/no question initially posed by the organization.

FIGURE 17.1 Behaviours metrics versus probability of change

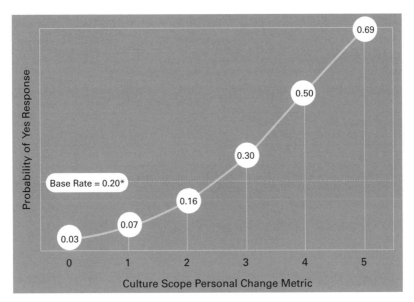

NOTE *20 per cent of sample responded yes

What are you seeing here? Well, we know that the base rate (the yes answers to that question) is around 20 per cent or one in five employees. But that base rate masks an underlying metric that clearly distinguishes between very low disposition to personal change (0 on the horizontal axis) and a very high disposition to personal change (5 on that horizontal axis).

What Figure 17.1 also shows is that those who are highest on the underlying metric (5) are 23 times more likely to commit to behavioural change than those lowest on that underlying metric (0).

37 per cent of employees were identified as showing positive likelihoods of being able to change their own behaviours (3 and above on the metric). That still showed that the odds in favour of employees having a positive disposition to personal change were 1.7:1 against, but that was a significant improvement on odds of 4:1 against.

The good news for the organization was that those behavioural profiles could be identified and the metric could be used to identify not only those with a substantially higher likelihood of being effective change champions, but also to identify those who, with the right support from those change champions, would be able to embrace the change programme.

FIGURE 17.2 The behaviours for the change metric

⬆ **Personal Change Metric**	⬇ **Personal Change Metric**
Expressive and more likely to voice an opinion	**_Neutral_** and less likely to voice a thought or opinion
Flexible and more likely to value the ability to work flexibly	**_Standardized_** and more likely to place importance on processes and systems
People Focus and more likely to focus on people rather than just outputs	**_Delivery Focus_** and more likely to focus on outputs rather than people
Team Focus and more likely to value team working	**_Self Focus_** and more likely to value individualism and individual reward

The behavioural profiles driving that metric

Our modelling showed that there were eight behavioural factors that, together and either positively or negatively, drove that metric. Figure 17.2 summarizes those behavioural factors.[6]

Those employees who were more likely to embrace behavioural change and to commit to change programmes, were those who were more likely to focus on the impacts of change on people, as well as how change programme goals could be incorporated in the way teams work more effectively together. They were also those who were more likely to adapt their approach to the demands of different situations and challenges, and were more likely to share their opinions and views on how best to approach change and whether change programmes were achieving their goals or not.

In contrast, those who were less likely to embrace behavioural change and to commit to change programmes were those with a stronger tendency to focus on process for the sake of process rather than the impacts on other employees. They were also more likely to focus on what change programmes offered for them as individuals and were also less likely to voice their opinions on whether change programmes were achieving their goals or not.

Putting the metric into practice

Unpacking these behavioural profiles offers value in two ways. One flows from data analytics, the other flows from providing more qualitative insight to change programme leaders as well as equipping change champions to deliver on change programme goals.

From a data analytics perspective, the metric enables further analysis by employee segment (seniority, tenure, gender and age) as well as by business function, department, team and location to identify where effective change champions are more likely to be found in the organization. Simply put, why look to find champions where they are less likely to be committed to personal change and to the change programme, particularly when the starting odds are 4x against any employee selected at random fitting the bill of an effective change champion?

At a more qualitative level, the behavioural profiles pose clear questions that need to be addressed to ensure that change initiatives are being landed. For example, how can we promote employee voice to flag issues and course correct as change programmes unfold? How can we promote team goals that support change programme goals and reward and recognize team rather than individual successes in achieving change goals? How do we frame change programme communications to ensure that they reflect the people aspect of change as well as the achievement of process and structural improvements?

How we crunched the numbers

The question about disposition to change was framed as a closed 'yes' or 'no' question. Given that the response was binary, we used logistic regression to identify which behavioural dimensions predicted whether employees were more likely to respond positively and with a yes.

Logistic regression was developed to predict binary outcomes. Logistic regression models serve to identify which of a set of non-binary and binary predictors are most strongly related to an outcome such as a 'yes' response in this particular application. The result of a logistic regression provides the building blocks for constructing metrics that measure the likelihood of the outcome being observed (e.g. a 'yes' response to the personal change question). Those metrics can then be used to predict the odds or probabilities of that outcome being observed.

We tested a number of nested models to arrive at the most efficient model that offered the strongest predictions of a 'yes' response to the question posed to employees of whether they would be willing to change their behaviours. The strongest predictors of that 'yes' response formed the basis of the behavioural profile described in the main body of this piece.

In terms of model fit and for those more familiar with linear methods such as correlations and least squares regression models, two indicators of fit allied to those obtained from linear methods are available from logistic regression – as explained by Cox and Snell.[7] Taking the square root of these fit indices yields indicators that approximate the multiple R obtained from linear regression or the correlation between two variables.

The multiple Rs associated with our final model for predicting a yes response to the survey question from behavioural factors were 0.43 (Cox & Snell) and 0.53 (Nagelkerke). The Place size of the relationships found in our model at or above the 75th percentile for research into employee attitudes and intentions such as commitment to change programmes.[8]

Part 2: Sizing the 'ask' of your organization when you ask it to change

In this part, we turn to the work environment, or Place, and how to use behavioural diagnostics to understand the size of the challenge that a change programme may present in asking the organization to operate and behave differently.

The growing realization that effective change means understanding the People and the Place

Recent research published by McKinsey shows that using behavioural diagnostics to guide change programmes delivers a fourfold increase in their odds for success.[9] That research also shows that behavioural diagnostics is not just about understanding the behaviours of employees. The success of change programmes also requires an understanding of how the workplace influences employee behaviour.

Why? The work context or Place influences how employees act by providing a strong set of stimuli which frames the behaviour of employees. Employees tend to act to satisfy what they see as the expectations of the Place even if those expectations go against how they would normally behave in non-work settings.

Another benefit from using behavioural diagnostics to guide change programmes flows from the simple axiom that to know where you are going, you need to know where you are starting from. That starting point might be very different across an organization. To borrow from a sports analogy, while organizational leaders might see change as a 200-metre sprint, it may feel more like a long-distance haul for some parts of the organization while other parts of the organization might actually be confounded by the need for a change programme as they see themselves as already standing at the finishing line.

This variation in where different parts of an organization start their change journeys also points to an all-too-often-missed opportunity to proactively identify where the desired behaviours may already exist, offering opportunities to tap into effective behaviours that already exist in the organization to promote learning and support. This is not just setting up groups through which experiences can be shared and diffused. This is about clarity in terms of specific strengths and weaknesses in different parts of the organization and using those specifics to design tangible and effective exchanges between employees and workgroups targeted on specific behaviours.

A case in point

I will briefly describe a project with this organization in the financial sector to illustrate the power of behavioural insights into the Place. This organization was embarking on a change programme focused on strengthening three key pillars of its organizational culture – Customer Focus, Simple is Best and Succeeding Together.[10] They wanted to ensure they had a clear understanding of where they were, their start position, and commissioned behavioural diagnostics using CultureScope to gain that understanding.

Delivering actionable insight from behavioural diagnostics requires more than just a survey and analytics know-how; it also requires a deep understanding of the context. To gain that understanding, I ran a series of workshops with senior members from the organization using the CultureScope behavioural taxonomy of 30 factors.[11]

The process for the workshops began with an open-ended question: 'How would you know that Customer Focus, Simple is Best and Succeeding Together were being truly lived in the organization?' To surface the specific organizational context, debate and even disagreement were encouraged while maintaining appropriate respect for the opinions of others. The workshops then progressed to mapping the 30 CultureScope behavioural factors to each of the three organizational pillars to establish tangible behavioural markers for the success of the organization's change programme.[12]

Those mappings framed how data from the CultureScope diagnostic were used to create metrics and establish where the Place was acting to promote desired behaviours and where the Place was acting against those desired behaviours.[13] So, what did the data show?

*How variation in behavioural profiles of the Place
provides insight into the ask of change programmes*

While organizations strive to promote consistent values and behaviours, our experience shows again and again that the 'Place' may actually promote very different employee experiences depending on where employees work. This was the case with this organization.

We identified eight clusters from the data on how employees saw their workplace. These eight clusters were obtained with the help of K-means clustering using indices to measure the between-cluster differences as well as within-cluster variation. The between-cluster differences indicate the extent to which the clusters represent distinct profiles across the three pillars. The within-cluster variation indicates the extent to which the overlap between clusters is low and, therefore, the extent to which the boundaries between clusters are distinct.

As a quick introduction, K-means clustering is a type of unsupervised learning, which is used when you have unlabelled data (i.e. data without defined categories or groups). The goal of this algorithm is to find groups in the data, with the number of groups represented by the variable K. The algorithm works iteratively to assign each data point to one of K groups based on the features that are provided. Data points are clustered based on feature similarity. The results of the K-means clustering algorithm are:

- the centroids of the K clusters, which can be used to label new data
- labels for the training data (each data point is assigned to a single cluster)

Rather than defining groups before looking at the data, clustering allows you to find and analyse the groups that have formed organically.

We ran a series of cluster analyses ranging from two to 12 clusters; all cluster solutions bar one showed significant differences for metrics for the three pillars between clusters. The within-cluster variation reduced with increasing number of clusters and reached a lower limit at eight clusters. As such, eight clusters were chosen as the most parsimonious solution meeting the criterion for differentiating behavioural profiles with lower overlap in cluster membership.

Using those clusters, we could show the organization how much variation there was in terms of the starting point for different groups of employees in their change journey.[14]

FIGURE 17.3 The three organizational change pillars versus behavioural alignment

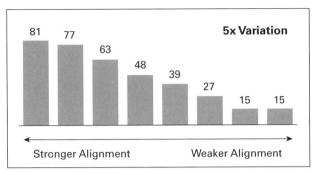

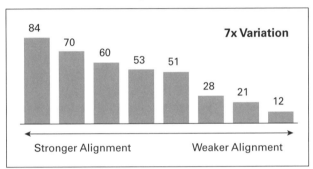

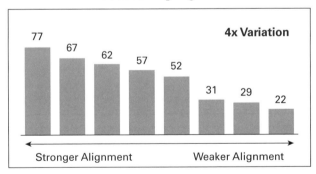

Figure 17.3 shows the variation for behavioural alignment for the three change pillars. The data demonstrated that a one size-fits-all approach to change was less likely to succeed. As we will see a little later, a given cluster might show strengths in some areas and need for improvement in others. Adopting a one-size-fits-all approach would have ignored the nuances in the

cluster profiles as well as the simple fact that all three pillars act together to define the context in which any given group of employees work.

The organization saw that a more tailored approach offered a better opportunity to guide change based on the differences in the starting points for different clusters and specifics on what behaviours those clusters should focus on.

Figure 17.4 shows the resulting profiles of the eight clusters and why a deeper dive into the data supported a more nuanced and tailored approach to launching and supporting the change programme.

That deeper dive into the data also showed that there were parts of the organization where strong alignment with the goals of the change programme already existed and where stronger alignment could be leveraged to support learning at the very earliest stages of the change journey.

Using behavioural diagnostics to support and strengthen the learning

Let's explore those eight clusters in Figure 17.4 in more detail. The left side of Figure 17.4 shows a ranking of the clusters relative to their general strength of alignment across the three pillars of Customer Focus, Simple is Best and Succeeding Together, the focus of the change programme. This takes into account where each cluster stands across the three pillars and shows the highs and lows in terms of alignment for each cluster.[15]

The bar charts to the right of Figure 17.4 shows how each cluster scored on each pillar in terms of alignment and conveys the start positions for each cluster. Clearly, the ask of Cluster 6 and Cluster 2 is substantial. In contrast, Cluster 8 and Cluster 5 show strong alignment, suggesting that these clusters offer potential for tapping into tangible day-to-day experiences that are benefitting the organization today and that can be leveraged to the benefit of other parts of the organization in supporting stronger alignment for tomorrow.

The clusters identified from behavioural data on the Place provide a frame for data analytics to identify which Places (e.g. business function, location, team) are likely to show stronger or weaker alignment with the change programme's goals, and answer the question of where the ask of the change programme is more achievable in the shorter term and where meeting that ask is more likely to be a longer-term effort.

I am not suggesting that those clusters showing weaker alignment and a bigger ask should be ignored. However, in the immediate term, these may represent Places within the organization that pose a risk to current performance in the organization. They clearly need to be monitored.

FIGURE 17.4 The profiles of the eight clusters and the alignment by pillar

What I am saying is that a failure to recognize these as Places where the ask is considerably more challenging is also a failure to proactively address potential risks to the success of a change programme.

Understanding the ask of change is a key factor but not the only factor to consider

We have focused on how behavioural diagnostics of the Place can help an organization to understand the ask demanded by change programmes and provide insight to enable an organization to think ahead of the launch of a change programme by knowing where that programme is more likely to gain traction and where that programme is more likely to struggle.

My experience tells me that data on the Place is not enough to build a robust plan of action that supports the success of change programmes. Building that robust plan also required data on the People and their appetite for change – as I have already demonstrated in Part 1.

Bringing together behavioural diagnostics on the People and the Place is what we will explore in Part 3 of this case study.

Part 3: Building a behavioural roadmap to drive effective change

Let's address how organizations can use cultural diagnostics and behavioural analytics to avoid failure of change programmes, the unfortunate outcome that decades of research documents as the fate of those programmes.

In my view and that of others,[16] behavioural analytics is emerging as a critical tool in enabling organizations to improve the odds that their change programmes will deliver. In Part 1, we explored how behavioural analytics on the people in the organization helps organizations to understand which employees have what it takes to embrace and respond positively to change. In Part 2, we explored how behavioural analytics on the work environment helps organizations to understand the size of the challenge that change programmes pose in asking an organization to operate and behave differently.

To create impact, I must show how insights into the People and the Place can be combined to develop a behavioural roadmap for proactively planning and managing change. That behavioural roadmap not only gives organizations a better means of implementing change strategy and tactics, but also the means to promote the organizational learning that serves to strengthen the achievement of change programme goals.

But how do you persuade people to engage in learning and to change their behaviour? Or, more specifically, how do you design programmes and interventions that increase the likelihood that a desired and beneficial behaviour will be adopted and sustained? These questions have led to the emergence of a new thinking in the field of design, namely persuasive design which will target capability building.

The principles that underpin persuasive design represent a mode of thinking that those charged with designing and implementing change programmes would do well to adopt. Framed by a roadmap developed using behavioural analytics, we see this mode of thinking as a step change in how organizations approach the challenge of change. So, let's briefly explore those principles of persuasive design before we move onto a case study that describes the application of a behavioural roadmap for guiding change.

Applying the principles of persuasive design to organizational change programmes

The first step in applying persuasive design is to identify a target behaviour. This is no different to the first step in designing a change programme. Whether it is the introduction of new systems and practices or improving the performance of existing systems and practices, success lies in changing People's behaviour and setting and reinforcing new norms for that behaviour. That, in turn, requires a clear, tangible and commonly understood definition of the target behaviour.[17] We gave an example in Part 2 of how an organization used cultural diagnostics, specifically CultureScope, to define the target behaviours they set as goals for their change programme.

Once that target behaviour is identified, the next step in persuasive design is to understand what might prevent people from performing the target behaviour. Is it a lack of motivation – are people unwilling or simply uninterested in adopting the target behaviour? Is it a lack of capability or ability – do people lack the means or resources to adopt the target behaviour, or, correctly or not, see the target behaviour as too ambitious for them to perform? Or is it a lack of a well-timed trigger to perform the behaviour (the opportunity) – is the organization asking the wrong people at the wrong time to perform the target behaviour?

Persuasive design advocates clear thinking about the goals set for people, as well as how those goals improve motivation and promote the sense that people are able to achieve them. Much of that effort is centred on promoting incremental learning and, with learning as a central focus, persuasive design advocates an incremental approach to behavioural change.

Applied to change programmes and the level of individual and groups of employees such as work teams, persuasive design advocates for a careful sizing of the goals set for individuals and teams, whilst also providing a clear understanding of their motivation for change and their ability to achieve the change that the organization is asking for. At the programme level, persuasive design advocates for smaller-scale experiments conducted in targeted parts of the organization and where the opportunities for learning are stronger. Ultimately, the success of change programmes depends on knowing where in the organization work practices are stronger and exploiting opportunities for the diffusion of those stronger work practices across the wider organization.[18]

Whilst I see the thinking represented in persuasive design as offering a step change in how organizations approach change, implementing that thinking raises a challenge and a question – how do you identify where in the organization those opportunities for learning are stronger? This is where the behavioural roadmap that we will describe next comes into play.

In order to understand where those learning opportunities are more likely to be stronger, we have argued that you need to have two pieces of intelligence on an organization. First, you need to know which employees are more likely to be more open to change and more likely to adopt the behaviours a change programme seeks to promote.[19] Through the lens of persuasive design, addressing the question of 'who' through diagnostics on the People addresses the issue of motivation.

Second, you need to know how big an ask a change programme is making of the organization and, more specifically, where in the organization that ask is more likely to be achievable and where it isn't. Through the lens of persuasive design, addressing the question of 'what' through diagnostics on the Place addresses the issue of ability.

That, from the perspective of persuasive design, leaves the issue of well-timed triggers and, from a change programme perspective, that raises the question of where an organization should think about starting their change journey and where the opportunities for learning are strongest.

This is where a behavioural roadmap offers value to change programmes. By combining insight into the what (the Place) and the who (the People), organizations can have a much better stab at identifying where they are likely to yield better returns on starting their change journey. So, let's explore what we mean by a behavioural roadmap for guiding change.

Building a behavioural roadmap from insights on the People and on the Place

Let's briefly reprise where we landed in Part 1 and Part 2. In Part 1, I described how we built an index that measured employee propensity for change. Those employees who ranked highest on whether they would voice an opinion, be more flexible, be more people- and team-focused were 3.5 times more likely to champion change than the average employee, irrespective of whether those employees are afforded the title of change champion. That behavioural index defines the horizontal axis of our behavioural roadmap and speaks to the inherent motivation of employees to engage with change positively.

In Part 2, I showed how analytics applied to the Place surfaced eight clusters or profiles in terms of the gap between where they were at the start of the change process and where the change programme wanted the organization to be. This data defines the behavioural roadmap and speaks to the size of the challenge that different parts of the organization face in adopting and demonstrating the behaviours promoted by the change programme.

Figure 17.5 summarizes how combining insight into the who (the People) and the what (the Place) helps determine where opportunities to start the change journey lie in an organization. The question of where is answered in terms of where change is more or less feasible, and feasibility is driven taking into account the size of the ask from change across the organization and combining that insight with knowledge of the propensity of employees to engage positively with change.

Back to our case study, where the organization had to come to the realization that effective change is dependent on learning, that an incremental approach was required to enable the learning, and looked to behavioural analytics to provide the intelligence it needed to tell it where in the organization the change journey was more feasible and where starting that journey could result in failure.

Putting a behavioural roadmap to work

Let's see what the starting position for that organization looked like when we mapped the organization, by combining analytics on the People and the Place. Note that once the map is defined, we can dig deeper into each cluster and segment by employee demographic to understand what membership of each cluster represents in terms of employee age, gender, tenure, job level, business function, work team and location.

FIGURE 17.5 Combining the insight of the Place defining the size of the ask vs the People defining the propensity for change

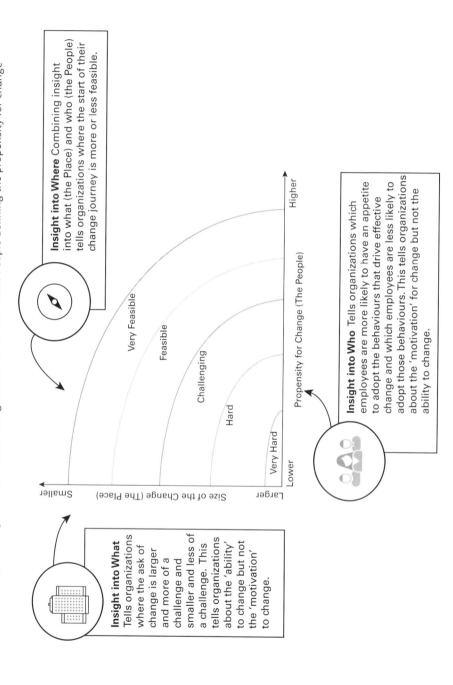

FIGURE 17.6 The eight-cluster mapping analysis within the size of the ask (Place) vs propensity for change (People) metrics

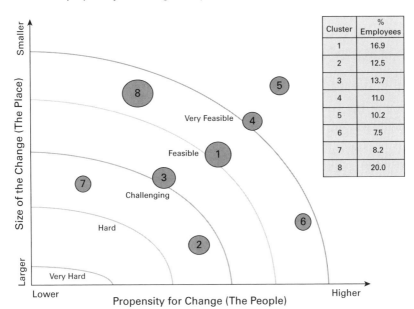

Cluster	% Employees
1	16.9
2	12.5
3	13.7
4	11.0
5	10.2
6	7.5
7	8.2
8	20.0

Refer to Figure 17.6, which maps where the eight-cluster lay within the size of the ask (Place) vs propensity for change (People) metrics. This mapping tells us that around 20 per cent or one in five employees represented by Cluster 8 already showed strength in the behaviours the organization wanted to strengthen.[20] There was still scope for improvement for this cluster, but note that this cluster ranks among the lowest for propensity for change (basically, present at Place, absent for People). That tells us that Cluster 8 was a potential resource for the organization to draw on in understanding what it is at that Place in that cluster that is going right and that could then be shared with other clusters to facilitate organizational learning.

Whilst Cluster 6 shows the highest propensity for change, it sits in the mapping as one of the clusters facing the largest challenges in the Place adopting the target behaviours. That told us that while employees and parts of the organization represented by that cluster might be willing, it was highly unlikely that they would be able to achieve the goals of the change programme if the Place continues to be the inhibitor Perhaps not the best Place to start the change journey if you cannot change the Place, or in other words, if the size of the ask is too difficult to change the Place; again, it's about making informed targeted choices to build on data and evidence.

What we can see from the mapping in Figure 17.6 of the organization is a series of clusters towards the top right that represent employees and parts of the organization where there is scope for improvement, where change is feasible and where the propensity for change is relatively strong. These are Cluster 5, 4 and 1, and here is where we begin to turn our map into a roadmap as per our Figure 17.7.

So, what is Figure 17.7 actually showing? Let's start with the doughnut charts at the bottom of that figure, which show internal benchmarks for each of three target behaviours drawn from analytics on the Place: B1 represents behavioural markers for Customer Focus, B2 represents behavioural markers for Simple is Best and reflects a desire to remove internal barriers to organizational performance, and B3 represents behavioural markers for Succeeding Together and an aspiration to break down internal silos and promote shared commitment to achieving organizational goals.[21]

As I have already described, Cluster 8 represents a profile where there is scope for improvement but lower inclination to change. My view was that this is a segment of the organization that offers a resource to support other segments given its relatively strong profile across all three target behaviours. They may not be inclined to change themselves, but they do offer the opportunity to understand what is driving their current strength to facilitate learning elsewhere in the organization. There is also a reciprocal benefit to leveraging Cluster 8 in this way. By observing the learning in other clusters, it is reasonable to assume that this will reduce any reticence to change shown by those in Cluster 8 at the start of the organization's change journey.

My suggested direction of travel at the start for this organization's change journey is centred on Cluster 5, Cluster 4 and Cluster 1 as these represent employees and parts of the organization with a stronger propensity for change and where there is specific rather than general scope for strengthening the target behaviours.

Diving into the detail of the doughnut charts for these three clusters shows where they can share learning from their respective strengths to address target behaviours where a cluster is weaker; for example, compare the bench strength of Cluster 1 on Succeeding Together with the bench strength of Cluster 4, and the bench strength of Cluster 4 on Customer Service and Simple is Best with the bench strength of Cluster 5 for these target behaviours.

Iterating with and learning from these clusters offers a bridge to other parts of the organization as the change programme demonstrated that change is feasible, builds success stories and leverages shared learning across

FIGURE 17.7 The translation of target clusters as the starting point of the change programme into the three pillar benchmarks

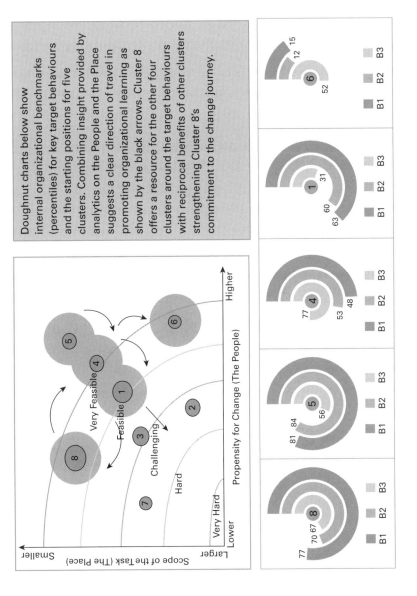

and beyond these clusters. And where would that change journey move next? Armed with those tangible examples, leveraging the strong propensity for change of those in Cluster 6 becomes not only feasible but also significantly more achievable.

Addressing three root causes for the failure of change programmes

More than 83,000 books on change management can be counted on Amazon,[22] and that number is growing I am sure, yet despite all of that published wisdom, the statistics on the success of change programmes continue to disappoint.

I do believe that organizations can beat the odds of failure for change programmes by addressing three root causes driving that failure:

1 A lack of insight into the employees who are the true champions of change and have what it takes to be effective in delivering change programme objectives.

2 A lack of insight into the size of the change task – the 'ask' of employees and work teams – that their change programmes demand and how much the size of that ask varies across an organization.

3 A lack of tools and specifically a behavioural roadmap that enables them to promote shared learning through change and to understand where in the organization they are most likely to gain early traction with their change initiatives.

So, the key learning is not to leave change to chance!

Notes

1 B Ewenstein, W Smith and A Sologar. Changing change management, McKinsey & Co, 2015, www.mckinsey.com/featured-insights/leadership/changing-change-management (archived at https://perma.cc/298Y-WVE9)

2 P Strebel. Why do employees resist change? *Harvard Business Review*, May–June 1996, https://hbr.org/1996/05/why-do-employees-resist-change (archived at https://perma.cc/XKT7-BT84)

3 B Gleeson. Leading change: 6 reasons change management strategies fail, Forbes, 7 December 2016, www.forbes.com/sites/brentgleeson/2016/12/07/leading-change-6-reasons-change-management-strategies-fail/ (archived at https://perma.cc/VC9Y-3CNM)

4 E Lawson and C Price. The psychology of change management, McKinsey, 1 June 2003, www.mckinsey.com/capabilities/people-and-organizational-performance/our-insights/the-psychology-of-change-management (archived at https://perma.cc/Q94M-WTHL)

5 For an example of how the impact of context such as the workplace is now being recognized in research on organizations see G Johns (2006) The essential impact of context on organizational behaviour, *Academy of Management Review*, **31**, pp. 386–408

6 These behavioural dimensions are consistent with broader research on the characteristics of people who are more open to personal change and more likely to commit to organizational change programmes. For an example of this research see M Vakola, I Tsaousis and I Nikolaou (2004) The role of emotional intelligence and personality variables on attitudes towards organizational change, *Journal of Managerial Psychology*, **19**, pp. 88–110

7 D R Cox and E J Snell (1989) *Analysis of Binary Data* (2nd ed), Chapman & Hall

8 For details of benchmarks associated with different lines of organizational research, see F A Bosco, H Aguinis, H, K Singh, J G Field and C A Pierce (2015) Correlational effect size benchmarks, *Journal of Applied Psychology*, **100**, pp. 431–49

9 S Keller and B Schaninger. Getting personal about change, *McKinsey Quarterly*, 21 August 2019, www.mckinsey.com/capabilities/people-and-organizational-performance/our-insights/getting-personal-about-change (archived at https://perma.cc/4G4J-FE4Z). This paper shows that executives in organizations that use insights into the mindsets of employees to guide their change programmes are four times more likely to rate those programmes as successful.

10 To maintain organizational confidentiality, the titles used in this piece are approximations of the actual titles used by this organization.

11 These workshops follow the principles outlined by Kurt Lewin for action research with a specific focus on the 'Changing' aspect of change. That is, diagnosing the impetus for change and exploring and testing new models of behaviour.

12 These behavioural markers act as pre- and post-intervention indicators or Key Development Indicators (KDIs) that enable the organization to know where they are starting from and how much variation there is in those starting points across the organization, as well as the basis for metrics for measuring where the change programme has achieved its objectives and where more investment is required to achieve the change desired.

13 CultureScope provides data on both the People and the Place. In this chapter, we focus on the data from the Place. In the third piece in this series, we show how data on the People and the Place are used to develop a behavioural roadmap to guide change programmes.

14 The metrics shown in this chapter are calibrated in percentiles using an internal benchmark based on this organization's employee responses to the CultureScope behavioural diagnostic.

15 This plot shows the spread between the highest and lowest scores for any pillar. The box for any cluster shows the main concentration of scores across pillars while the vertical lines indicate where the highest and lowest scores for any pillar lie for each cluster.

16 S Keller and B Schaninger. Getting personal about change, *McKinsey Quarterly*, 21 August 2019, www.mckinsey.com/capabilities/people-and-organizational-performance/our-insights/getting-personal-about-change (archived at https://perma.cc/X34U-3HZY). This paper shows that executives in organizations that use insights into the mindsets of employees to guide their change programmes are four times more likely to rate those programmes as successful.

17 There may be more than one target behaviour that sets the objectives and goals of a change programme. In Part 2 of this chapter, we show how three business objectives for the organization were distilled through a systematic process into a set of behavioural markers that served to provide a clear and tangible definition of each behaviour. Those behavioural markers also served to provide the organization with benchmarks against which it could see where it was prior to implementing its change programme and for measuring progress towards its business aims.

18 For an example of how an incremental approach to change was adopted with measurable impact using 'implementation intentions' (having a plan to achieve a goal – an 'implementation intention' – increases the chance that people will follow it up with actions), see the work supported by the Behavioural Insights Team in supporting the people back to work programme. This (pages 7 to 11) and other examples are provided in the Behavioural Insights Team: Update Report 2013-2015, www.behaviouralinsights.co.uk/wp-content/uploads/2015/07/BIT_Update-Report-Final-2013–2015.pdf

19 As this part argues, a key factor in anyone adopting a target behaviour is the obvious one of how goals are set for them to achieve the behaviour in question. Irrespective of how challenging a target behaviour may be for an individual or group of employees, adopting or changing behaviour is only possible if that behaviour is defined in a clear and tangible way, and when there is consensus on how that behaviour is defined and experienced.

20 Cluster numbering simply follows the numbering of the clustering programme we used rather than any ranking or ordering by cluster number.

21 To maintain organizational confidentiality, the titles used in this chapter are approximations of the actual titles used by the organization.

22 R Ashkenas. Change management needs to change, *Harvard Business Review*, 16 April 2013, https://hbr.org/2013/04/change-management-needs-to-cha (archived at https://perma.cc/LZ8D-F5C3)

18

Are your HR processes supporting alignment between culture and strategy?

*Using culture and behavioural analytics
to find whether the answer is 'Yes' – or where
to intervene when the answer is 'No'*

As any wise organizational leader knows, organizations perform better when they acquire, develop and retain the best talent, but simply claiming 'best practice' HR processes is not enough. This is because value grows fastest when those processes align with business strategy.

As the global economy becomes increasingly knowledge-based, firms need to acquire and nurture the best and brightest human capital available and keep these investments in the firm.[1]

HR processes improve operational effectiveness and financial performance[2] when they build skills, motivate employees and empower employees to use their skills and motivations to achieve organizational outcomes.[3]

When you align culture with strategy, you transcend the limits of traditional business conduct. You still need to crunch numbers, but the data holds a more profound meaning – one that informs multiple departments working together toward cultivating something greater than the company itself.[4] In fact, in one study focused on the five-year benefits for alignment between culture and strategy vs lack of alignment, has revealed a positive impact of 17 per cent on financial profit and a 30 per cent positive impact on growth:[5] 'The particular strategy a company employs will succeed only if it is supported by the appropriate cultural attributes', yet over 56 per cent of the surveyed leaders in the study reported low to moderate alignment between workplace culture and strategy.[6]

The plethora of HR metrics in use today do not ask or answer this question: 'Are our HR processes strengthening the alignment between strategy and culture?' Or, as another research study asks, 'Is your talent strategy rooted in your business strategy? Culture can't just be an assortment of well-meaning HR practices… There can be no talent strategy without a compelling business strategy.'[7]

Organizations ignoring this question risk failing to anticipate operational issues and diluting or destroying the value that they seek to create.

Most HR metrics are focused on the following:

- attract and acquire
- onboard and develop
- motivate and retain

Ultimately, the alignment between workplace culture and strategy will be a strong predictor for the above metrics, as this case study will shortly demonstrate.

To create alignment between workplace culture and strategy, organizations should have:

- a valid approach for measuring their organizational culture
- a valid method for measuring their intended outcomes
- a metric to measure alignment between culture and strategy as well as the impact of the adopted HR process
- an action plan to inform ongoing HR investments to achieve targeted culture for serving the strategy

These approaches and methods bring together effective behavioural diagnostics and culture analytics, showing organizations to what degree their HR processes are aligned to strategy, and, critically, where to intervene to improve the alignment.

You may be asking, 'Why this approach?', and I will show you why by making the following key points:

1 The most tangible evidence for an organization's culture is observable behaviour – the day-to-day actions of the organization and its employees, and how they behave in this organization.
2 Metrics for alignment must address two questions:
    o What behaviours drive the success or failure of business strategy?
    o How aligned are the expectations of the organization with the behaviour of its employees?

3 Culture and behaviour analytics must deliver actionable insight into:
   o the measurable impact of HR processes on alignment
   o which processes to focus on to ensure investments do strengthen alignment
4 It is not enough to know which HR processes to focus on; any action plan must also identify specific employee segments where action will deliver the dividends from strengthening alignment between workplace culture and strategy.

So how do we get to understanding fit, misfit and impacts of HR processes? Data on organizational expectations for behaviour (the Place) and how employees naturally behave (the People) provide clear metrics for levels of fit, misfit and misalignment, which can be categorized as follows:

- **Virtuous Alignment**: Expectations of the Place and the behaviour of the People are aligned with strategic goals.
- **Double Negative**: Clear lack of alignment (misfit) between culture and strategic goals for both the People and the Place.
- **Strong Foundation**: Distinct type of misalignment, pointing to the need for capability-type interventions for the People.
- **Suppressed Talent**: Another distinct type of misalignment, pointing to the need for opportunity- and motivation-type interventions for the Place.

Figure 18.1 illustrates these categorizations using the quadrant distribution method by showing the behavioural alignment between Place and People.

FIGURE 18.1 The behavioural defined alignment categorization zones

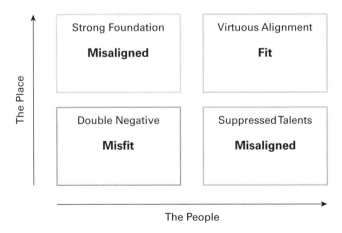

Using this categorization, organizations can discover how HR processes affect alignment and invest appropriately and effectively.

Figure 18.1 is only showing the behavioural alignment, which on its own may be meaningless. However, with analytics you can now add HR outcome metrics just as I described earlier. I will now provide metric definitions as follows:

- **Attract and acquire**: Hiring process, methods and conversion rates and metrics. Are you attracting and hiring talent for your target culture in line with the critical behaviours you will need in the organization?
- **Onboard and develop**: Where there is misalignment, what should you focus on? Is it the Place or the People? Are there any particular employee segments that you need to focus on?
- **Motivate and retain**: Is staff turnover weakening the alignment between culture and strategy? Are there key points in the employee journey that you need to improve?

Let's get into the details of how behavioural measurement and culture analytics actually make sense of workplace culture alignment with strategy. The process can be articulated as follows:

1 **Define**: What are the intended outcomes metrics that you have – are they valid? Do you have any gaps? Review your strategy and define or translate it to outcomes that you can measure.
2 **Measure**: Deploy valid behavioural diagnostics organization-wide, with a target to achieve a statistically relevant sample size.
3 **Identify**: Through the predictive analytics and path analysis process already outlined in Part 1 of this book, you will get to the behavioural leading indicators needed to drive your thematic outcomes and achieve your strategy.
4 **Design, plan and implement targeted interventions**: You will now be able to examine the behavioural alignments across the entire organization and design, plan and implement interventions by demographic segments.
5 **Validate**: As before, remeasure at sensible intervals measuring the behaviours targeted, the alignment between Place and People and the outcomes.

Let us now test this approach on our next case study. This organization is a large professional services business that was interested in hiring and

FIGURE 18.2 Multiple countries analysis hiring against the targeted five behaviours

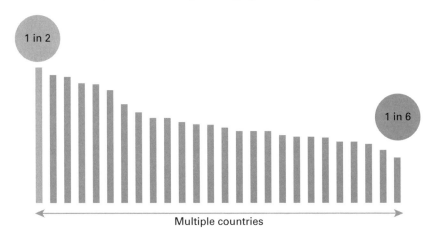

retention success in line with five behaviours that predicted all their targeted outcomes and strategy. The behaviours are: Collective, Empower, Standardized, Conformity and Innovate.

Figure 18.2 shows a multiple countries analysis where alignment to the targeted behaviours of recent hires is lower despite stronger available talent pools. Is this due to a blind spot in hiring practices, complacency, or both?

Analysing Figure 18.2 reveals that there is a three times variance across the countries for talent acquisition. At the top end, one in two candidates have the behaviour Virtuous Alignment; that drops to one in six at the other end of the scale.

Combining behavioural alignment data between Place and People with additional employee metrics for tenure, gender and job level (seniority) reveals the following trends:

- One-year tenure is a key pivot point in terms of alignment, with longer tenure correlated with Suppressed Talent or Double Negative.
- Gender is correlated with distinct patterns of misalignment, with females more likely to represent Strong Foundation and male employees Suppressed Talent.
- Job level (grade) correlated with misalignment (Suppressed Talent) and misfit (Double Negative).

Figure 18.3 shows the above demographic type insights versus the alignment zones and the likelihood of occurrence.

FIGURE 18.3 Employee demographic insights versus the alignment zones and the likelihood of occurrence

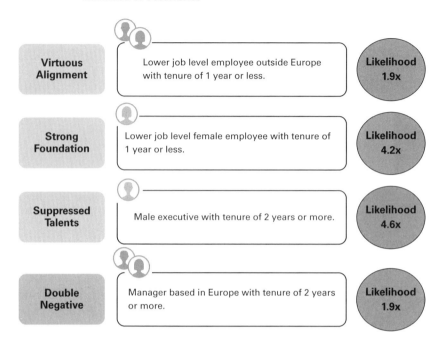

For clarity, the narrative for Figure 18.3 goes like this (remember, the alignment refers to the five critical behaviours that predict their targeted outcomes and ultimately their strategy):

- For Virtuous Alignment (the target zone), I am almost two times more likely to be an employee outside of Europe, with a tenure of one year or less and within a lower job grade.
- For Strong Foundation (focus interventions on People capability), I am four times more likely to be female, with a tenure of one year or less and within a lower job grade.
- For Suppressed Talent (focus interventions on opportunity and motivation), I am four and a half times more likely to be male with a tenure of two years or more.
- For Double Negative (focus interventions on capability, opportunity and motivation), I am almost two times more likely to be a manager in Europe with a tenure of two years or more.

In addition to answering the question for this organization 'Are our HR practices strengthening our alignment to strategy?', the culture fit metrics also provide the analytics framework for identifying actions and interventions where the answer is 'maybe' or 'no'.

Employee behavioural profiles associated with levels of fit provide clarity as to what investments are required for HR practices to strengthen alignment and where those investments should be targeted. Those profiles enabled the organization to design and implement interventions that are tailored to specific employee segments and to set up actions with clear goals and measures of success.

Having gained the behavioural actionable insights along with the demographic segmentations, the following were recommended as key action points for this organization:

- Attract and acquire:
  o Action: Key organization-wide issues are centred around the variation in the impact of the hiring practices across countries, manifesting in the lower fit of hires in countries with stronger talent pools; immediate review of the selection process; perhaps learn from the one country that got it right.
  o Action: Key employee segment is the managerial hires with higher levels of Double Negative and where hiring and promotion criteria will benefit from immediate review.
- Onboard and develop:
  o Action: For male executives, onboarding should focus on leveraging their talents and soft skills to build stronger alignment between the Place and the People.
  o Action: For female employees, development programmes should focus on the positives of the Place and address soft skills gaps among employees.
- Motivate and retain:
  o Action: Pivotal retention point is just after one year of tenure, with alignment weakening for longer tenures; is there an issue with employee experience over time? The trick is to learn what is happening in the first year of tenure that is favourable and find a way to maintain it after the first year in the employee journey.

o Action: Risks of employee turnover in Europe are driven by management employees who feature in the Double Negative zone. Immediate programmes/interventions should be designed and implemented to work on capability, as well as opportunity and motivation; these interventions must target the five critical behaviours.

Additionally, those demonstrated profiles defined by demographics also serve to challenge working assumptions that may be misplaced and fail to surface operational issues and risks.

Before we move on, I want to address an interesting question related to tenure that I often get asked. That is, 'Can the behavioural alignment or tension between People and Place be a predictor of tenure?' To answer the question fully, I would develop a full saturated regression model resulting in restricted nested behaviours, with odds ratio, based on tenure to answer a primary question, 'Can the behavioural profile predict which tenure group a person is likely to belong to?' The answer for one of the organizations that asked this question is demonstrated in Figure 18.4.

FIGURE 18.4 The tenure odds ratio for five behaviours: Disenfranchise, Delivery Focus, Collective, Consolidate and Conformity

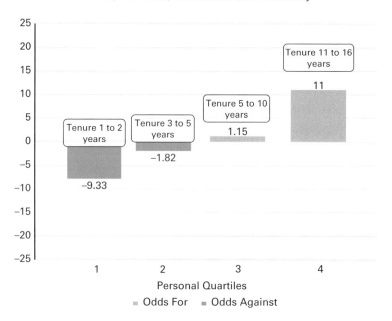

NOTE N=8,588 and R=0.359

Analysing the model in Figure 18.4 reveals that the five behaviours are the predictor of tenure; these are Disenfranchise, Delivery Focus, Collective, Consolidate and Conformity. You can see that the longer the tenure, the more likely that employees will have these behaviours as present. In fact, employees that have been with the organization for 11 to 16 years are 11 times more likely to have these behaviours as present, and employees that have been with the organization for up to two years are nine times less likely to have these behaviours as present.

Having developed the model, we can now look at the tension between Place and People for the five behaviours. That yields a dramatic insight for two of the behaviours:

- Disenfranchise tension for lower tenures is at 40 per cent between People and Place, decreasing to 23 per cent for higher tenures
- Consolidate tension for lower tenures is at 38 per cent, decreasing to 10 per cent for higher tenures

Basically, the higher the tenure, the more likely employees are aligned to the Place for the two behaviours.

This organization also examined employee departure historic data, showing that employees are 38 times more likely to leave when the tension between People and Place, for the two behaviours, is above 18 per cent.

Now for the complication with this case. Two of the predictive behaviours that are part of the model for the intended outcomes to achieve the strategy are opposite to the retention model – Empower vs Disfranchise and Innovate vs Consolidate. This organization is actually hiring talent fit for their strategy; however, this talent is not likely to stay as the issue is with the Place. So action is needed in two ways:

1 Intervention design targeted at the Place for the desired two behaviours, Empower and Innovate (dichotomous to Disenfranchise and Consolidate) for all tenure groups, to address the need for opportunity and motivation.
2 Intervention design targeted at the People for the desired two behaviours, that is Empower and Innovate (dichotomous to Disenfranchise and Consolidate) for tenure of five years and above, to address the need for capability.

This second case tells an interesting story about how you simply cannot drive change by just hiring. You will need to create the environment as well, as the two will work in tandem.

Notes

1. T R Crook, S Y Todd, J G Combs, D J Woehr and D J Ketchen (2011). Does human capital matter? A meta-analysis of the relationship between human capital and firm performance, *Journal of Applied Psychology*, **96**, pp. 443–56
2. B E Becker and M A Huselid (1998) High performance work systems and firm performance: A synthesis of research and managerial implications, *Research in Personnel and Human Resources Management*, **16**, pp. 53–101
3. K Jiang, D P Lepak, J Hu and J C Baer (2012) How does human resource management influence organizational outcomes? A meta-analytic investigation of mediating mechanisms, *Academy of Management Journal*, **55**, pp. 1264–94
4. W Craig. What happens when you align culture with strategy, Forbes, 29 May 2018, www.forbes.com/sites/williamcraig/2018/05/29/what-happens-when-you-align-culture-with-strategy/ (archived at https://perma.cc/B4LZ-JQF9)
5. B Jaruzelski, J Loehr and R Holman. Booz & Company Global Innovation 1000: Why culture is key, strategy+business, 25 October 2011, www.strategy-business.com/article/11404 (archived at https://perma.cc/46UQ-RWSG)
6. Institute for Management Development (2017) IMD World Talent Rankings 2017
7. B Taylor. 5 questions to ask about corporate culture to get beyond the usual meaningless blather, *Harvard Business Review*, 1 June 2017, https://hbr.org/2017/06/5-questions-to-ask-about-corporate-culture-to-get-beyond-the-usual-meaningless-blather (archived at https://perma.cc/EP94-KDY7)

19

Going beyond diversity metrics to actionable insights on DE&I

It's the behaviours that matter

While the business case for diversity, equity and inclusion (DE&I) has been made by those such as Dixon-Fyle, Dolan, Hunt and Prince (2020),[1] doubts are growing about whether DE&I programmes are having a real and positive impact. In an online BBC article, Nathoo (2021) cites research showing that the kinds of training that organizations tend to favour the most are short, one-shot sessions that can be completed and the requisite diversity boxes ticked, are unlikely to make a difference in the long-term behaviour of participants.[2]

Friedersdorf (2023) in an article in *The Atlantic* comments: 'While its advocates claim that "diversity workshops can foster better intergroup relations, improve the retention of minority employees, close recruitment gaps and so on" ... in practice there is little evidence that many of these initiatives work. And the type of diversity training that is currently in vogue – mandatory trainings that blame dominant groups for DEI problems – may well have a net-negative effect.'[3]

These doubts are supported by a US survey conducted by WebMD Health Services (2023) showing that, while 89 per cent of respondents report their organization has a DE&I programme and while 72 per cent report wanting to work for an organization that supports it, 46 per cent report that their organization is not doing enough, with around a half of respondents reporting experience of work situations inconsistent with a DE&I culture.[4]

Could the root problem be behaviours and organizational culture?

From their survey, WebMD concludes 'the DE&I focus should be on shifting workplace culture so that the programs meet the needs of employees and are supported through all levels of management'. I agree, but the notion of 'culture' is a rich one with a wealth of theories and models (e.g. Denison; Hofstede; Schein; Trompenaars and Hampden-Turner[5]). To frame our approach to understanding culture, let's consider the notion of 'unconscious bias' that many DE&I programmes aim to address.

Unconscious bias, by definition, is bias that we are unaware of. The former US Secretary of Defence Donald Rumsfeld captured this when he stated 'Reports that say that something hasn't happened are always interesting to me because, as we know, there are known knowns; there are things we know we know. We also know there are known unknowns; that is to say we know there are some things we do not know. But there are also unknown unknowns – the ones we don't know we don't know. And if one looks throughout the history of our country and other free countries, it is the latter category that tend to be the difficult ones.'[6]

So, how can organizations get to something that is an 'unknown-unknown'? In our view, maybe they can't. What they can do is determine what people should consciously experience day-to-day that evidences a real commitment to DE&I. In that spirit, our approach to culture can be summed up as clusters of behaviours that reflect the beliefs and values of individuals and organizations, and the questions we seek to answer are: what behaviours demonstrate a true commitment to DE&I, and to what extent are those behaviours present in an organization today? From the answers to those questions, we then work back to explore how targeted behaviours can be developed to provide a platform for broader organizational learning and change.

A similar definition has been adopted by the UK's Financial Conduct Authority (FCA), important to the context of this case study, who define culture as 'the habitual behaviours and mindsets that characterize an organization'.[7] The FCA goes on to state: 'Simply put, culture is "the way things are done around here" … This includes the norms, values and practices which are revealed by how people think and behave … as well as our behaviour when no-one is looking.'

What's the elephant still in the room? Maybe it's real commitment to DE&I programmes!

Recently we have been hit with a tsunami of DE&I-related news items that begs several questions about whether we have achieved a truly DE&I-friendly workplace culture. This is the elephant that may still be in the room. Whilst DE&I programmes are seen as a must-do, are organizations really gaining traction with those programmes? From that question follows another for the analytics community – how is the investment in analytics helping organizations understand the impact of their DE&I programmes, and what do organizations need to do to strengthen that impact?

The ask of DE&I programmes is not an easy one; if organizations want diversity, then they have to be able to embrace difference, even divergence, and recognize the value in doing so. If they want inclusion, then they have to accept the sharing of opinions even if, at first sight, that may appear to bring the additional complexity of including others in making decisions and in acting on those decisions.

Let's take a step back from demographics and take a moment to think about what DE&I programmes are really asking organizations and their employees to do. A little reflection takes us inevitably and logically to a simple proposition: if the proof for whether DE&I programmes are gaining traction lies in how people behave rather than the demographic they represent, then surely organizations need to understand whether their culture encourages or discourages the behaviours aligned with DE&I initiatives.

Whilst most organizations are frantically chasing the diversity metrics, and there are so many to focus on, they often miss that one must primarily and critically create the environment of acceptance and equality, else all that diversity will leak out. It's a bit like trying to eat soup with a fork!

Before we move on, I want to provide basic definitions for diversity, equity and inclusion:

- Diversity: being mindful of all dimensions of human differences at organizations. It often translates to a deliberate process for how many different types of people, by demographics, are hired and promoted.
- Equity: having an egalitarian environment and the policies that service equality where people of all differences, genders, races and ethnicities are treated in an equal manner. This results in equal opportunities for all.
- Inclusion: the act of including people regardless of their differences. This act leads to an environment where everyone feels respected and valued.

Seven behaviours of a DE&I-friendly workplace culture

How do you know if the culture of your organization is DE&I friendly? As part of the research I conducted, outlined in Chapter 4, I managed to extract seven behavioural dimensions for the Place that talk to how inclusive an organization is:

1 **Collective**: Goals achieved through partnership and alliances.
   o Inclusion impact: Shared obligations are clear. Goals are set and agreed within the organization and with external stakeholders in a spirit of partnership and through alliances.

2 **Empower**: Decisions are delegated to lower levels with supportive guidance.
   o Inclusion impact: Decision-making is a cascade, not a directive. They are effective at delegating decisions to lower levels within the organization and provide supportive guidance on how those lower down should exercise judgment.

3 **Expressive**: People do not hesitate to express their feelings and openness is valued.
   o Inclusion impact: They want to know what employees really think and feel. Employees are encouraged to share and express their opinions and concerns.

4 **Team Focus**: Work is delivered through collaborative effort and team results are prioritized over individual results.
   o Inclusion impact: Teamwork is valued as much as individual contributions. Managers recognize that goals are achieved through collaborative effort.

5 **Active Learning**: Active steps are taken to improve employees' skills and careers, and employee growth is considered an integral part of the job.
   o Inclusion impact: They ask the question 'How are people growing through the work they do?' Employees grow through their jobs and their work is actively recognized in reward and in career progression.

6 **Conformity**: People try to deal fairly with each other based on clear rules, values and mutual obligations.
   o Inclusion impact: The rules for dealing with differences are clear. Employees are encouraged to resolve issues based on clear expectations for interpersonal behaviour and mutual obligations.

7 **Achievement**: People are valued for the contribution that they make, irrespective of status.

   o Inclusion impact: Accountability is based on contributions made. People are valued for the contribution they make, irrespective of the status they hold in the organization.

Essentially, once the CultureScope diagnostic is deployed organization-wide, measuring the above listed behaviours, an inclusion index can be obtained. However, as I am regularly reminding all organizations, workplace culture is unique – so one should not rely purely on that index. Through the addition of DE&I outcome measures to the analytics, each organization can obtain their own inclusion behavioural index.

The context for the case study

The organization is a private financial institution subject to the regulatory framework for the financial sector in the UK, and specifically the Financial Conduct Authority (FCA).[8]

An audit by the FCA triggered by concerns over the company's risk exposure and volatility in its core markets had identified a number of additional concerns related to working practices that they felt reflected issues with the organization's culture. As a consequence, the FCA instructed the company to commission a report by what the FCA refers to as a 'skilled person', which they define as 'appearing to the regulator to have the skills necessary to make a report on the matter concerned'.

In short, the organization was required to respond to the FCA's concerns in a meaningful way and to demonstrate that it understood what it needed to fix by producing a tangible plan for doing so.

Whilst the organization had an existing employee survey, it and the FCA felt that this survey did not provide clarity around employee engagement and did not provide the basis for tangible actions. As an example of the type of negative workplace culture indicator referred to by the FCA, and for which the existing employee survey did not provide clear diagnostics, one data point shared by the organization with me before CultureScope was deployed indicated potential DE&I issues.

While the employee split across the organization's workforce by gender was approximately 50:50, the average tenure of female employees was 2.2 years compared to an average tenure for male employees of 6.8 years, more than three times lower. The CEO had some key questions: 'What behaviours exist in the organization, and how do these specifically relate to their DE&I agenda? And what are the relevant outcomes to consider?'

Thus, with the FCA's approval, CultureScope was commissioned at a time when the company appointed a new CEO to lead the transformation of the organization. That CEO, in turn, created a new position of Communications and Culture staffed by a C-suite appointee with a strong background in corporate communications.

These appointments signified a broader intent of the company in deploying a behavioural approach to change. While we have referred to the FCA's interest in organizational workplace culture underpinning the effective conduct of financial firms and therefore, in their view, business performance and customer confidence, the new CEO with Board approval had also established a need to develop and implement a new people strategy.

To respond to the FCA's concerns, the organization had identified a clear need to undertake a business transformation to address rebalancing its portfolios and its systems for managing its customer transactions as well as tighter controls over its day-to-day finances. To achieve that business transformation and to demonstrate to the regulator that it could address what might be referred to as the hard and soft factors key to successful transformation, the organization was also conscious of the need to ensure it had a stable supply of talent to deliver the transformation. This included retaining the talent it had as well as attracting strong talent where it needed to strengthen its workforce. A new people strategy was therefore seen as key to the overall success of a broader business transformation.

The project was supported by the appointment of an independent transformation consultant to work alongside my team. In line with the principles of change management described earlier, the appointment of the transformation consultant served to combine a data-driven approach with the insights offered by someone experienced in working at Board and C-suite levels, in business change and transformation as well having experience at a senior level in financial services including commercial and retail banking, brokerage and Fintech.

The focus of the transformation consultant's role was to work with the organization's leaders in translating behavioural and actionable insights from CultureScope into achievable goals, to work with human resources and organizational development specialists in the organization to help shape communications in support of achieving those goals, as well as working alongside my team in identifying where good practice already existed in the organization that could be used to provide concrete examples for sharing and strengthening desired behaviours across the organization.

This specific case for DE&I began with the organization asking our team to investigate broader issues related to an organizational transformation programme which was part of an organizational development (OD) initiative.

One of the OD initiatives was to explore barriers to employee engagement, seen as essential to shifting the client organization from where it had been to a healthier inclusive culture and demonstrating a commitment to this shift in culture to the financial regulator.

To truly answer the 'why' of why DE&I was not working, and just before CultureScope diagnostics deployment, I worked with the OD consultant to design specific outcome measures. We decided to add in our deployment two sentiment-type questions related to the feeling of belonging, as belonging is one key outcome of DE&I. The questions were:

Outcome 1: I feel I am a valued member of our organization.

1 Strongly agree
2 Agree
3 Neither agree nor disagree
4 Disagree
5 Strongly disagree

Outcome 2: I feel I am a valued member of my team.

1 Strongly agree
2 Agree
3 Neither agree nor disagree
4 Disagree
5 Strongly disagree

Insights generated

The CultureScope diagnostic was deployed, and data collection yielded a completion rate of 1,565, representing a 75 per cent response rate within three weeks, providing a substantial effect size. The high response rate reflected the company's commitment to culture measurement, including a video by the CEO explaining the purpose and importance of the project, daily reminders with links to the survey and dedicated time to complete the survey allotted to employees as part of their work schedules.

To develop the full insights for DE&I, I used two approaches: firstly using the seven behaviours inclusion index, and secondly developing an outcome-based model then delivering insight on absent and present behaviours.

Using the seven behaviours inclusion index, the data was analysed by gender and ethnicity with breakdowns for various parts of the organization, notably for client-facing 'front office' operations. The results showed the following:

Substantial variance by gender

To illustrate the difference at the Place, and to provide another diagrammatic method to present analytics, I will use radar graphs. With this type of graph you will be able to see the targeted behaviour and its dichotomous pair.

Figure 19.1 shows the master inclusion index as well as the behavioural factors driving the results of the overall index. For each behavioural dichotomous pair, the target behaviours are underlined for ease of reference and clarity. The inclusion index includes a percentage ruler, which is the outermost rim, and, for each benchmark, an inner strength rim denoting in percentage terms how inclusive the organization is. Anything beyond 50 per cent for a benchmark denotes that inclusion is present, and less than 50 per cent indicates that for the specific benchmark inclusion is absent.

The overall gender split may look great at 52 per cent male vs 48 per cent female employees. The gender diversity agenda is working! However, the issue is with inclusion. Figure 19.1 shows significant variance by gender of the observed (at the Place) behaviours. To provide contextual analysis for two of the behavioural factors as an example:

- Conformity organizationally is absent for females, so fairness and rules based on equality are not working for me if I am female. However, if I am male then Conformity is relatively present.
- Team Focus is organizationally absent if I am female, meaning I am not invited to team collaborative work and I am expected to work alone. This is very different if I am male, when teamwork is happening at the Place.

The above behaviours are a Place issue. What I am articulating is that the opportunity and motivation for Team Focus and for Conformity are present for males, and absent for females.

The Place is working against providing an environment for inclusion, resulting in much higher female employee turnover (female average tenure is 2.2 years vs male average tenure of 6.8 years) and lower engagement, explaining the 'why' of poorer performance. By now, this example should illustrate how inclusion by behaviour is a leading indicator for tenure, engagement and performance.

I find it very interesting that most organizations tell me that they want to focus on performance. My response would be: performance is the outcome, and you need to focus on the culture and behaviours that drive the desired performance. This example goes further, as you will need to focus on behaviours that drive inclusion before you can influence performance.

To demonstrate the 'where' as an additional insight, we examined the Front Office since that is the function that is the most client-facing. Their behaviour organizational data (the Place) demonstrated a concerning variance.

Figure 19.2 shows a significant difference across a number of organizational behaviours. In the 'Place', in fact, for the Front Office, inclusion is working totally against females.

Whilst I was participating in a number of focus groups organized by the OD consultant with female employees to explore this further, the qualitative information obtained from these focus groups' substantiated CultureScope results which had also identified an unhealthy management environment in one of the customer-facing operations (Front Office).

When this unhealthy environment was uncovered, the Chief Executive Officer asked me why the female employees had not spoken up and expressed these significant issues. I was quick to share with the executive the females' own behavioural measurement for Expressive, as it is absent and shows significant difference from their male colleagues. See Figure 19.3 for the radar graph: behaviour peaks in the present zone for males for Expressive and is absent for females. This behavioural People absence is also combined with the organizational (Place) absence for Expressive along with other gender- and Place-related behavioural factors, namely Conformity, creating an environment in which female employees were unlikely to speak up.

Simply, in the Front Office, the environment does not support gender equality for speak up, and that has fully manifested in its absence for females.

FIGURE 19.1 Radar graph and inclusion index for the whole organization, organizational behaviours

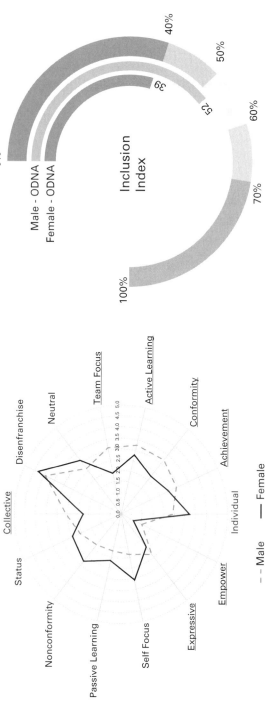

NOTE Total n=1565, M=811, F=754. ODNA = Organizational Culture Behavioural DNA

FIGURE 19.2 Radar graph and inclusion index for Front Office, organizational behaviours

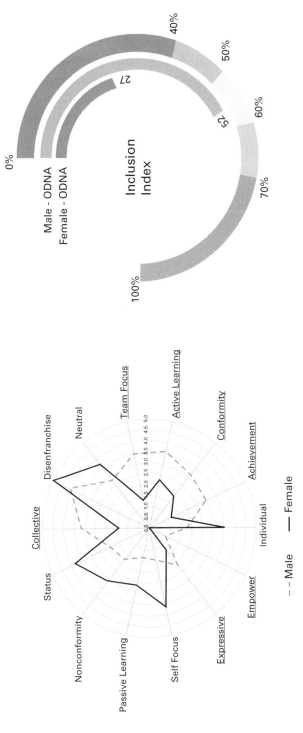

NOTE Total n=538, M=281, F= 257

FIGURE 19.3 Radar graph for Front Office, personal behaviours

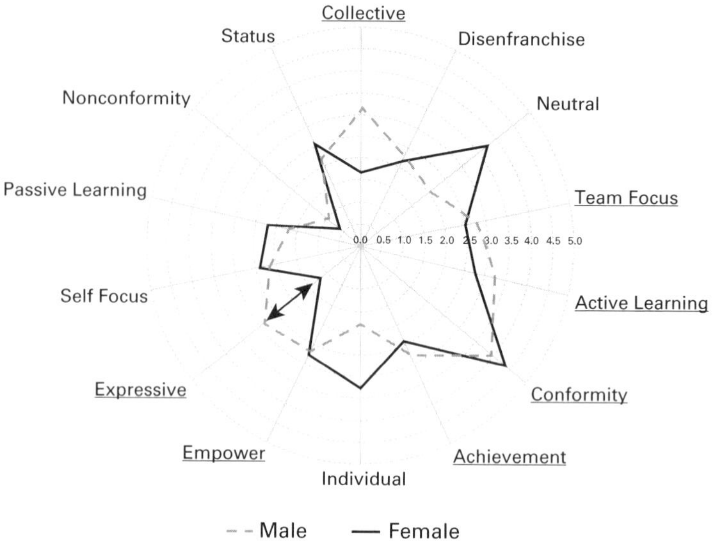

[Radar chart with axes: Collective, Disenfranchise, Neutral, Team Focus, Active Learning, Conformity, Achievement, Individual, Empower, Expressive, Self Focus, Passive Learning, Nonconformity, Status. Scale 0.0 to 5.0. Dashed line = Male, solid line = Female.]

NOTE Total n=538, M=281, F= 257

Substantial variance by ethnicity and racial discrimination uncovered

Let's examine ethnicity with the same behavioural lens. The data analysis showed a positive result for only one ethnic group tagged as 'White' (51 per cent) with another ethnic group in particular showing a concerning variance tagged as 'Black' (22 per cent). A further 27 per cent reported a different ethnicity and were classified for analysis as 'Mixed'. Interestingly, ethnicity diversity numbers again may look OK, but the inclusion index tells a different story.

This illustrated a particular ethnic cohort with significantly absent organizational behaviours for the inclusion index, suggesting that the organization treats this group differently.

These differences conjure up contrasting styles of interaction depending on the ethnicity of the employee, but what does data on the Place suggest for behaviours encouraged by the workplace? Figure 19.4 shows Black employees and employees classified as Mixed see the workplace as discouraging for Collective, Team Focus, Expressive, Active Learning and Conformity when compared to White employees. Particularly concerning is the significant behavioural difference between the White ethnicity and Black ethnicity employees at the Place, resulting in the inclusion index being absent for the Black ethnicity and by contrast somewhat present for the White ethnicity.

FIGURE 19.4 Radar graph showing the organization (Place) behavioural differences and the inclusion index for different ethnic groups for the whole organization

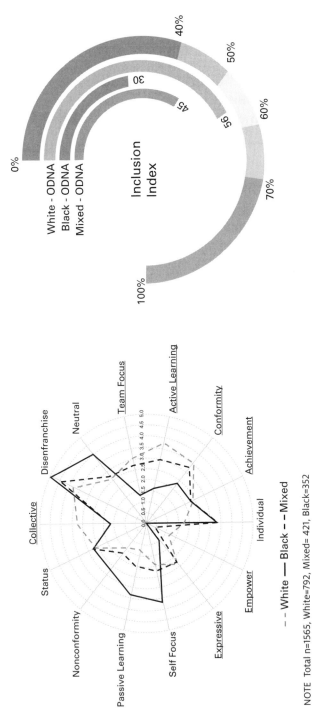

NOTE Total n=1565, White=792, Mixed= 421, Black=352

Going back to the outcome measures to understand 'how' to fix inclusion

As with any organization and research project, the process through which I developed the model shared in this book followed a number of iterative steps. Ultimately, choosing a model comes down partly to what the data says. So, to develop an inclusion index and behaviours specific to this organization as leading indicators, let us now run an analysis for the two outcome measures: 'I feel I am a valued member of our organization' and 'I feel I am a valued member of my team'. The outcomes are broadly seen as indicative for the feeling of belonging.

At the aggregated data level, I completed a maximum likelihood factor analysis with oblique rotation of the two outcome questions. I then used a series of hierarchical regressions to explore the relationships between CultureScope behavioural measures for the 'People' and the 'Place' for each outcome model. I used a fully saturated model with all 15 CultureScope dimensions as the baseline to test more restricted and nested models with fewer CultureScope dimensions to arrive at our final predictor set of CultureScope behaviours.

To illustrate the strength of each model, I further calculated the odds ratio for each outcome as odds ratio is an easy way to represent the likelihood of an outcome based on the absence and/or presence of nested behaviour models to show how good the predictive model is.

To apply the odds ratio method, we have arranged the behaviours into four quartiles, and count the number of outcome occurrences per nested model quartiles.

If it occurs that the odds ratio is lower than 1, this indicating an odds against relation, hence the negative reciprocal of this value, and therefore it would be plotted on the negative y-axis.

Based on the methodology above, let's explore the first outcome:

Outcome 1: I feel I am a valued member of our organization.

1. Strongly agree
2. Agree
3. Neither agree nor disagree
4. Disagree
5. Strongly disagree

FIGURE 19.5 Regression analysis odds ratio for the first outcome, employees being valued by the organization

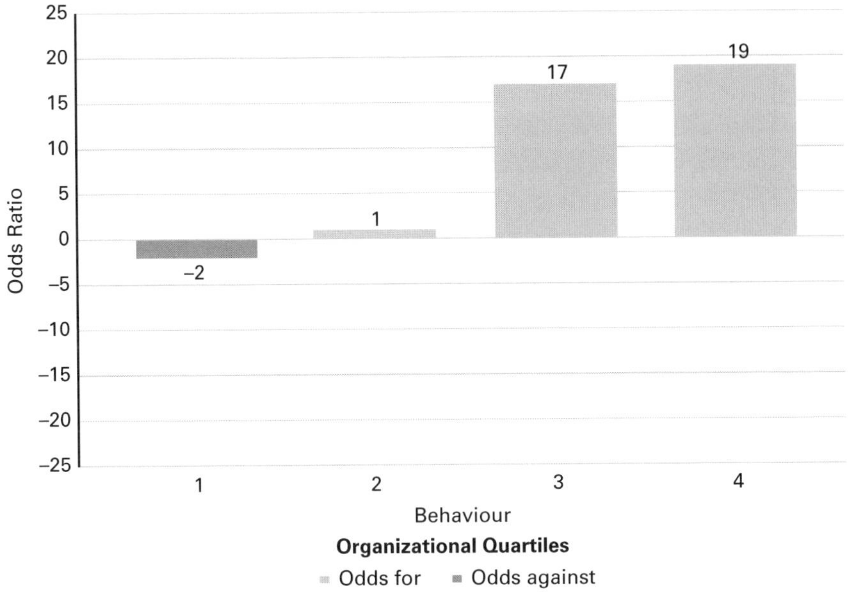

[Bar chart: Odds Ratio on y-axis (-25 to 25), Behaviour Organizational Quartiles 1-4 on x-axis. Values: Q1 = -2, Q2 = 1, Q3 = 17, Q4 = 19. Legend: Odds for, Odds against]

NOTE n=1,565. Probability of behaviours' presence or absence. Behaviours are Conformity, Expressive and Team Focus

Figure 19.5 shows that the absence or presence of three organizational behaviours, Conformity, Expressive and Team Focus, predict the first outcome with a multiple R=0.5614. For this effect size that is beyond the 80th centile for predictive,[9] and results in the following odds ratio: employees are 19 times more likely to feel valued at the organization when Conformity, Expressive and Team Focus are present at the 'Place', and two times less likely to feel valued when the said behaviours are absent.

Again, based on the methodology above, let's explore the second outcome:

Outcome 2: I feel I am a valued member of my team.

1 Strongly agree
2 Agree
3 Neither agree nor disagree
4 Disagree
5 Strongly disagree

FIGURE 19.6 Regression analysis odds ratio for the second outcome, employees being valued by their team

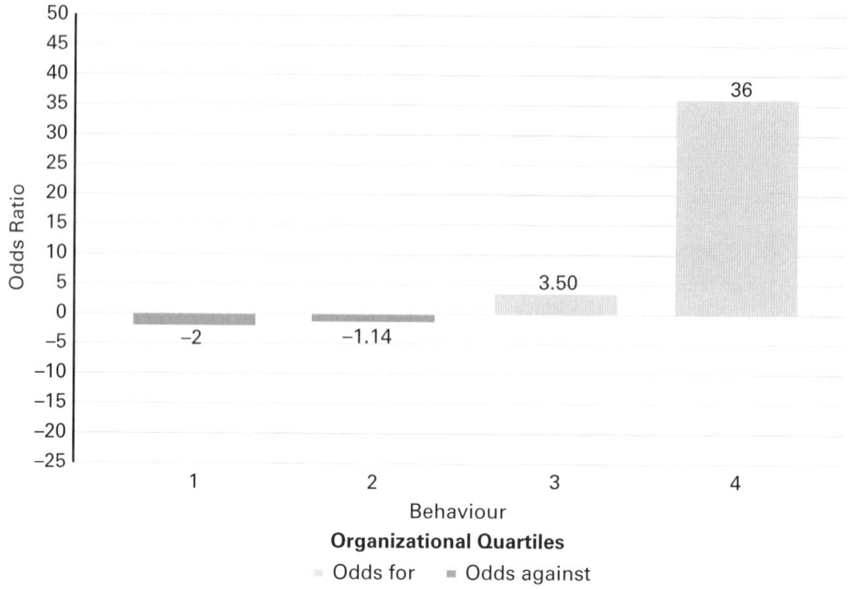

[Bar chart showing Odds Ratio on y-axis (from -25 to 50) versus Behaviour Organizational Quartiles on x-axis (1-4). Values: 1 = -2, 2 = -1.14, 3 = 3.50, 4 = 36. Legend: Odds for, Odds against.]

NOTE n=1,565. Probability of behaviours' presence or absence. Behaviours are Conformity, Expressive, Achievement and Team Focus

Figure 19.6 shows that the absence or presence of four organizational behaviours predict the second outcome with a multiple R=0.6211, that is Conformity, Expressive, Achievement and Team Focus, resulting in the following odds ratio: employees are 36 times more likely to feel valued by their teams when Conformity, Expressive, Achievement and Team Focus are present at the 'Place', and two times less likely to feel valued when the said behaviours are absent.

Having explored both models, you can now see that three behavioural factors exist in both models. In fact, with simple path analysis it can be deduced that the organization will not achieve outcome 2 if they can't solve outcome 1, and since outcome 1 relates to being valued at the organization, I think that makes perfect sense. If belonging is not driven across the entire organization, then teams are unlikely to deliver it.

So, what does this mean? Focusing on the inclusion context, it means that regardless of gender, ethnicity, seniority and so on, the Place must provide all employees with the opportunity to express their opinions and views. The rules must apply fairly and equally to all (this will be a critical checkpoint for any organizational policies, as some can work against inclusion), and team contribution should be encouraged and welcomed as every team member matters (it's about what you do rather than who you are).

Having built a cluster of the behaviours for outcomes 1 and 2 respectively, we can further investigate how significant the issue is by gender and ethnicity and then focus on the absent behaviours for intervention design and planning.

Figure 19.7 shows the three behavioural clusters generated by the first outcome model applied to the gender benchmark, and this illustrates that at the Place, interventions are needed for opportunity and motivation for the female population. The inclusion index for these three behaviours provides further evidence on the gap, showing how differently females are treated by the Place compared to their male colleagues.

Figure 19.8 shows the four behavioural clusters and inclusion index for the second outcome generated model; that is, being valued by teams within the organization. As the second model encompasses all three behaviours from the first model, it will not come as a shock that variance between the genders is significant; however, the fourth behaviour, which is Achievement, does not have such a stark difference. This does simplify matters as interventions directed at the three behaviours that exist in both models will go a long way to solve the inclusion issues.

For completeness, let us apply the same lens for the generated behavioural cluster models for both outcomes to generate ethnicity benchmarks.

Figures 19.9 and 19.10 show the ethnicity benchmarks for the outcome 1 and 2 models respectively, exhibiting organizational behaviours and the inclusion index. These figures indicate that similar interventions are needed as per the gender insights, and should be directed at the Place for three behaviours: Conformity, Team Focus and Expressive. The key demographic that would benefit from such interventions is the 'Black' ethnic group.

A better approach to illustrate the 'where' is by using quadrant dispersion analysis, so let us apply the quadrant dispersion method for the model 1 and model 2 behaviours. It can be seen from the analysis in Figure 19.11 that the three behaviours can be learnt from the Treasury and IT functions, and in particular if we can understand the environmental difference between the two functions and Front Office, we can design interventions that are likely to work. If they are working for you already, then the question becomes: how can we replicate that?

FIGURE 19.7 Gender behavioural radar graph and inclusion index for model one outcome, employees valued at the organization

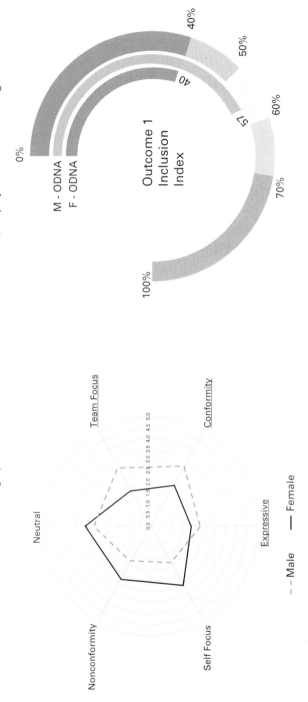

NOTE Total n=1,565

FIGURE 19.8 Gender behavioural radar graph and inclusion index for model two outcome, employees valued by their teams

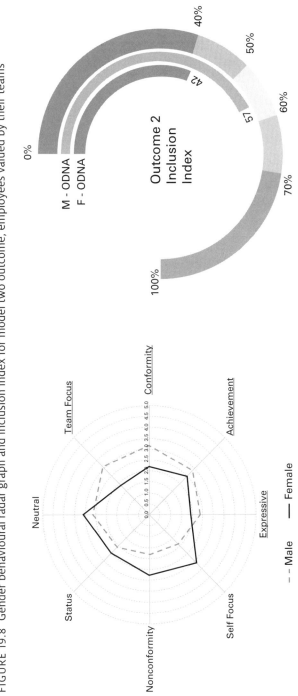

NOTE Total n=1,565

FIGURE 19.9 Ethnicity behavioural radar graph and inclusion index for model one outcome, employees valued at the organization

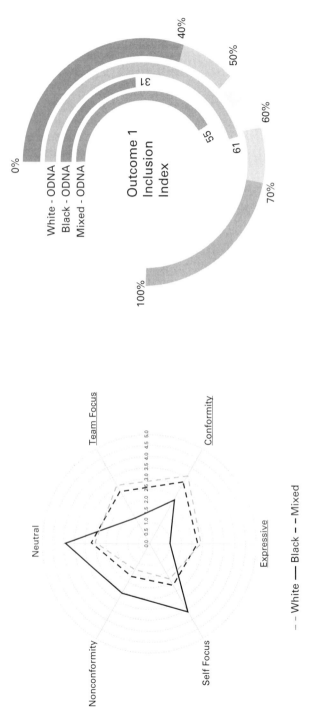

NOTE Total n=1,565

FIGURE 19.10 Ethnicity behavioural radar graph and inclusion index for model two outcome, employees valued by their teams

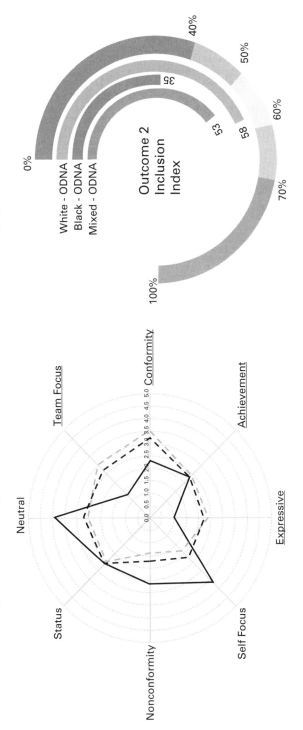

NOTE Total n=1,565

FIGURE 19.11 Quadrant distribution of the three targeted behaviours: Conformity, Team Focus and Expressive

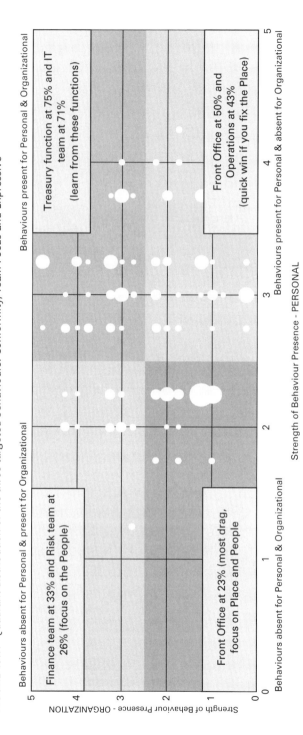

From a return-on-investment perspective, it is interesting to note that the targeted three behaviours resolve inclusion and boost all diversity demographics.

What actions were taken?

Turning insights into action for this organization involved both quantitative and qualitative elements, and the behavioural quadrant alignment matrix as shown in Figure 19.12 developed for this organization was used to guide the OD transformational consultant in conducting further interviews and workshops. That alignment matrix identified which business functions showed stronger alignment and which, like the Front Office, showed weaker alignment, giving the OD transformational consultant a map to work from to compare employee experience where alignment was stronger and weaker.

The deeper dives led to a number of targeted interventions ranging in scope from companywide communication to those focused on the company's executive committee's actions and to how existing use of technology, such as collaboration platforms, in one business function could strengthen DE&I behaviours in other functions.

These deeper dives were led by the OD transformation consultant and identified that where alignment was higher between the People and the Place for Expressive, there was a stronger capability among leaders to make the time to engage in two-way communication. Furthermore, that willingness to encourage open communication whilst showing respect also enabled trust in the use of technology for more open communication between employees. In contrast, and where alignment was lower, the contrasting pole of Neutral was more likely because leaders and managers felt they did not have the time or the physical space for them to be Expressive, and those leaders and managers also felt uncomfortable about where the limits were to be Expressive, indicating an issue of psychological safety.

Further deeper dives led to interventions aimed at promoting a sense of psychological safety from the top down in the organization, to using corporate communications to provide examples of how Expressive and other behaviours could be incorporated and encouraged in day-to-day interactions, and how issues of physical space could be addressed through using the virtual space provided by technology.

FIGURE 19.12 Behavioural quadrant alignment matrix and descriptions per quadrant

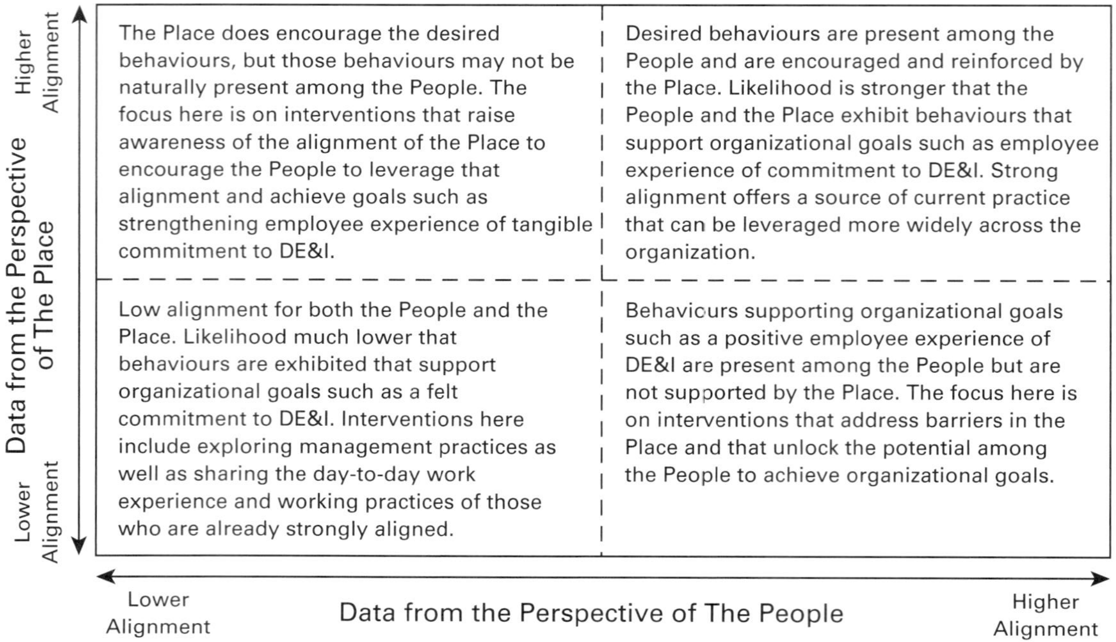

	Lower Alignment ← Data from the Perspective of The People → Higher Alignment
Higher Alignment (Data from the Perspective of The Place)	The Place does encourage the desired behaviours, but those behaviours may not be naturally present among the People. The focus here is on interventions that raise awareness of the alignment of the Place to encourage the People to leverage that alignment and achieve goals such as strengthening employee experience of tangible commitment to DE&I.	Desired behaviours are present among the People and are encouraged and reinforced by the Place. Likelihood is stronger that the People and the Place exhibit behaviours that support organizational goals such as employee experience of commitment to DE&I. Strong alignment offers a source of current practice that can be leveraged more widely across the organization.
Lower Alignment (Data from the Perspective of The Place)	Low alignment for both the People and the Place. Likelihood much lower that behaviours are exhibited that support organizational goals such as a felt commitment to DE&I. Interventions here include exploring management practices as well as sharing the day-to-day work experience and working practices of those who are already strongly aligned.	Behaviours supporting organizational goals such as a positive employee experience of DE&I are present among the People but are not supported by the Place. The focus here is on interventions that address barriers in the Place and that unlock the potential among the People to achieve organizational goals.

Here are three examples of the interventions introduced by the organization using data to guide the qualitative inquiry pursued by the OD transformation consultant:

- Companywide communications. Review of existing communications showed that they rarely touched on the three DE&I behaviours. The Head of Communication and Culture took the remit with her team to establish guidelines to frame future communications and reinforce the seven behaviours, singly or together as the nature of the communication allowed. These guidelines were first used in company-wide messaging and then, once the guidelines had been concretely modelled, cascaded to business unit-level communications.
- Executive Committee. One example of interventions at this level was framed around psychological safety and included workshops as well as one-to-one coaching focused on two behaviours, Team Focus and Expressive, to build understanding among leaders on how these behaviours foster trust and their role in modelling those behaviours for the wider organization.
- Use of Microsoft Teams channels. This was already used effectively in a back-office function to promote and reinforce three of the behaviours in the normal course of work activities; Conformity (what fairness and applying the rules fairly to all means and how to apply it day-to-day), Expressive (encouraging sharing of opinions and feelings) and Team Focus (fostering collaboration). The deeper dive showed that training and usage of Teams was variable across the company, and few in some functions knew of or even thought they could use the chat function to explore ideas and opinions with their colleagues.

So, did the needle move?

CultureScope measurement was redeployed as planned after 10 months from the first measurement to check if the planned interventions were working. To what degree were they having a positive effect on the intended behaviours, and had the outcomes improved?

Having analysed the newly collected data with n=1,586, the following can be observed:

- Expressive has increased by 22 per cent and is now a present behaviour for females. Interestingly it has also slightly improved for males, and we now have alignment at the Place regardless of gender. Expressive presence

is also showing alignment for different ethnic groups. Personal behaviours also showed an improvement by 19 per cent and 21 per cent.
- Conformity has had a significant change from very absent for females to present with a 32 per cent change, and is now showing alignment with male colleagues for the Place. Conformity at the Place has also improved to only present for the 'White' ethnicity to present for all ethnicities.
- Team Focus has also shown an improvement from somewhat absent to somewhat present for females, and although not totally aligned with male colleagues yet, it's not far behind. Ethnicity also shows similar improvement at the Place.
- Achievement has increased by 20 per cent for females and is now aligned with males, which has also impacted ethnicity by 16 per cent improvement.

Although these demonstrate a moderate gain, they are encouragingly in the right direction.

So what? What about the outcome?

A further deployment of the organization's employee survey in the same timeframe also showed a positive shift in employee outcomes. Table 19.1 compares the percentage variance for employees responding favourably (agree or strongly agree) to the two outcome items discussed previously by gender and ethnicity with favourable responses to the items increasing substantially for Female employees and for ethnically Black employees and those classified as Mixed, with little or no change for Male and ethnically White employees (total n = 1,565).

TABLE 19.1 The two outcomes comparison before and after interventions by gender and ethnicity demographics

	1st Measurement (before interventions) *n=1565*		2nd Measurement (after interventions) *n=1586*	
	Valued at the Place	Valued by the People	Valued at the Place	Valued by the People
Gender: Male positive response	68%	71%	72% (var 4%)✱	74% (var 3%)✱

(*continued*)

TABLE 19.1 (Continued)

	1st Measurement (before interventions) n=1565		2nd Measurement (after interventions) n=1586	
Gender: Female positive response	33%	36%	59% (var 26%)*	56% (var 20%)*
Ethnicity: White positive response	75%	80%	75% (var 0%) →	78% (var 5%)*
Ethnicity: Mixed positive response	52%	57%	66% (var 14%)*	67% (var 10%)*
Ethnicity: Black positive response	48%	38%	61% (var 13%)*	59% (var 21%)*

The behavioural and outcome measurement data shows improvement, but the organization still has a way to go, now that they have the evidence that their targeted interventions are working.

The data was also shared with the financial regulator (the FCA), and the big question is: what did the regulator think when this data and the interventions designed by the OD transformation consultant were shared with them? The FCA was satisfied that the company had identified where the gaps in its workplace culture were and had taken concrete actions to address those gaps, which is a great result considering the starting point for this organization.

Additionally, the organization has also reported an improvement in employee openness and wellbeing. It is also interesting to note the organization effectiveness measures have also improved, and in particular at the Front Office; such measures included customer workflow effectiveness and issue resolutions. Clearly an inclusive organization will be creating an inclusive Place and brand for their employees and customers alike! As the saying goes, 'Look after your employees and they will look after your customers.'

Implications for the research approach focused on inclusion

As those cited in the introduction to this chapter either state directly or imply, current DE&I practice appears to have run ahead of research on what interventions are more likely to promote a lived experience of DE&I in the workplace. So, what does this case study say about where future research on DE&I might focus?

First, I suggest it offers one way to respond to the observations made by WebMD Health Services on the back of their 2023 survey in investigating cultural factors underpinning employee experience of DE&I as it is and as it could be.[10] Second, I hope it offers a model for how both quantitative data using an empirically tested behavioural framework can be combined with qualitative lines of inquiry to build a deeper understanding on where there are levers to promote a stronger sense of DE&I among employees and where there are barriers to employees having a positive sense of an organization's commitment to DE&I.

From the perspective of the practitioner, this case study is offered as one example of how a behavioural framework drawing on practical research can be applied to generate testable hypotheses about what promotes or hinders employee experience of DE&I within a given organizational setting, hypotheses that can be tested in terms of whether there is a consensus about what the tangible experience of DE&I should be and whether that consensus translates into meaningful and substantive predictions of whether employees feel valued or not.

The case study is also offered to show how quantitative data analytics can be combined with qualitative inquiry to better understand the employee experience as it is and as it could be, but also to leverage behavioural frameworks by translating them into practical interventions that can, in turn, be tested as to whether they are having an impact and moving the needle.

Many DE&I practices appear to have erred on the side of efficiency at the expense of meaningful applications of research on behaviours and behavioural change. I really hope that I have provided an example of how behavioural science and culture analytics can not only help promote meaningful support to DE&I initiatives through organizational applied research and data-guided insight, but also achieve tangible results efficiently through an evidence-based approach.

Notes

1 S Dixon-Fyle, K Dolan, V Hunt and S Prince. Diversity wins: How inclusion matters, McKinsey, 18 June 2020, www.mckinsey.com/~/media/mckinsey/featured%20insights/diversity%20and%20inclusion/diversity%20wins%20how%20inclusion%20matters/diversity-wins-how-inclusion-matters-vf.pdf (archived at https://perma.cc/F37S-ZWP7)

2   Z Nathoo. Why ineffective diversity training won't go away, BBC Worklife, 17 June 2021, www.bbc.com/worklife/article/20210614-why-ineffective-diversity-training-wont-go-away (archived at https://perma.cc/BC4E-LUJ8). This article cites a 2019 qualitative review of 30 studies of interventions aimed at reducing implicit bias (C FitzGerald, A Martin, D Berner et al. Interventions designed to reduce implicit prejudices and implicit stereotypes in real world contexts: a systematic review, *BMC Psychology*, 7 (29), https://doi.org/10.1186/s40359-019-0299-7 (archived at https://perma.cc/VFX2-4D6C)). These authors found inconsistent impacts from these interventions and comment on the lack of substantive empirical research in this area.

3   C Friedersdorf. The paradox of diversity trainings, *The Atlantic*, 18 January 2023, www.theatlantic.com/newsletters/archive/2023/01/diversity-training-paradox-intolerance/672756/ (archived at https://perma.cc/96YS-L9E8)

4   WebMD Health Services. Efforts to promote diversity, equity, inclusion, & belonging in the workplace falling short, new WebMD Health Services survey finds, PR Newswire, 2 February 2023, www.prnewswire.com/news-releases/efforts-to-promote-diversity-equity-inclusion--belonging-in-the-workplace-falling-short-new-webmd-health-services-survey-finds-301736551.html (archived at https://perma.cc/K6NC-C7DA)

5   See examples of some research by these authors:

   o   N Fondas and D Denison (1991) Corporate Culture and Organizational Effectiveness, *The Academy of Management Review*, **16**, p. 203, https://doi.org/10.2307/258613 (archived at https://perma.cc/2VQM-9232)

   o   G Hofstede (2011) Dimensionalizing cultures: The Hofstede model in context, *Online Readings in Psychology and Culture*, 2 (1), https://doi.org/10.9707/2307-0919.1014 (archived at https://perma.cc/LJA4-G8GT)

   o   E Schein (1990) Organizational Culture, *American Psychologist*, **45**, pp. 109–19, https://doi.org/10.1037/0003-066X.45.2.109 (archived at https://perma.cc/B6S5-LW29)

   o   F Trompenaars and C Hampden-Turner. Riding the Waves of Culture, January 1998, www.researchgate.net/publication/238710832_Riding_the_Waves_of_Culture (archived at https://perma.cc/HXG2-5CWU)

6   Transcript – US Department of Defense News Briefing – Secretary Rumsfeld and Gen Myers, 12 February 2002, https://web.archive.org/web/20160406235718/http://archive.defense.gov/Transcripts/Transcript.aspx?TranscriptID=2636 (archived at https://perma.cc/R5EV-XFHG)

7   FCA, Culture and governance, www.fca.org.uk/firms/culture-and-governance (archived at https://perma.cc/U6NK-9YKB)

8   For more information about the role and mandate of the FCA, see www.fca.org.uk/publications/corporate-documents/regulatory-framework-reforms (archived at https://perma.cc/HGS6-AKCV)

9 F A Bosco, H Aguinis, K Singh, J G Field and C A Pierce (2015) Correlational effect size benchmarks, *Journal of Applied Psychology*, **100**, pp. 431–49

10 C Muldoon. The future is inclusive: What a culture of diversity, equity, inclusion & belonging looks like, WebMD Health Services, 14 February 2023, www.webmdhealthservices.com/blog/the-future-is-inclusive-what-a-culture-of-diversity-equity-inclusion-belonging-looks-like/ (archived at https://perma.cc/X9PS-PV5K)

20

A tale of two organizations: Why innovation needs the letter 'C'

Day in, day out, we read, hear and see breakthroughs that are changing the way we live and work. The Apple iPhone, the Internet of Things and robotic treatments that have dramatically increased the survival rates from disease, not to mention the ubiquitous impact of big data and artificial intelligence. So, we may think that innovation is alive and well. But is it?

Companies are still spending heavily on research and development (R&D), with PwC reporting that the 1,000 largest corporate R&D spenders globally increased their R&D spend by 3.2 percent in 2017 to $702 billion (over £500 billion).[1] As that article states, there is still a shared belief among executives that 'innovation today is a key driver of organic growth for all companies – regardless of sector or geography'.

The latest report for the global R&D market stipulates that R&D is poised for substantial growth in the coming years, driven by increasing investments in various industries and technological advancements.[2] The predicted Compound Annual Growth Rate (CAGR) for this market ranges between 14.1 per cent and 17.2 per cent from 2023 to 2027. This growth is attributed to several factors, including the emergence of cutting-edge technologies, the rise of innovative startups, and the increased focus on R&D by governments and private organizations worldwide. The pharmaceutical and life sciences sector accounts for a significant share of the R&D market, given the growing demand for novel treatments and therapies. Additionally, the information technology and electronics sectors are also witnessing considerable R&D investments due to rapid advancements in areas such as Artificial Intelligence (AI), the Internet of Things (IoT) and 5G technology.

Clearly the budgets and investments are there, but return on investment is still the elephant in the room. So, is innovation getting harder or are we just getting worse at innovation? This was the question posed in a *Harvard Business Review* article as to whether those investments in innovation are seeing a sustainable return.[3] The data suggests not, with returns to companies' R&D spending declining by 65 per cent since the late 1980s – a decline that mirrors the worrying decline in productivity that continues to vex economists.

Is it simply that innovation has become harder as scientists, engineers and those engaged in R&D struggle to find ever more incremental ways to add value to the processes and technologies already in place? Or is it that some companies are better at innovation than others? And, if that is the case, what is it about those companies that enables them to be better than others at innovation?

A deeper dive into the data indicates that the decline in returns from R&D spend is not necessarily true of all companies. The not-so-good news is that many companies are making it harder for themselves to achieve a return from the spend on R&D, and they are just not very good at innovation.

It's not just about smarts and process: Why the letter 'C' is important

Whilst returns from R&D spend have been declining, organizations, private and public, have expended enormous efforts in processes for managing R&D, not least in change management. The problem with these efforts is that all too often they have ignored one fundamental factor in successful change – workplace culture. And, yes, that's where the letter 'C' comes in – it's not about yet another change management programme.

This became clear at a recent meeting of 100 CEOs organized by IBM's Ginni Romerty. Representing 17 different industries and some $2 trillion (£1.5 trillion) in revenues, the meeting was confident that technology was about to see a new wave of disruption by helping companies leverage their core expertise through more effective management of data. Upbeat though this meeting was, *Time* magazine found a challenge shared among CEOs in realizing this opportunity: 'The biggest problem they face is not technology, but rather creating a workplace culture that can embrace and adapt to technological change'.[4]

This isn't surprising when you consider that innovation is principally about new futures – new products, new services and new ways of doing things. It is about future states. While those charged with innovation are pursuing those future states, their colleagues are focused on business as usual, the current state they have been trained and socialized to understand and work with. Bridging these two states – current and future – is the crux of the problem recognized by those CEOs attending the IBM event.

Context and methodology

Following the 2008 financial crisis, banking competition was increased by the opening of the financial market. Banking now operates in an increasingly competitive environment, which makes innovation an important strategy for organizational survival.

A combination of regulatory changes and public dissatisfaction with traditional banking practices led to the proliferation of new entrants of various structures and offerings into the banking market.[5]

These new entrants into the market have been grouped into a single category by the media: challenger banks. Therefore, customers now have increased choices about where they can do their banking and are no longer limited to the big traditional banks for their banking needs.

Has regulation improved innovation by virtue of introducing competition? This case study aims to give a snapshot of both a challenger and a traditional bank's journeys with innovation, and can also show whether regulation enables or hinders innovation. Both banks underwent a qualitative and quantitative cultural analysis to understand the characteristics in each bank that enable and/or inhibit innovation.

I will aim to demonstrate the connection between organizational culture and innovative capabilities driving the competitive advantage.

To understand and analyse the workplace culture of these two banks, CultureScope behavioural diagnostic and analytics was used. However, for the purposes of this study only seven behaviours driving innovation were analysed, which will I refer to as the culture innovation index. This index was developed during the significant research outlined in Chapter 4 as well as recent ongoing research. As I have articulated in previous chapters, we should never rely exclusively on a predeveloped framework, and you must research your own workplace culture and the outcomes it drives to build your own unique model and framework. However, I will use this index for this research as the insight into the cultural differences and impact on innovation returns.

You may be wondering why I am doing so despite the 'health warning' I just provided. As the purposes for this case study suggest, I only want to create the connection between R&D investment, workplace culture and the return on investment, hence any organizations seeking to drive change should do their organization-specific research.

For qualitative analysis, semi-structured interviews were conducted with employees from both the banks. In the traditional bank, participants from various departments including the innovation centres, asset management, investment banking, systems and sales were interviewed. In the challenger bank, participants from the departments of recruitment, private banking, regional banking, innovation, learning and development, and retail management were interviewed.

The seven behaviours defining the innovation index

Before we dive into the differences between the two organizations, it would be good to define those seven behaviours in the context of innovation as follows:

1 **Flexible**: People value variability and deal with each situation afresh, vs **Standardized**: People value working within clear processes and systems.

2 **Innovate**: New and creative ideas are pioneered; intelligent risk taking is encouraged and praised, vs **Consolidate**: Predictability and control are preferred; risk taking is avoided until it is absolutely necessary; tried-and-tested methods are encouraged.

3 **Radical**: Continuous improvement and evolving ideas are valued; there is an emphasis on responding differently to different situations, vs **Moderate**: Individuals value working steadily within assigned and streamlined processes favouring stability.

4 **Synchronous**: People see the past, present and future as interwoven periods; they often work on several projects at once, in a fast-paced manner, and view plans and commitments as flexible, vs **Sequential**: People like events to happen in order; they place a high value on punctuality, quality, planning and staying on schedule; in this culture, 'time is money,' and people don't appreciate it when their schedule is thrown off.

5 **Outer Focus**: People believe that their environment controls them; they want to work within their environment to achieve goals; at work or in

relationships, they focus their actions on others, vs **Inner Focus**: People believe that they can control nature or their environment to achieve goals; this includes how they work with teams and within organizations.

6 **Conformity**: People place a high importance on laws, rules, values and obligations; they try to deal fairly with people based on these rules, but rules come before relationships, vs **Nonconformity**: People believe that each circumstance, and each relationship, dictates the rules that they live by; their response to a situation may change based on what is happening in the moment, and who is involved.

7 **Strategic**: Emphasis is on long-term delivery and results, and focus is on the wider impact, vs **Tactical**: The emphasis is on short-term delivery and results.

The traditional bank (TB)

This is a well-established global bank that has been trying to drive innovation particularly in their retail and business banking. The focus has been on researching, developing and delivering innovative products and solutions that are technology-based. For that purpose, a research and development (R&D) function was established that included the creation of an innovation board to manage a significant billion-dollar investment – a well-funded R&D centre.

This innovation centre was established within the bank's normal operational environment and is governed and managed the same way as all other 'business as usual' functions. Unfortunately, the bank had very little success to show off! Hardly any innovative products or solutions have been delivered, and any product improvements that did go live had significant issues, leading to a barrage of customer complaints.

Qualitative analysis

Based on 38 semi-structured interviews conducted with employees at the traditional bank, and after analysing the data through a bottom-up approach, a thematic map was generated to describe the organizational culture. The resulting map has been crystalized in three themes: power and hierarchy, importance of internal risk management, and external moderators to innovation.

Let's dive into each theme.

THEME 1: POWER AND HIERARCHY

- **Top-down decision-making:** The bank is highly bureaucratic and values the importance of power and hierarchy. Top-down decision-making is the normal course of action in deciding what innovation means for the organization and who decides and implements functions related to it.
- **Information exclusivity:** Another output of the hierarchical structure is that very senior executives had exclusive knowledge of how innovation is propagated and maintained in the organization, and the teams driving innovation were simply information-blind about what is next and the direction of travel or even strategy.
- **Tradition:** The bank was often described as 'old' and 'slow' by employees. Participants spoke of an organization where 'everything moves slowly' and referred to the technology and ways of thinking as 'outdated' or 'passé'. The value TB places on tradition and 'the way things are done' also seemed to inhibit the implementation of new ideas.

See Figure 20.1 which provides a diagrammatic summary for this theme.

THEME 2: IMPORTANCE OF INTERNAL RISK MANAGEMENT

- **Pockets of experimentation:** It is within the bank's innovation functions that employees are encouraged, by their remit, to experiment and are provided this space to try different approaches, occasionally creating a 'two-speed' organization.
- **Playing it safe:** Although employees are encouraged to speak up if they have new ideas, these were usually contained to small changes that would not risk the efficient running of the organization as a whole.

FIGURE 20.1 Power and hierarchy theme

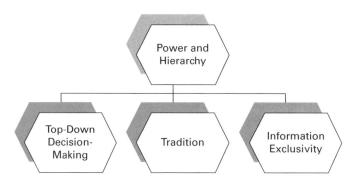

- **Sharing and collaboration:** Being a large organization, various communication channels are needed to make relevant employees aware of the potential risks and benefits of new products or ideas. 'Tech fests' and 'innovation showcases' are places where information about new technology can be shared amongst members of the organization. Ideas are then reported upward and implemented if management believes they can provide value for the business.

Figure 20.2 provides a diagrammatic summary for this theme.

THEME 3: EXTERNAL MODERATORS TO INNOVATION

- **Competitor effects:** If competitor banks have done it, then we can – it's about borrowing innovation. Certain innovative solutions can also be progressed quickly, but only if there is a perceived threat to the bank's reputation or market share.
- **Regulatory roadblocks:** A highly competitive marketplace is a key accelerator for innovation; however, there was a perception by employees that regulatory roadblocks and security concerns, such as cybersecurity and customer data protection, inhibit or limit the level of innovation.
- **Security concerns:** Security concerns are a key factor that could stop the business from innovating in the ways it would like. Historically, TB has garnered media attention for their involvement in various scandals that created a loss in reputation and a resulting loss in stakeholder trust and market share. The bank seeks to protect both its reputation and existence as an organization by prioritizing cyber-security and allowing innovation to 'take a back seat' in the day-to-day functioning of the organization. The focus was total risk avoidance rather than risk awareness.

FIGURE 20.2 Importance of internal risk management theme

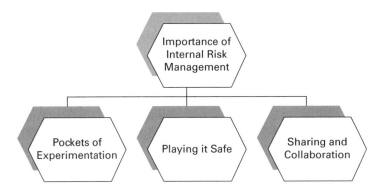

FIGURE 20.3 External moderators to innovation theme

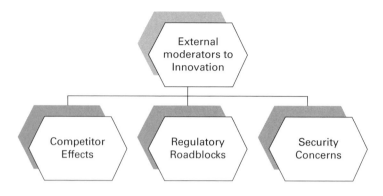

Figure 20.3 is the diagrammatic summary for this theme.

Quantitative analysis

In the thematic qualitative analyses, we built a picture of what is hindering innovation. Let's validate further by now adding the behaviours to articulate 'why' the qualitative outcomes are so.

Figure 20.4 shows the master innovation index as well as the radar graph showing the seven behaviours that combine to drive the index. As for each behavioural dimension, both dichotomous factors are shown; however, the targeted behaviours are underlined for ease of reference.

Analysing the innovation index yields the first headline news, essentially that the organization is working against innovation. Why? The Place is about Consolidating, being Moderate, being Standardized, and without analysing further we can see this is a culture for preserving the status quo and business as usual. A workplace like this is unlikely to support multiple experimentation or pioneering ideas, or support doing things differently. We just met the 'enemy', and it's the Place!

What about the People? The bank has been hiring a team dedicated to innovation and R&D – has the bank got its hiring strategy right? To answer this question, we can now look the behavioural insights using the same index for the People hired to be dedicated to R&D.

Figure 20.5 looking at the innovation index indicates that the bank is indeed hiring talent aligned to a culture for innovation. Why? Again, look at the Innovate, Radical, Flexible and Synchronous behaviours to name a few. However, the innovators are incubated in an environment that would seem to inhibit what they are hired for, hence significant tension. I can tell you

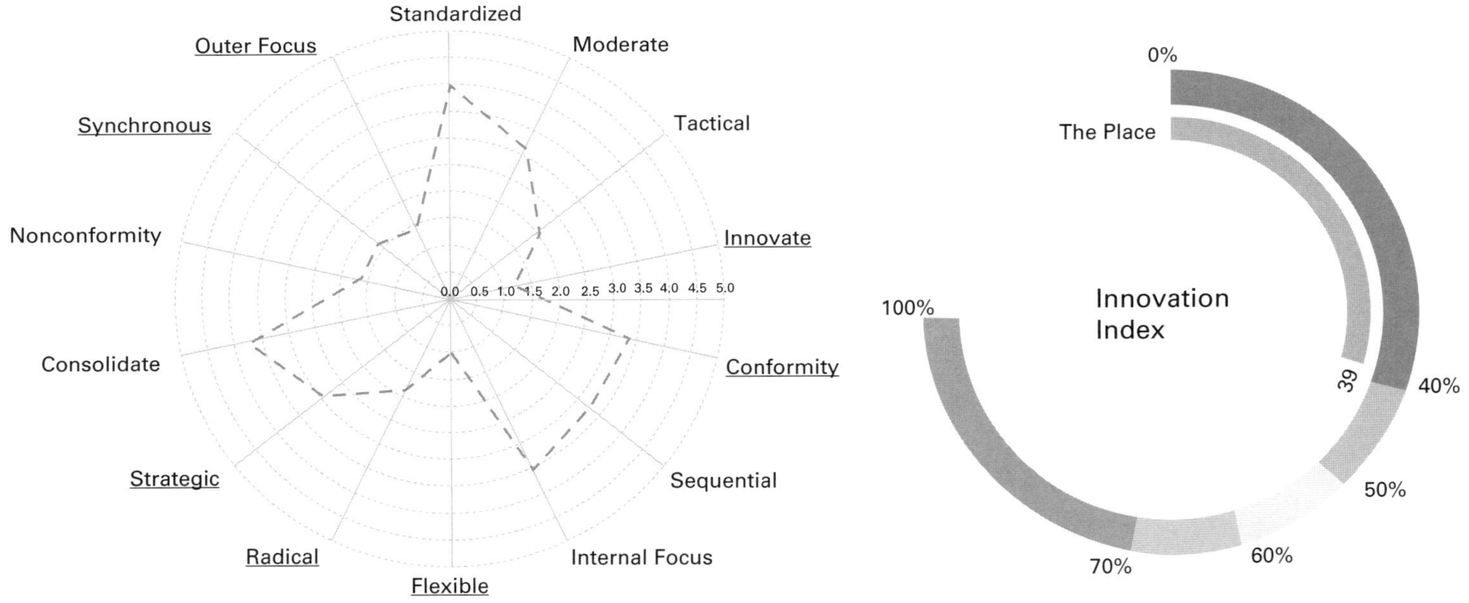

FIGURE 20.4 The innovation index indicator and a radar graph for the seven behaviours that drive it for the Place

that this tension has two outcomes: these innovators have a maximum tenure of 16 months, and as the Place is acting as the inhibitor, although the programme is very well funded, there are no tangible outcomes and return on the bank's investment.

The key action is to create a separate environment to incubate the innovators away from the business-as-usual operations within the bank.

The challenger bank (CB)

This is a relatively new bank, having gained their license in 2018/19. The bank is all about driving innovation in both technology and modus operandi. Smaller than a typical traditional bank, with significantly lower financial muscle power available to invest in R&D for innovation, this bank is winning awards for product innovation and is making significant gains in new customer acquisition, customer retention and organizational growth.

Qualitative analysis

Based on 32 semi-structured interviews conducted with employees at the challenger bank, and after analysing the data through a bottom-up approach, I generated a thematic map to describe the resulting organizational culture. To compare like with like, I managed to establish three themes: however, they are very different themes to the traditional bank, which is to be expected if they do have a fundamentally different workplace culture.

The themes are: creating the best customer experience, importance of collegial relationships, and external perceptions.

Let us dive into each theme as follows.

THEME 1: CREATING THE BEST CUSTOMER EXPERIENCE

I can summarize the qualitative evidence for this theme resulting from the semi-structured interviews as follows: (words in bold show relevance to the thematic Figure 20.6):

- All participants interviewed spoke about innovation at CB as their **commitment to customer service**. Employees believe the banking experience should be simple and friendly and employees are encouraged to **go above and beyond for the customer**.

- **Customers are also encouraged to give feedback** both online and face-to-face on their banking experience, which is then incorporated into **further innovative offerings**.

FIGURE 20.5 The innovation index indicator and a radar graph for the seven behaviours that drive it for the Place and the People – traditional bank

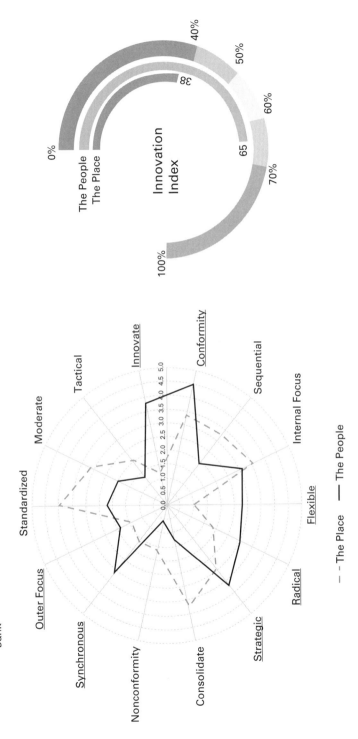

FIGURE 20.6 Creating the best customer experience theme

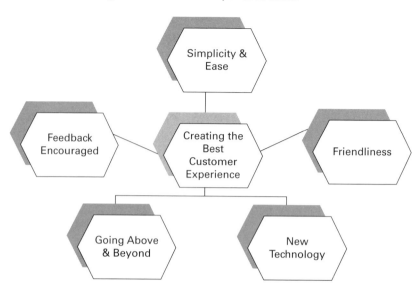

- Part of creating the best customer experience also depends on providing top-of-the-line new **technological offerings to customers**. Due to financial and human resources constraints, CB does not have the ability to provide in-house created offerings. The organization reconciles this challenge by partnering with third-party vendors.

Figure 20.6 is the diagrammatic summary for this theme.

THEME 2: IMPORTANCE OF COLLEGIAL RELATIONSHIPS
Again, I can summarize the evidence for this theme as follows:

- Employees place a high value on **customer relationships,** but they also place equal value on **collegial relationships,** stating that 'our colleagues are our customers'. The resulting work culture is **friendly, nurturing and structurally not hierarchical.**
- CB's employees are actively encouraged to come up with new ways to make the organization better, whether it's a new idea to solve an internal problem or a new customer proposition.
- This **informal 'roll up your sleeves' attitude** is also solidified in the formal performance review process, where employees are asked to recount what tangible actions they had taken to make sure the organization is gradually improving.

FIGURE 20.7 Importance of collegial relationships theme

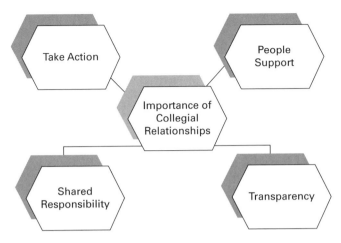

- Tying the collegial relationships theme together is a **shared responsibility to make the organization better**, with everyone **taking ownership to make improvements** in the organization. When asked where new ideas come from, answers were similar: 'The onus is on everyone, we all play a part', and 'Everyone is responsible'.

Figure 20.7 is the diagrammatic summary for this theme.

THEME 3: EXTERNAL PERCEPTIONS
The theme's demonstrated narrative summary is as follows:

- The bank is **perceived as new** by the public and has an untarnished reputation due to the fact that it was established after the financial crisis. When asked about how the bank's ability to innovate is affected by this, one employee answered: 'People trust you as a brand. It's not necessarily **perceived as being as risky** as it might be for a [traditional bank] that have got legacy issues.'
- Therefore, the bank **feels enabled to provide new customer technologies and innovations** without fearing that customers may be wary of such a change.
- The bank also believes that it is **perceived by the public to be risk-averse**, due to its low lending rates and purely retail-based offering. Employees believe customers view CB as a 'safe and stable lender' and, thus, a trusted brand.

FIGURE 20.8 External perceptions theme

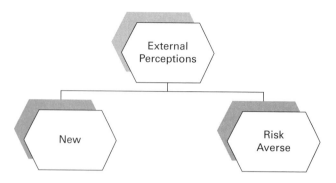

- There are certain technology affordances that are available to the bank that stem from the fact that CB was created with technology already embedded in its structure, unlike traditional banks that have had to add on technological structures as society has moved into a technology age.
- Having a modern 'tech stack' enables innovation at CB since technological changes can be implemented quickly and widely throughout the bank.

Figure 20.8 is the diagrammatic summary for this theme.

Quantitative analysis

Buckle up and hold on to your seat as I will now show the quantitative behavioural insights explaining the 'why' of the CB workplace culture and the great outcomes that they are achieving.

Figure 20.9 shows the master innovation index as well as the radar graph showing the seven behaviours that combine to drive the index. I have combined the benchmarks for both the People and the Place in one figure, and what a difference compared to the traditional bank! The innovation index shows the behavioural presence and alignment between the Place and the People 'ready made' to serve and drive effective innovation.

The Place is enabling the behaviours of Innovate to be pioneering, Flexible to be able to respond to operational change and Synchronous providing the ability to work on multiple innovative trials and experimentations, to name a few behaviours. The People are aligned to Place and, if anything, there is some positive mild tension as the Place is ahead in some of the behaviours.

FIGURE 20.9 The innovation index indicator and a radar graph for the seven behaviours that drive it for the Place and the People – challenger bank

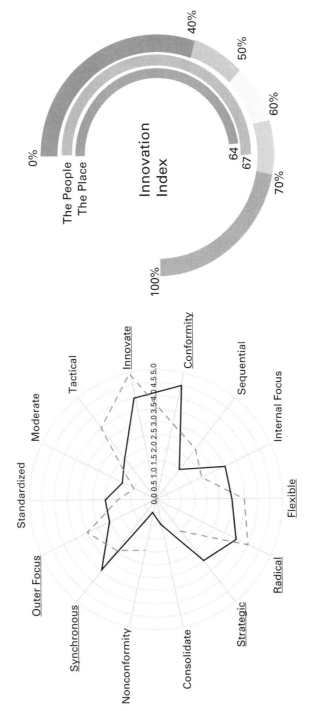

Do we need the letter 'C' in Innovate?

Well, I can't change the English language, but I really hope I have illustrated the importance of workplace culture to drive Innovate. For this case study, I can also argue that regulation is not a blocker – both banks are operating in the same regulatory environment, and you can see from the behavioural diagnostic that both have Conformity as a present behaviour, hence you can still innovate while abiding by the regulations and rules.

Another key takeaway is that pouring money into innovation is not the only solution. One needs to create the environment though workplace culture; in fact, I would go as far as saying do not fund it until you are sure the environment exists, or you are working to create it. Remember what I previously called this approach: 'Culture by Design'.

For large, well-established organizations, innovation can become a survival issue, and I would argue that creating a completely separate environment away from the day-to-day business will be important. Creating such an environment means a different culture, with different operating model, agile organizational structure, different policies and processes and ways of working. Just think of it as creating and funding your own competitor to your current organization, and the good news is that it still belongs to your organization and brand.

Another question that I posed at the beginning of this case study: is innovation getting harder? It would seem that it is for many organizations as they are making it harder for themselves by either ignoring the importance of culture or because they lack the insight they need into whether their workplace culture is enabling or disabling their efforts to innovate.

That's why I believe that effective innovation needs the letter 'C', and the letter 'C' is for culture.

Notes

1. PwC. The Global Innovation 1000 study: Investigating trends at the world's 1000 largest corporate R&D spenders, strategy&, https://www.strategyand.pwc.com/gx/en/insights/innovation1000.html (archived at https://perma.cc/DVN8-6SG6)
2. Research And Development in Global Market Overview 2023–2027. Market Overview Report – August 2023
3. G O'Connor. Real innovation requires more than an R&D budget, *Harvard Business Review*, 19 December 2019, https://hbr.org/2019/12/real-innovation-requires-more-than-an-rd-budget (archived at https://perma.cc/37B9-BMU6)

4   A Murray. Get ready for the new disrupters, *TIME*, 2 November 2017, https://time.com/5006970/get-ready-for-the-new-disrupters/ (archived at https://perma.cc/27CF-3Q8Q)
5   R Bennett and R Kottasz (2012) Public attitudes towards the UK banking industry following the Global Financial Crisis, *International Journal of Bank Marketing*, 30 (2), pp. 128–47, https://doi.org/10.1108/02652321211210877 (archived at https://perma.cc/KS5D-JLS4)

21

Safety culture and risk management

Nuclear power generation stands at the intersection of advanced technology, energy production and safety considerations. In this context, cultivating a robust safety culture is paramount to ensure the reliable and secure operation of nuclear power plants.

Safety culture in nuclear power generation refers to the shared values, beliefs and behaviours that prioritize safety above all else. Given the potential risks associated with nuclear energy, maintaining a strong safety culture is not just a regulatory requirement but a moral and operational imperative. A robust safety culture is built on a foundation of accountability, transparency and continuous improvement.

Key attributes for nuclear generation safety workplace culture:

- **Leadership commitment:** Safety culture starts at the top. Leaders in the nuclear industry must demonstrate an unwavering commitment to safety, setting the tone for the entire organization. This involves fostering a proactive approach to identifying and addressing safety concerns.
- **Employee empowerment and accountability:** An effective safety culture empowers every member of the organization to actively participate in ensuring safety. Employees should feel comfortable reporting concerns, suggesting improvements and contributing to a culture where safety is everyone's responsibility.
- **Continuous training and learning:** The dynamic nature of the nuclear industry necessitates ongoing training and education. Keeping employees abreast of the latest safety protocols, technological advancements and lessons learned from past incidents contributes to a culture of continuous improvement.
- **Open communication:** Open and transparent communication channels are fundamental to a strong safety culture. Employees should feel

encouraged to express safety concerns without fear of reprisal. Regular safety meetings, reporting mechanisms and feedback loops play a crucial role in maintaining an open dialogue.

Regulatory bodies play a pivotal role in ensuring that nuclear power plants adhere to strict safety standards. Regulatory oversight helps maintain accountability and provides an external layer of scrutiny to complement internal safety measures. For that purpose, the World Association of Nuclear Operators (WANO) has established the Nuclear Leadership Effectiveness Attributes.[1]

Given the global nature of nuclear energy, international collaboration is essential. Countries and organizations share best practices, conduct joint safety assessments and participate in forums to collectively enhance safety measures and address common challenges.

Context

For this case study, we will visit a nuclear power generation organization as we address the important topic and theme of safety culture.

The organization's aim is to prove their ability to demonstrate to the World Association of Nuclear Operators (WANO) that they have established a workplace culture for safety. In line with the key attribute of the safety workplace culture for the nuclear operations, I worked with the organization to design the following key outcome questions (this will act as the lagging outcome indicators).

Psychological Safety:

- We hold each other to account and challenge appropriately.
- I am always able to speak up and challenge deviations.

Inclusion:

- I feel like I can be myself at work.

Questioning Attitude:

- During an unexpected event, my line manager encourages stopping and seeking advice.
- When faced with an unclear procedure, I pause work and try to resolve the issue.
- I am expected to consider undesired consequences before starting work.

Safety Communication:

- I always have briefings to capture safety issues and concerns when handing over work.
- Line manager communicates desired and undesired safety behaviours with examples.

Continuous Learning:

- We often seek support from OPEX to enhance safety before carrying out work.
- My department proactively conducts self-assessments to improve nuclear safety.
- My department proactively benchmarks to improve nuclear safety.
- I proactively and regularly check that I am compliant with training to be qualified and experienced to do my job.
- The training I receive enables me to perform at my best.

Accountability:

- The decisions I make affect our performance.
- I am consistently held to account for the delivery of actions.
- Leaders use the formal accountability process to monitor performance and delivery.
- Leaders hold each other to account for delivery and performance standards.
- There are clear consequences for non-delivery or displaying poor behaviours.

The generated actionable insights

The CultureScope behavioural diagnostic was deployed in October 2023 for the entire organization. After two weeks of data collection, a 48 per cent completion rate was established, providing a large enough sample size for statistical and analytics validity as described in Chapter 6.

After closing data collection, the analytics for actionable insights work commenced with a clear objective of establishing a behavioural (leading indicator) predictor for each theme and for each outcome within a theme.

This was achieved by combining the outcome measures to the saturated 30 factors (15 dimensions) behavioural measurement and conducting the hierarchical regression analysis to establish the best parsimonious model for a restricted nested behavioural model. The odds ratio method was then used to articulate the model bench strength.

Having established the leading indicators for each outcome and theme, a path analysis was established using the methodology described in Chapter 10.

I will provide you with outcome examples for each theme to demonstrate the findings before we put the entire picture together using the path analysis method.

PSYCHOLOGICAL SAFETY

Figure 21.1 shows that people are 19 times more likely to be psychologically safe when the behaviours of Active Learning, Standardized, Collective and Sequential are in the upper quartile of presence.[2]

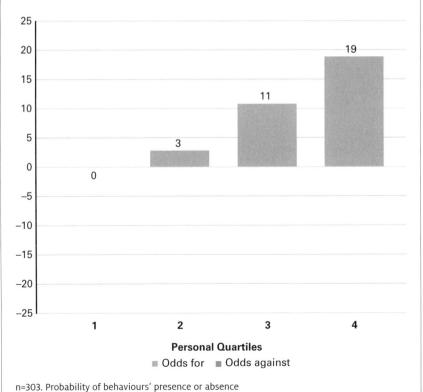

FIGURE 21.1 The odds ratio for Psychological Safety where Active Learning, Standardized, Collective and Sequential behaviours are present

n=303. Probability of behaviours' presence or absence

INCLUSION

This is predicted and driven by Active Learning, Conformity, Relationship and People Focus. When these behaviours are in the upper quartile of their presence, this organization is 34 times more likely to gain inclusion at their Place.

Referring to Figure 21.2, if these behaviours are absent, this organization is five times less likely to gain inclusion at the workplace.

FIGURE 21.2 The odds ratio for Inclusion at work where Active Learning, Conformity, Relationship and People Focus behaviours are present

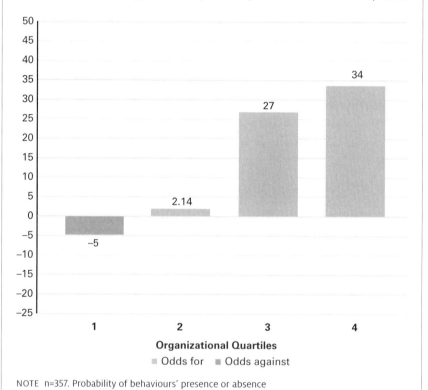

NOTE n=357. Probability of behaviours' presence or absence

QUESTIONING ATTITUDE

Three behaviours are the leading indicators for questioning attitude: they are Active Learning, Sequential and Team Focus. Where the People have these three behaviours as present, they are 61 times more likely to have a questioning attitude, as Figure 21.3 shows.

If that was not compelling enough, consider this – employees are two times less likely to have a questioning attitude when these three behaviours are absent.

FIGURE 21.3 The odds ratio for Questioning Attitude at work where Active Learning, Conformity, Sequential and Team Focus behaviours are present

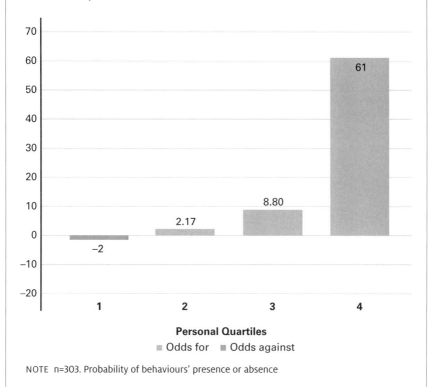

NOTE n=303. Probability of behaviours' presence or absence

SAFETY COMMUNICATION

For this organization, as Figure 21.4 indicates, they are 54 times more likely to achieve safety communication outcomes where four behaviours are present; they are Standardized, Sequential, Conformity and Team Focus.

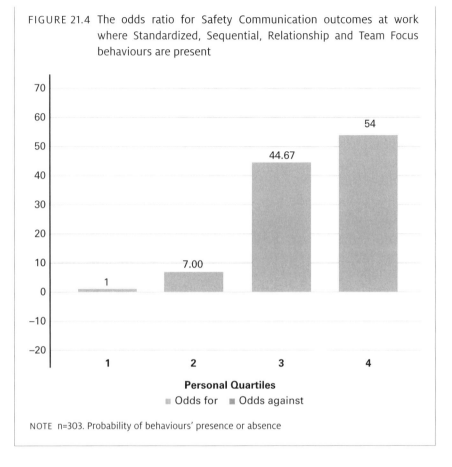

FIGURE 21.4 The odds ratio for Safety Communication outcomes at work where Standardized, Sequential, Relationship and Team Focus behaviours are present

NOTE n=303. Probability of behaviours' presence or absence

CONTINUOUS LEARNING

For this theme, it's good to see the very first behavioural leading indicator is Active Learning. Additionally, Strategic, Team Focus, Sequential and People Focus are key behaviours, and where these five behaviours are in the upper quartile of their presence, this organization is 24 times more likely to achieve a workplace culture for continuous learning.

Referring to Figure 21.5 you can also see that this organization is six times less likely to achieve a culture for continuous learning where the five behaviours are absent.

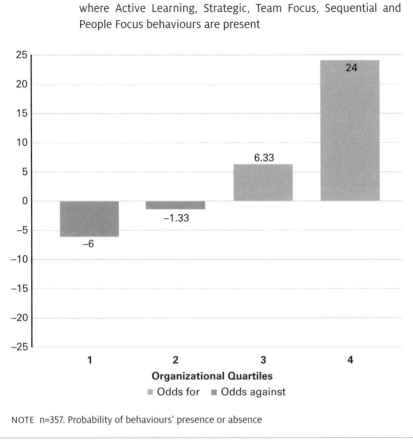

FIGURE 21.5 The odds ratio for driving a Continuous Learning culture at work where Active Learning, Strategic, Team Focus, Sequential and People Focus behaviours are present

NOTE n=357. Probability of behaviours' presence or absence

ACCOUNTABILITY

For this last theme, we have a very interesting odds ratio as Figure 21.6 reveals. This organization is seven times more like to drive accountability where the behaviours of Strategic, Conformity, Team Focus and Sequential are in the upper quartile of their presence.

The flip side of this story provides for an interesting insight as well; if these four behaviours are absent, this organization is 17 times less likely to drive a culture of accountability, and even if these four behaviours are only slightly absent, this organization is 9 times less likely to drive the desirable culture of accountability.

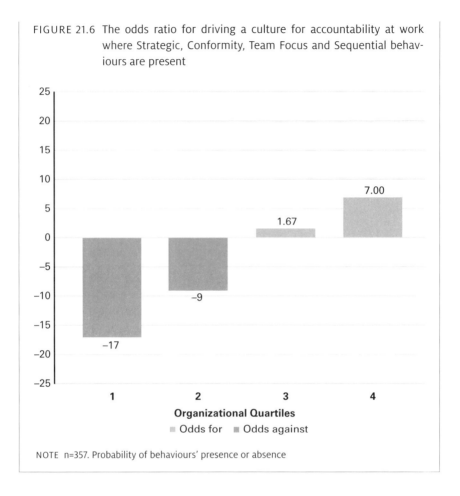

FIGURE 21.6 The odds ratio for driving a culture for accountability at work where Strategic, Conformity, Team Focus and Sequential behaviours are present

NOTE n=357. Probability of behaviours' presence or absence

Let's just take a breather and think about what this is telling us; if the People do not think and act in line with the long-term needs and action consequence, if they do not follow the rules and regulations, they do not plan accurately and precisely and let's not forget team orientation (it seems accountability in nuclear generation is a team sport!), even the slight absence of these behaviours can spell disaster.

Already we can see a few behaviours existing in many of the predictive models, but for good measure we should now turn our attention to the path analyses to see if all the themes hang together and what is the path to greatness.

Path analysis

The next step is to use the structural equation modelling approach as described in Chapter 10 to discover if these outcomes are connected, and in what order.

The result of the analyses has provided two paths. I have named these paths for easy of reference. Path 1 is the Accountability path, and I will present it in two ways, simplified as demonstrated in Figure 21.7 and a more detailed path as shown in Figure 21.8.

The starting point behaviours that are critical for driving the Accountability path are Strategic, Sequential, Conformity, Team Focus and Outer Focus. The first two behaviours are present at the Place and for the People, so no interventions are needed. However, Conformity, Team Focus and Outer Focus are absent behaviours, so intervention design is needed as we cannot drive down that path if the starting point is not achieved. Once that is achieved, we can target People Focus and Empower to achieve the rest of the path outcomes. Note that Active Learning is needed, but it is already a parent behaviour.

To clarify what this means: the focus now must be on clear accountability. Currently this organization has issues with abiding by the rules and regulations. Accountability at team level is not happening, so each team

FIGURE 21.7 The Accountability path, also showing the behaviours' presence needed to drive that path

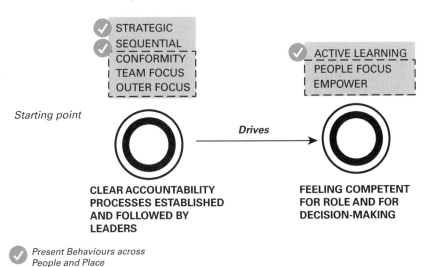

FIGURE 21.8 The full outcome details for the Accountability path and the R value illustrating the strength of the relationship between the outcomes

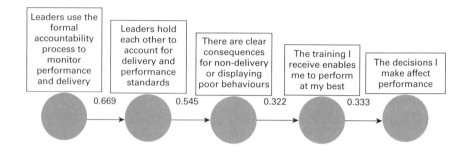

FIGURE 21.9 The Proactive Safety Management path, also showing the behaviours' presence needed to drive that path

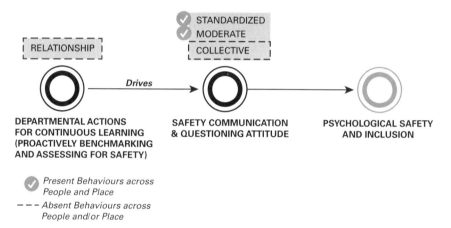

member will end up making lone decisions rather than team decisions, and I do want to remind you that in critical environments team decisions are better for risk management. Finally, the organization is not considering the impact on others as part of their accountability.

Let's turn our attention to the second path, which is Proactive Safety Management. The simplified path is illustrated in Figure 21.9 and the detailed path with the outcomes is shown in Figure 21.10.

It is interesting to note that inclusion is part of the Proactive Safety Management path, something that has often been cited by researchers as critical for good safety and risk management. I support this theory as it makes good common sense – if a certain cohort of people do not feel that they matter with no sense of belonging, they are unlikely to take part in the safety culture. If we analyse the behaviours of the second path, you can see that the starting point is yet to be achieved as the Relationship behaviour is absent.

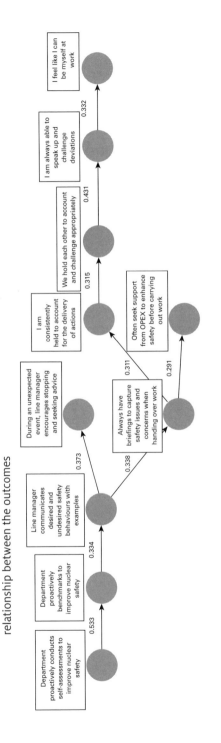

FIGURE 21.10 The full outcome details for the Proactive Safety Management path and the R value illustrating the strength of the relationship between the outcomes

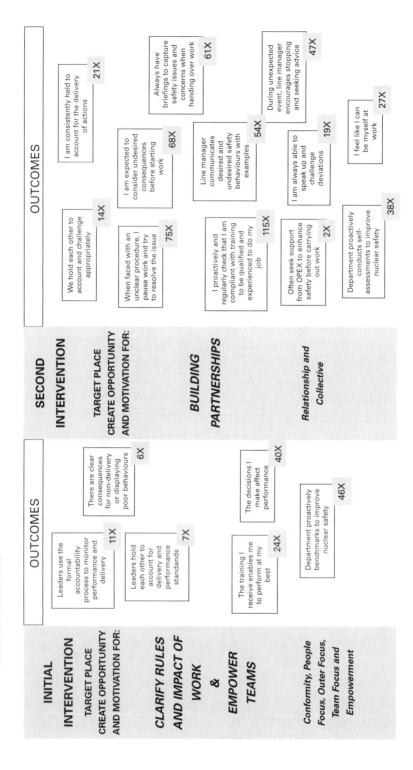

FIGURE 21.11 The behaviours that need intervention design, planning and implementation as well as the odds ratio for impacting the outcomes' return on investment

NOTE Each outcome box shows the likelihood of this outcome manifesting from the intervention (i.e. 46 X = 46 times more likely to manifest if you have the presence of behaviours and other outcomes

In order to demonstrate the behavioural intervention design needed and the return on investment, we should bring the entire system together as illustrated in Figure 21.11.

To enable change, this organization should design two sequential intervention programmes. The first should focus on the following behaviours:

- **Conformity** (valuing clear rules and laws, and treating people fairly according to these): The Place is seen to not consistently value rules, laws and obligations, whereas the People value rules and obligations at work. How can we create opportunities to clarify what the rules and laws are and ensure employees consistently follow these within the organization?
- **Outer Focus** (focusing on the impact of work on the wider environment): The Place is seen to be more internally focused and does not consider the wider impact of work on the environment in which it operates. How can we create opportunities to focus on the wider impact of work on the external environment?
- **People Focus** (focusing on people rather than purely on tasks and outputs): The Place tends to focus more on tasks and outputs than on the people – leading to the unintended consequence of making people feel like they don't matter. How can they ensure the organization and its ways of working elevate the impact of work on people rather than only focusing on tasks and output?
- **Empower** (delegating decisions to lower levels with supportive guidance): The Place is encouraging hierarchical ways of working where leaders tend to retain decision-making power. How can we create more opportunities and motivation for better delegation and empowerment?
- **Team Focus** (collaborating group efforts and team results are prioritized over individual results): The Place is seen as encouraging high individual performance rather than valuing achieving goals through partnerships and alliances. How can we create opportunities to focus on collective efforts and team results within the organization?

I am sure you noticed that the above behaviours targeted for change are all related to the Place. The interventions should be focused on opportunity and motive.

The deliberate focus on driving these behaviours will get this organization off the blocks for their starting points in their respective paths, and will directly and significantly impact six outcomes as shown in Figure 21.11.

The second intervention programme should work on the following behaviours:

- **Relationship** (valuing building strong relationships to meet work objectives): The Place doesn't value building relationships as part of achieving work objectives. People believe that they can work without having good relationships. How can we create more opportunity and motivation for building relationships to get work done?
- **Collective** (valuing building strong relationships to meet work objectives): The Place doesn't value building partnerships and networks to achieve goals. It seems to elevate winning and individualism over collective effort. How can we create more opportunity and motivation for building partnerships and alliances to achieve work?

The first behaviour in the second intervention should target the People and the Place, hence interventions should work on capability, opportunity and motivation. The second behaviour is related to the Place only, and the interventions should focus on opportunity and motivation.

As with some previous case studies, you may well be wondering what the 'size of the ask' for change is. As they mostly need to target the Place, the best and quickest way to demonstrate that is using the quadrant distribution graph. Figure 21.12 illustrates the size of the entire ask, and the critical seven absent behaviours.

Only 31 per cent of the entire organization exists in the top right-hand side of the quadrant – the is where both the People and the Place have these behaviours as present. This is low, but at least we have a Place to learn these behaviours from. They are the champions, if you like.

The lower right-hand side of the quadrant should be an interesting target. Just over 51 per cent of the total sample exists here, and since the People have the capability, if the organization targets the Place for change they are onto a winner. That population will move on up to the top right-hand side of the quadrant, and the result will be 82 per cent of the entire sample size in that quadrant, relatively low-hanging, and just like that they would have significantly improved their chances to gain 18 outcomes. Another demonstration of the power of targeting the leading indicators for change.

Behaviours form the bedrock of conduct and safety workplace culture at nuclear generation organizations. The World Association of Nuclear Operators is very aware of this fact, and has dedicated much research to it.

FIGURE 21.12 Quadrant distribution for the entire sample size for the seven absent behaviours: Conformity, Team Focus, Collective, Relationship, Outer Focus, People Focus and Empower

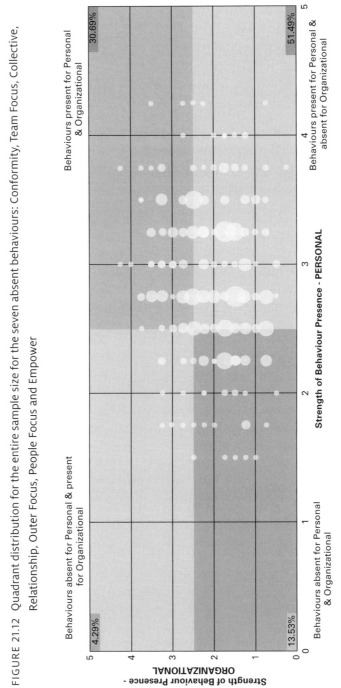

Applying the correct behavioural interventions and, critically, knowing which behaviours each organization should uniquely target, will significantly increase the chances for proactive risk and safety management while maximizing effectiveness.

The best evidence I can point to for this approach is the 1986 Chernobyl disaster which is still negatively impacting the environment today. The lack of transparency and a culture of authority caused a disaster and inhibited learning.[3] The root causes can be summarized as:

- A fear of authority and the need to please political masters resulted in a fear- and compliance-driven culture.
- A pervasive culture of secrecy and denial bred in part by a desire to preserve national pride obstructed the acceptance of external help, stalling recovery efforts and exacerbating the disaster's effects.
- A lack of psychological safety, resulting in operators not speaking up about their concerns, was fundamental to the causal chain of events that led to the disaster. Had operators, decision-makers and politicians felt safe and able to raise concerns and make decisions, the disaster may not have occurred, or had it occurred, the impact could have been mitigated.

Notes

1 WANO. Nuclear leadership effectiveness attributes, December 2019, www.wano.info/resources/nuclear-leadership-effectiveness-attributes (archived at https://perma.cc/3Z92-6C7R)
2 Refer to Figure 11.1 as a reminder of how to read this graph.
3 T Geraghty. Chernobyl: Safety cultures and secrecy, *Psychological Safety*, 23 June 2023, https://psychsafety.co.uk/chernobyl/ (archived at https://perma.cc/QME9-VN2H)

22

What about agile culture? Does that need the letter 'C'?

Should you be embracing agility by nurturing an agile organizational culture? If so, why? What is agile going to do for you, and how do you even achieve agile?

In today's fast-paced and dynamic environment, the concept of agility has emerged as a critical factor for organizational success. An agile organizational culture is characterized by adaptability, collaboration and a continuous learning mindset.

Typical key questions for seeking an agile organization are the benefits of an agile organizational culture, the key elements that contribute to its development, and how organizations can successfully transition to and then sustain agility.

Let us focus on the characteristics to articulate what each means.

Flexibility and adaptability

At its core, an agile organizational culture is marked by the ability to quickly respond to change. This involves being flexible, adaptive and embracing uncertainty as an opportunity rather than a threat. Agile organizations are adept at adjusting strategies and operations in response to shifting market dynamics.

A very useful exercise is to develop an opportunistic behavioural model, as behaviours are the leading indicators, by doing a behavioural mapping exercise similar to what you have learnt in Chapter 4. This can be done as follows:

- 'Ability to quickly respond to change': The mapped behaviour is **Flexible** (people value variability and deal with each situation afresh) rather than **Standardized** (people value working within clear processes and systems).

- 'Embracing uncertainty as an opportunity': The mapped behaviour is **Radical** (continuous improvement and evolving ideas are valued; there is an emphasis on responding differently to different situations) rather than **Moderate** (individuals value working steadily within assigned and streamlined processes favouring stability).
- 'Adjusting strategies and operations in response to shifting market dynamic': The mapped behaviour is **Outer Focus** (people believe that their environment controls them; they want to work within their environment to achieve goals; at work or in relationships they focus their actions on others); rather than **Internal Focus** (people believe that they can control nature or their environment to achieve goals; this includes how they work with teams and within organizations).

And remember to keep reading this characteristic title to validate the mapping. In this instance the three mapped behaviours, Flexible, Radical and Outer Focus, are a good match for flexibility and adaptability.

Collaboration and cross-functional teams

Collaboration is a cornerstone of agility. Agile organizations break down traditional silos and encourage cross-functional teams that bring diverse skills together. This fosters a workplace culture of shared responsibility and collective problem-solving.

Let's do the mapping exercise as follows:

- 'Break down traditional silos and encourage cross-functional teams': The mapped behaviour is **Team Focus** (work is delivered through collaborating group efforts and team results are prioritized over individual results) rather than **Self Focus** (individualism and independence are encouraged and rewarded).
- 'This fosters a workplace culture of shared responsibility and collective problem-solving': The mapped behaviour is **Collective** (goals are achieved through partnerships and alliances) rather than **Individual** (maintaining high individual performance and winning prevail over working relationships).

Iterative and incremental approach

Agile workplace culture embraces an iterative and incremental approach to work. Rather than waiting for a perfect, fully developed solution, agile teams deliver incremental value regularly, allowing for continuous improvement and adjustment based on feedback.

The behavioural mapping exercise gives us:

- **Synchronous** (people see the past, present and future as interwoven periods; they often work on several projects at once in a fast-paced manner and view plans and commitments as flexible) rather than **Sequential** (people like events to happen in order; they place a high value on punctuality, quality, planning and staying on schedule; in this culture 'time is money' and people don't appreciate it when their schedule is thrown off).

- **Radical** – again, which indicates the importance of that behaviour (continuous improvement and evolving ideas are valued; there is an emphasis on responding differently to different situations) rather than **Moderate** (individuals value working steadily within assigned and streamlined processes favouring stability).

Customer-centricity

Agile organizations prioritize customer needs and feedback. This customer-centric focus ensures that products and services are developed with a deep understanding of user requirements, fostering stronger customer satisfaction and loyalty.

The behaviours are:

- **Outer Focus** (people believe that their environment controls them; they want to work within their environment to achieve goals; at work or in relationships, they focus their actions on others) rather than **Internal Focus** (people believe that they can control nature or their environment to achieve goals; this includes how they work with teams and within organizations).

- **Strategic** (the emphasis is on long-term delivery and results, and focus is on the wider impact) rather than **Tactical** (the emphasis is on short-term delivery and results).

To bring the mapping into one view, see Table 22.1.

TABLE 22.1 The resulting behavioural map for agile organizational characteristics

Mapped Behaviours	Flexibility and Adaptability	Collaboration and Cross-Functional Teams	Iterative and Incremental Approach	Customer-Centricity
Flexible	X			
Radical	X		X	

(continued)

TABLE 22.1 (Continued)

Mapped Behaviours	Flexibility and Adaptability	Collaboration and Cross-Functional Teams	Iterative and Incremental Approach	Customer-Centricity
Outer Focus	X			X
Team Focus		X		
Collective		X		
Synchronous			X	
Strategic				X

Seven behaviours drive the four agile characteristics, and it is interesting to note that Innovate is not one of those behaviours. I note this as generally people tend to link agile with innovation, but that's not always true – you can drive agile with or without the need to innovate for new products and services. Hence the importance of understanding the difference, and this is exactly why I did this mapping exercise as an illustrative exercise.

Although these four characteristics and the behaviours are a good base model, never purely borrow a 'straight out of the box' model for your organization. As with previous examples, always develop your own model for your own unique situation and desired outcomes. I will shortly demonstrate why with the next case study.

Before we turn to the case study, I would like to address the 'why bother?' question. What can agile do for you? Well that depends on what you want to achieve that your current modus operandi is perhaps not delivering, and possibly even working against. However, general benefits can include:

- **Faster time to market**: With a focus on iterative development and quick response to changing requirements, agile organizations can deliver products and services to the market more rapidly, gaining a competitive edge.
- **Enhanced customer satisfaction**: By prioritizing customer needs, gathering feedback regularly and adapting products or services accordingly, agile organizations are better positioned to meet and exceed customer expectations, leading to improved satisfaction and loyalty.
- **Improved efficiency**: By simplifying complex processes and procedures while being risk aware rather than risk-evasive.
- **Increased creativity**: Although innovation is not directly linked, you can design an agile organization to benefit from faster creativity as the environment will encourage experimentation and learning from both successes and failures.

- **Improved employee engagement:** Agile cultures promote a sense of purpose and autonomy among employees, contributing to higher levels of engagement and job satisfaction. When individuals feel empowered and valued, they are more likely to contribute meaningfully to the organization.

Context

A global oil and gas organization driving a major transformation programme wanted to target an agile methodology as part of their transformation. The organization targeted 2,652 employees for this approach to evaluate the effectiveness before a wider rollout.

The targeted employees were selected from several countries to fully validate a global agile approach. The countries included were the USA, Canada, Mexico, Trinidad and Tobago, the UK, Azerbaijan, Georgia, Oman, the United Arab Emirates, Egypt, Angola, India, Indonesia, Malaysia, China, Australia and New Zealand. The total sample size per county is shown in Table 22.2.

TABLE 22.2 The sample size per county targeted for the agile methodology

Country	Sample Size
USA	356
Canada	192
Mexico	172
Trinidad and Tobago	156
UK	295
Azerbaijan	126
Georgia	113
Oman	120
United Arab Emirates	151
Egypt	108
Angola	98
India	137
Indonesia	110
Malaysia	120
China	186
Australia	123
New Zealand	89

TABLE 22.3 The organizational current state vs the target agile characteristics

From individualism		To team collaboration working towards a common purpose	
Hierarchy & siloed thinking	• Multiple layers between work being done and decisions being made lack of integration & collaboration across teams • Competing functional & regional priorities • Leaders feeling they need to have the answer	**Empowered teams**	• **Reduced layers** to simplify and ease decision-making • **Leaders** create a safe environment, setting direction & enabling action. **Teams** feel and are trusted to make decisions • **Collaboration** in and between teams • Instil ethos of **what's right for the business**
Holding back	• Caution of speaking up • Fear of 'not meeting expectations' • Being frustrated and holding things in • Loudest voices winning • Groupthink	**Honesty & Transparency**	• Be honest & inclusive, be open and make work **transparent** • **Courage** to share opinions, rationale and raise concerns • **Diversity of thought**: Value every voice & seek diverse views • Acknowledge tensions in decision-making: **Disagreement does not mean disrespect**
Limited ownership	• Culture of 'us' and 'them' • No end-to-end accountability for outcome • Not knowing who owns activity & who owns decisions. • 'Who reports to me' & 'who I report to' more important than 'what we deliver'	**Accountability**	• Take **ownership** of issues and outcomes • **Customer First**: Be specific about who the customer is and what success looks like for them • 'Roll up your sleeves' culture • Leaders to **role model** right behaviours and **coach**
Fixed mindset	• Avoiding giving and receiving constructive feedback • Avoiding change - 'We have always done it like this' & 'this is the way things are' • Knowing all the answers	**Growth mindset**	• Continuously give and **be receptive to honest feedback** • **Failure is a learning opportunity** – learn, improve, innovate – every innovation counts no matter how small • Ok to say 'I don't know' – **be authentic** • Leaders **create** an environment for **people to grow and encourage innovation**

TABLE 22.4 The behavioural mapping for both the current organizational state as well as the targeted agile state

CultureScope Dimensions	From individualism				To team collaboration working towards a common purpose			
	Hierarchy & Siloed Thinking	Holding Back	Limited Ownership	Fixed Mindset	Empowered Teams	Honesty & Transparency	Accountability	Growth Mindset
Disenfranchise Vs Empower	Disenfranchise		Disenfranchise		Empower		Empower	
Active Learning Vs Passive Learning				Passive Learning				Active Learning
Collective Vs Individual	Individual		Individual		Collective		Collective	
Innovate Vs Consolidate		Consolidate		Consolidate		Innovate		Innovate
Conformity Vs Nonconformity		Nonconformity				Conformity		
Team Focus Vs Self Focus	Self Focus				Team Focus			
Achievement Vs Status	Status	Status	Status		Achievement	Achievement	Achievement	
People Focus Vs Delivery Focus		Delivery Focus		Delivery Focus		People Focus	People Focus	
Neutral Vs Expressive		Neutral		Neutral		Expressive	Expressive	
Moderate Vs Radical				Moderate				Radical

The organization developed their own theoretical concept for an agile characteristics framework. This was developed via a collaborative effort utilizing a number of qualitative workshops that included a significant representation from the above targeted participants per country. The framework output from these collaborative workshops included the current as well as the targeted characteristic, a very useful exercise for all participants to understand and evaluate the 'size of the ask' which can be compared against the actual quantitative measurement.

The participants also completed a behavioural mapping exercise which cemented 'how' we get there, now that they know the 'what'. As with previous case studies, I will shortly reveal the 'why' as I share with you their targeted outcomes.

Table 22.3 shows the developed agile characteristics, and Table 22.4 shows the behavioural mapping.

To build a behavioural predictive model and a path to achieving an agile workplace culture relevant to their target framework in Table 22.4, the organization designed a number of outcomes that will be used in the analytics to build the quantitative behavioural model. These outcomes are:

- As a team we are transparent about how we work.
- The organization is developing my skills for the future.
- I am able to speak up if something is bothering me without the fear of negative consequences or retribution.
- I feel supported by my line manager to push back when I face challenges related to workload.
- I trust and respect the management team.
- Often my colleagues and I wait until things have gone wrong before acting to manage the impacts.
- I apply my own judgement to the situation while following risk policies and processes.
- My manager emphasizes the importance of doing the right thing even when working under pressure.
- When faced with a difficult situation, I have confidence in using my own judgement for decision-making.

- Our policies are centred around helping me achieve my goals and be effective.
- I have regular opportunities to ask questions, give my point of view and get my voice heard.

These outcomes have been tracked on a quarterly basis using a Likert scale to measure them, up to the full deployment of the CultureScope behavioural diagnostic.

The CultureScope deployment yielded a completion rate of 68 per cent with all participating countries achieving at least 38 per cent, hence a statistically valid sample.

Analytics and actionable insights

CultureScope data collection closed within four weeks, achieving a total sample of n=1,803. The analytics then commenced to establish a behavioural (leading indicator) predictor for each outcome. This was achieved by combining the outcome measures to the saturated 30 factors (15 dimensions) behavioural measurement and conducting the hierarchical regression analysis to establish the best parsimonious model for a restricted nested behavioural model. The odds ratio method was then used to articulate the model bench strength.

I can share with you some examples of the predictive models as follows. You may have already noticed that the behavioural leading indicators are so far matching the behavioural mapping created for the agile framework in Table 22.4. This is indeed good news as it is validating the framework.

> **TRANSPARENCY**
>
> **Outcome: As a team we are transparent about how we work.**
>
> Figure 22.1 shows the resulting regression analysis and odds ratio. The organization is 60 times more likely to be transparent where Team Focus, Conformity, Empower and People Focus behaviours are in the upper quartile of their presence.
>
> Interpreting this model provides an interesting insight: transparency will happen when all abide by the common rules fairly for teams and the individuals within each team, and empowerment will play a significant part in that journey.

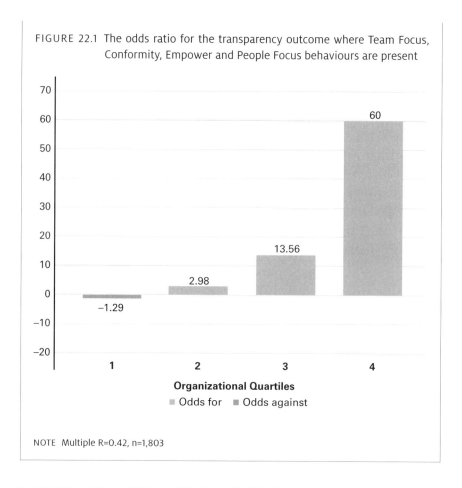

FIGURE 22.1 The odds ratio for the transparency outcome where Team Focus, Conformity, Empower and People Focus behaviours are present

NOTE Multiple R=0.42, n=1,803

GROWTH MINDSET

Outcome: The organization is developing my skills for the future.

The resulting regression and odds ratio is shown in Figure 22.2. This significant model shows that skills development for the future is 43 times more likely to occur where Active Learning, Team Focus, Conformity and Strategic are in the upper quartile of their presence. Additionally, the absence of these behaviours will mean that the organization is 13 times less likely to achieve a growth mindset.

The organization was very pleased to see both Active Learning and Strategic featuring in this model. Essentially, the organization has to create equal opportunities for all, and learning and development must serve the long-term strategy while also serving the team's needs.

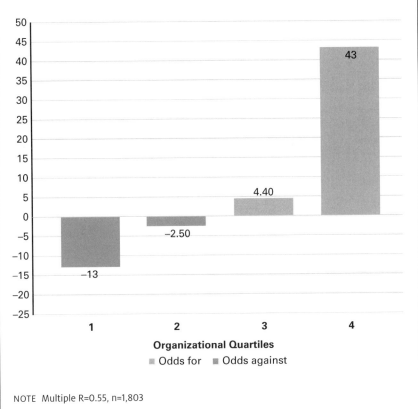

FIGURE 22.2 The odds ratio for the growth mindset outcome where Active Learning, Team Focus, Conformity and Strategic behaviours are present

NOTE Multiple R=0.55, n=1,803

EMPOWERED TEAMS

Let us examine two outcomes.

Outcome 1: Our policies are centred around helping me achieve my goals and be effective.

Four behaviours are the leading indicators; they are Active Learning, Conformity, Strategic and Outer Focus. This organization is 21 times more likely to drive effectiveness where their policies enable the presence of these behaviours, and 14 times less likely to drive effectiveness if their policies inhibit these behaviours.

290　CULTURE ANALYTICS: PART 2

FIGURE 22.3　The odds ratio for the driving effectiveness outcome where Active Learning, Conformity, Strategic and Outer Focus behaviours are present

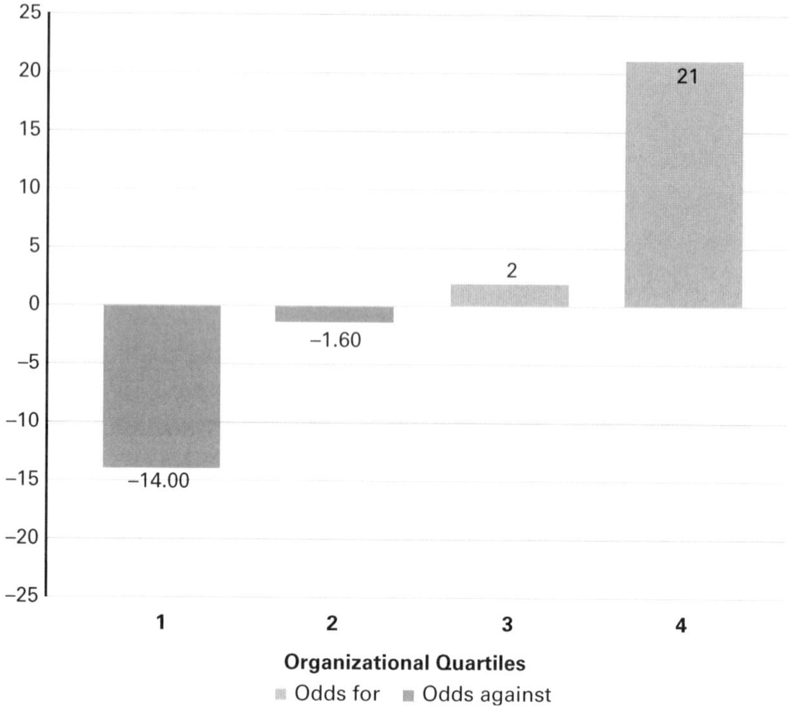

[Bar chart showing odds ratios across Organizational Quartiles 1-4: Quartile 1: -14.00; Quartile 2: -1.60; Quartile 3: 2; Quartile 4: 21. Legend: Odds for, Odds against]

Organizational Quartiles

NOTE　Multiple R=0.49, n=1,803

Outcome 2: I am able to speak up if something is bothering me without the fear of negative consequences or retribution.

Three behaviours are the leading indicators for psychological safety; they are Conformity, Expressive and People Focus. This organization is 47 times more likely to drive psychological safety where these behaviours are in the upper quartile of their presence, and 9 times less likely to drive psychological safety when these behaviours are absent.

Actually, it is reassuring to see Expressive behaviour being part of the leading indicators for psychological safety. Additionally, Conformity means that the rules are clear and applied fairly to all, and our people matter as they are the reason we will get to our outcomes. Hence, People Focus is the third leading indicator.

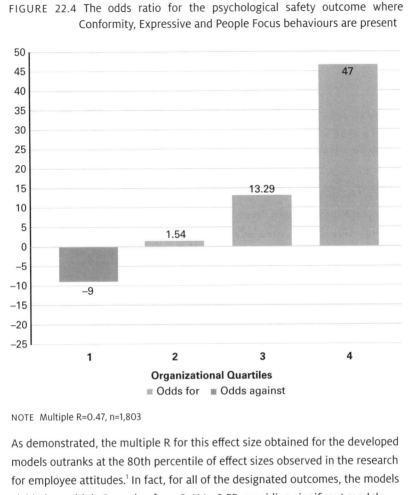

FIGURE 22.4 The odds ratio for the psychological safety outcome where Conformity, Expressive and People Focus behaviours are present

NOTE Multiple R=0.47, n=1,803

As demonstrated, the multiple R for this effect size obtained for the developed models outranks at the 80th percentile of effect sizes observed in the research for employee attitudes.[1] In fact, for all of the designated outcomes, the models yielded a multiple R ranging from 0.41 to 0.55, providing significant models.

Path analysis

Having established the leading indicators for each outcome, a path analysis was established using the structural equation modelling methodology as described in Chapter 10.

The methodology delivered one integrated path for agile; however, it can be described as two branches with a common starting point as demonstrated in Figure 22.5. The upper path is related to managing risks for agile workplace culture, and the lower path is about effectiveness and achievement for agile culture.

FIGURE 22.5 The full agile path analysis with the leading behavioural indicators

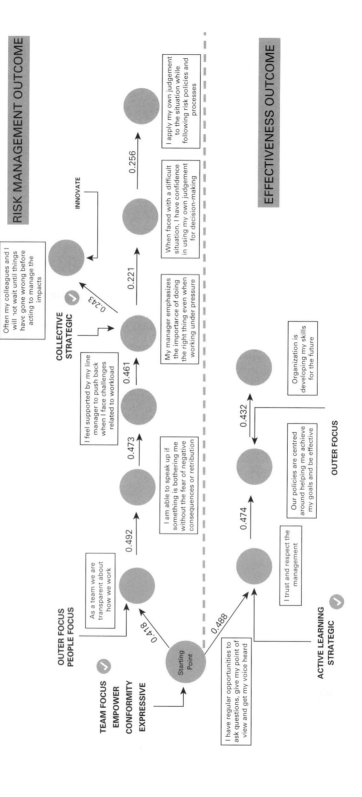

TABLE 22.5 The behavioural mapping for the current organizational state as well as the targeted agile state

CultureScope Dimensions	From individualism				To team collaboration working towards a common purpose				Predictive Behaviours
	Hierarchy & siloed thinking	Holding Back	Limited Ownership	Fixed Mindset	Empowered Teams	Honesty & Transparency	Accountability	Growth Mindset	
Disenfranchise Vs Empower	Disenfranchise	Disenfranchise ✓	Disenfranchise		Empower		Empower		Empower
Active Learning Vs Passive Learning				Passive Learning ✓				Active Learning	Active Learning
Collective Vs Individual	Individual		Individual ✓		Collective		Collective		Collective
Innovate Vs Consolidate		Consolidate		Consolidate ✓		Innovate		Innovate	Innovate
Conformity Vs Nonconformity		Nonconformity ✓				Conformity			Conformity
Team Focus Vs Self Focus	Self Focus ✓				Team Focus ✓				Team Focus
~~Achievement Vs Status~~	Status	Status	Status		Achievement	Achievement	Achievement		
People Focus Vs Delivery Focus	Delivery Focus	Delivery Focus ✓		Delivery Focus ✓		People Focus	People Focus	People Focus	People Focus
Neutral Vs Expressive	Neutral	Neutral ✓		Neutral ✓		Expressive		Expressive	Expressive
~~Moderate Vs Radical~~				Moderate				Radical	
Strategic Vs Tactical									Strategic ✓

NOTE This table includes the evidence-based predictive behaviours to achieve agile

The most interesting insight for this path is that psychological safety is a key starting point for this organization, without achieving the starting point. Additionally it is fascinating to see that the key behaviours of the starting point that will impact the entire agile path are Team Focus, Empower, Conformity and Expressive.

Let us think about what this is telling us. Empowered teams that are able to express their opinions openly and will abide fairly by the rules and regulations will have a significant impact on driving agile for this organization. This fact did 'myth bust', as some leaders in the organization told me: 'We bet you that Innovate will be a key starting behaviour'. The dangers of baseless assumptions!

This is a good point in the analysis journey to compare the evidence-based predictive behaviours versus the constructed agile framework mapped behaviours this organization constructed before the CultureScope diagnostic deployment. Table 22.5 shows the original mapping for current state versus future agile state; however, I have added a column for the predictive behaviours which does show a reasonably good match.

The organization needs to eliminate two behaviours from the mapping as these are not part of the unique journey for agile. The behaviours are Achievement and Radical, and they need to include Strategic behaviour. As the predictive analytics have specified, this behaviour should be mapped to 'Empowered Teams' and 'Accountability' in their agile framework.

Table 22.5 also indicates which behaviours are present, indicated by a 'tick' icon next to any present behaviours, and this illustrates that this organization is still at a very early stage in their agile journey. In fact, we know from the path analysis that the starting point is yet to be achieved; hence the left-hand side of Table 22.5 is well populated with 'tick' icons and the right-hand side of the table is rather bare.

To help this organization develop their behaviour-focused intervention design and planning, I refer you to Figure 22.6 which shows a three-stage sequential intervention plan as follows:

- Stage one: For the People, Expressive capability building. For the Place, opportunity and motivation to enable Empower and Conformity.
- Stage two: For the People and the Place, so capability, opportunity and motivation, to enable People Focus, Active Learning, Collective and Outer Focus behaviours.
- Stage three: For the People and the Place, so capability, opportunity and motivation, to enable Innovate behaviour. This behaviour has the most drag as it is significantly absent at the Place and for the People.

FIGURE 22.6 The three-stage sequential intervention plan and the odds ratio likelihood for the return on investment

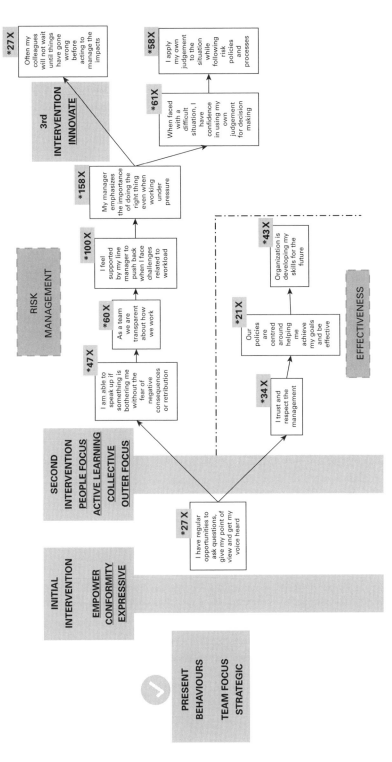

*Likelihood of this outcome manifesting from a behavioural intervention (i.e. 23 × more likely to manifest if you have the presence of behaviours and other outcomes)

These findings were provided to the dedicated organizational development function, and as I write this chapter, they are busy with the design and action planning. Indeed, they have found this to be both insightful and actionable as without this approach, it would have been impossible to evaluate or validate the mapped behaviours, or even know which behaviours they need to focus on and where in the organization, by virtue of the quadrant distribution method.

Another interesting learning in this case study is that I have demonstrated how one can develop a multiregional behavioural model yet still be able to provide a country-by-country intervention action plan uniquely designed for where each country is against the leading behaviours and the path model.

I can understand that you may think agile will be harder to deliver in large organizations and this can be further exacerbated by having multiple regions and locations. The methodology outlined in this case study should reassure you with the art of the possible.

As I have often stipulated, the uniqueness of each organization is driven by different circumstances, events and operating environments, so one must assess their needs for agile and what agile will do for them. However, the evidence is all around us that we are in a world where change is fast becoming a constant, driven by technology improvements such as artificial intelligence, shifting risk dynamics and talent needs. Fostering an agile organizational culture of some sort is not just a strategic choice; it may well be a necessity.

Revisiting the title for this chapter – I hope I have made my case for why agile also needs the letter 'C'.

Note

1 Many researchers use Jacob Cohen's correlations effect size benchmarks to gauge the strength of relationships. Those benchmarks are 0.2 for a small effect, 0.3 for moderate effect and 0.5 for a large effect. The results of our model for predicting employee voice would benchmark as a large effect size (R=0.496). More recent research suggests that the size of an effect varies depending on what is being studied and that different benchmarks reflecting different fields of study are required. We obtained our 80th percentile benchmark for research on employee attitudes from F A Bosco, H Aguinis, K Singh, J G Field and C A Pierce (2015) Correlational effect size benchmarks, *Journal of Applied Psychology*, **100**, pp. 431–49

23

The crucial role that workplace culture plays in shaping employee wellbeing

I have come across a plethora of wellbeing initiatives all claiming to improve employee wellbeing at work. Such initiatives can address physical wellbeing, mental wellbeing, social wellbeing and work/life balance. However, these initiatives fail to address the primary root cause, which is workplace culture.

Allow me to indulge you by providing an example. An organization may provide its employees with a gym membership claiming to improve both physical and mental wellbeing. Sounds like a great initiative, doesn't it? However, this organization is not adjusting workload so employees can actually take advantage of this the gym membership. In fact, this organization may well be expecting that employees should achieve more, now that they have provided them with an extra motivational perk. I will go as far as to say that if any employee complains about the amount that they are expected to achieve against unrealistic targets, they will be quickly reminded of how lucky they are to be part of an organization with such great perks like the gym membership.

Needless to say, and as an unintended consequence, employee wellbeing initiatives can be weaponized against individuals' ability to speak up, affecting their psychological safety.

In this case study, I want to demonstrate how workplace culture for wellbeing is about behaviours as the leading indicators for sustainable wellbeing, and should be your primary focus ahead of any non-evidence based initiatives. Any interventions that include employee perks should be planned and designed in line with intended workplace culture and behaviours.

There are several research studies connecting employee good wellbeing with increased productivity, employee retention, brand enrichment and so on, but what they do not focus on is 'how' to achieve an organizational culture for wellbeing.

Context

A competitive telecommunications operator, based in the Middle East and part of a large regional group, had been through a significant transformation programme that yielded great financial results and improved new customer acquisition and retention. This transformation and its results happened in a record time of just seven months, resulting in improved cash-flow and profitability.

The CEO knew that this may have taken its toll on employees, and wanted to see where they were at in terms of employee wellbeing and how to improve this through workplace culture.

Specifically, the objectives were as follows:

- Provide predictive analytics and a path analysis model on achieving psychological wellbeing and work/life balance.
- Design, plan and implement an actionable roadmap to drive sustainable wellbeing.

To achieve this, I worked with this organization to design a number of outcome measures which will help drive the analytics and behavioural insights. They were:

- I have regular opportunities to give my point of view and get my voice heard.
- Where I work, the same standards apply to everyone.
- Where I work, people can state their opinion without the fear of negative consequences.
- In my team, I feel safe voicing problems and tough issues.
- My manager emphasizes the importance of doing the right thing even when working under pressure.
- I feel supported by my line manager to push back when I face challenges related to workload.

- Our policies are centred around helping me achieve my goals and be effective.
- I feel my organization is sufficiently supporting my health and wellbeing in the current environment.
- I feel able to take time off work when I experience a physical health concern.
- I am often under constant strain at work.
- I feel able to take time off work when I experience a mental health concern or personal or family issues.

The outcome measure questions were deployed. At the same time, a CultureScope behavioural diagnostic was launched targeting the entire organization which totalled 756 employees. The diagnostic period was two weeks, and this achieved a 52 per cent completion rate; that is a total n=395, representing a good sample size for statistical and analytics validity.

Analytics and actionable insights

As soon as the CultureScope diagnosis was completed, the analytics work started by combining the 11 outcome measures with the saturated 30 factors (15 dimensions) behavioural measurement and conducting the hierarchical regression analysis to find the best parsimonious model to establish a restricted nested behavioural model for each outcome. As with previous case studies, the odds ratio method was then used to articulate the model bench strength per outcome.

The achieved multiple R ranged between 0.38 and 0.59 for all the outcomes which is an excellent model effect size.

I can share some example outcomes' odds ratio to demonstrate some of the behavioural predictive power as follows.

> **WHERE I WORK, THE SAME STANDARDS APPLY TO EVERYONE**
>
> Figure 23.1 indicates that where Conformity and Team Focus are in the upper quartile of their presence, this organization is 25 times more likely to apply the standards fairly to all.
>
> Seeing Conformity as part of this model is not a surprise, and is in fact reassuring. However, it's interesting to see Team Focus behaviour rather than

People Focus. So, for this organization, having an egalitarian system should be applied at team level rather than individual level.

Additionally, the absence of these two behaviours will mean that the organization is 38 times less likely to achieve this outcome. Note the significant multiple R of 0.59.

FIGURE 23.1 The odds ratio for applying the standards outcome where Conformity and Team Focus behaviours are present

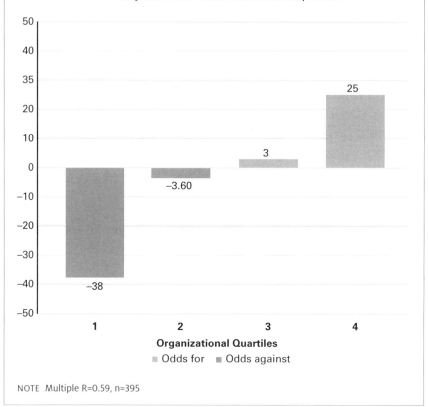

NOTE Multiple R=0.59, n=395

I FEEL MY ORGANIZATION IS SUFFICIENTLY SUPPORTING MY HEALTH AND WELLBEING IN THE CURRENT ENVIRONMENT

Three behaviours predict this outcome: Conformity, Team Focus and Strategic. The organization is 9 times more likely to achieve this wellbeing outcome where these behaviours are in the upper quartile of their presence, and 22 times less likely to achieve this outcome where they are absent.

As seen in Figure 23.2, it is interesting to note the significance of the achieved multiple R of 0.55 for this model. It is not surprising to see Conformity here; however, it's interesting that Team Focus, yet again, staged an appearance in this significant model. Perhaps this supports a recent study on the science of teamwork, which states the importance of Team Focus for wellbeing.[1]

It is also good to see Strategic behaviour as part of this model, as wellbeing should be part of the long-term and wider impact rather than a quick fix.

FIGURE 23.2 The odds ratio for supporting employee wellbeing outcome where Conformity, Team Focus and Strategic behaviours are present

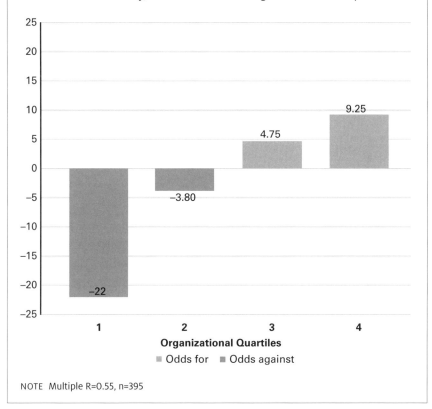

NOTE Multiple R=0.55, n=395

Path analysis for wellbeing

Having completed the predictive analytics for each of the outcomes, the path analysis was constructed using the structural equation modelling methodology. As a result two paths were developed: path 1 for Psychological Safety, and path 2 for Wellbeing.

Figure 23.3 shows the first path. The behaviours for that path are marked, and any present behaviours are also marked with a tick.

Interesting to see that the starting point for this path is the opportunity to be heard. However, the starting point behaviours are absent, hence this organization has not yet established the starting point for the first path.

The second path dedicated to Wellbeing can be seen in Figure 23.4. Although this path shares some behaviours with the Psychological Safety path, it has its own distinct existence. As can be seen, the starting point demonstrates exactly what I mentioned at the beginning of this case study: leaders and managers must think about workload as the root cause of wellbeing issues, and any employee perks will not resolve this issue.

Notice that two of the starting point behaviours for the Wellbeing path, that is Expressive and Team Focus, are shared with the Psychological Safety path, further emphasizing for this organization the role that these two behaviours play in achieving their optimal workplace culture.

The starting point behaviours for the Wellbeing path are all absent, hence this organization has yet to establish the first outcome in that path.

We can bring the entire system into one, as illustrated in Figure 23.5. This shows that the organization needs to design and deploy behavioural interventions in two stages. The first stage will focus on the following behaviours:

- **Expressive**: Capability-type interventions are needed as it is People-related.
- **Conformity**: Opportunity- and motivation-type interventions are needed as this is absent at the Place.
- **Team Focus** and **People Focus**: Capability-, opportunity- and motivation-type interventions are needed to act on the People and the Place as these two behaviours are absent for both.

These interventions will get this organization on their way down both paths, as these behaviours will work on both starting points.

These second stage will need to focus on the following behaviours:

- **Empower**: As this behaviour is absent at the Place, the inventions will need to be opportunity- and motivation-focused.
- **Innovate**: This behaviour is absent for the People and the Place, so the interventions design will need to address capability, opportunity and motivation.

I would like to point out that having the Innovate behaviour appearing as part of the wellbeing model is very unusual and unique to this organization. In this context it appeared as part of the 'the policies are centred around

FIGURE 23.3 The first established path for Psychological Safety along with the behavioural leading indicators

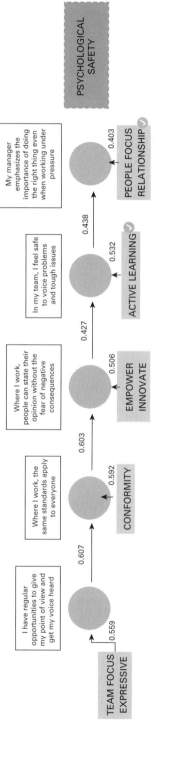

FIGURE 23.4 The second established path for Wellbeing outcomes as well as the behavioural leading indicators

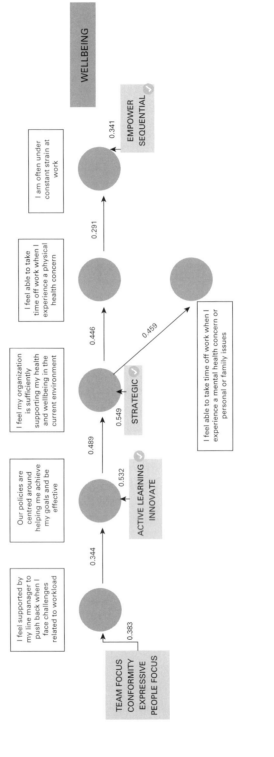

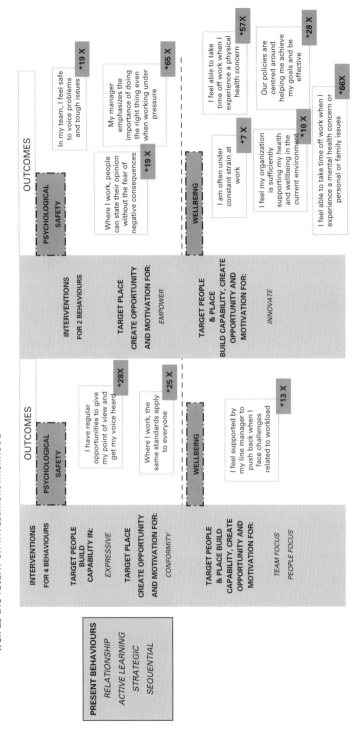

FIGURE 23.5 The absent behaviours, and the proposed behavioural intervention stages for the Psychological Safety and Wellbeing paths as well as the return-on-investment likelihood

helping me to be effective' outcome model. That made sense to this organization particularly as they want to implement innovative ways of working to help employees be more effective and have a better work/life balance.

Innovate behaviour did also appear in the Psychological Safety path, particularly for the 'People at work are able to state their opinion without the fear of negative consequence' outcome. Thought-provoking? I hope so; however, when I played this back to the organization, they were very pleased. In their context this is all about people's ability to bring new ideas and ways of working without fear. This type of speak-up culture is known as promotive rather than prohibitive. I define the two different types as follows:

- **Prohibitive** is defined as the ability to report concerns that may lead to negative outcomes. This could include speaking up about safety issues or whistleblowing; essentially, speaking up to prohibit undesired outcomes.
- **Promotive** is defined as the ability to speak up about ideas that will help progress with the intention of supporting desired outcomes.

I hope you will see why Innovate behaviour may well exist in the second type of speaking up.

Intervention design and planning

Having delivered the analytics and actionable insights, I had the opportunity along with one of my colleagues to get involved with the first-stage behavioural intervention design and planning, which I can share with you.

Before we get on with any design, and as I have regularly articulated, we need to examine the organizational 'where'. This will help target our approach by knowing 'where' to learn the behaviours from and 'where' to implement interventions.

To help demonstrate this approach, I have constructed a table that shows the four targeted starting point behaviours as a combined cluster and individually. You will be able to see the percentage behaviour presence distribution pre-function. See Table 23.1.

Let us examine Table 23.1. Look at the second row – this row will show us the behavioural champions by function. Expressive behaviour can be learned from HR & Corporate Affairs, Team Focus behaviour can be learned from HR & Corporate Affairs as well as IT. Conformity behaviour can be learnt from IT, Finance, Engineering and HR & Corporate Affairs, as well as Commercial. People Focus behaviour has no obvious champions.

TABLE 23.1 The starting point behavioural distribution per functional area within the organization

Starting Point	ALL Behaviours	EXPRESSIVE	TEAM FOCUS	PEOPLE FOCUS	CONFORMITY
Percentages of employees falling in the top-right green corner of the dispersion quadrant, where the behaviours are present both for the Place and the People (learn from these)	71% HR & Corp Aff. 45% Engineering 41% Commercial 41% IT 30% Finance	43% HR & Corp Aff. 33% IT 22% Commercial 21% Engineering 10% Finance	57% HR & Corp Aff. 52% IT 34% Commercial 33% Engineering 15% Finance	12% HR & Corp Aff. 15% Finance 10% Commercial 7% Engineering 0% IT	67% IT 60% Finance 59% Engineering 57% HR & Corp Aff. 57% Commercial
Percentages of employees falling in the bottom-right amber corner of the dispersion quadrant, where the behaviours are present for the People, but absent for the Place (implement here first to have a conducive environment) EXCEPT FOR EXPRESSIVE where it's the top-left corner of the quadrant approach, hence 'I don't', but the Place 'does'.	40% Finance 23% Commercial 20% Engineering 18% IT 7% HR & Corp Affairs	60% Finance 50% HR & Corp Aff. 49% Commercial 48% IT 47% Engineering	35% Finance 28% Engineering 26% IT 23% Commercial 7% HR & Corp Aff.	35% Finance 23% Commercial 19% Engineering 15% IT 7% HR & Corp Aff.	43% HR & Corp Aff. 40% Finance 34% Engineering 33% Commercial 18% IT

FIGURE 23.6 The quadrant distribution for the Expressive behaviour functionally across the organization

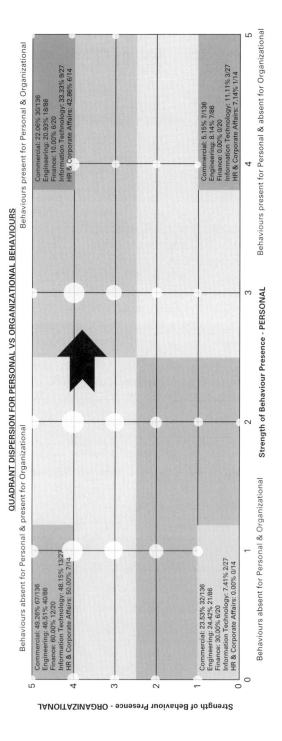

The third row of Table 23.1 would indicate 'where' we need to focus our interventions within the organization.

We must also examine the potential gain from targeting the interventions at the Place or the People using the quadrant distribution method. See Figure 23.6. For the Expressive behaviour, the idea is to move as many People as possible from the top left to the top right of the quadrant. That movement is shown by the superimposed arrow.

As an example, if we drive the Expressive behavioural change for the Commercial function, 49 per cent of that population will move to the top right side, joining the 22 per cent already in that zone, resulting in 71 per cent of the total population with Expressive behavioural presence for People and Place.

Figures 23.7, 23.8 and 23.9 demonstrate the same approach for Team Focus, People Focus and Conformity behaviours respectively.

Looking at these distribution quadrants can really help to demonstrate the gain from the intended interventions, but will also illustrate the behaviours that may have the most significant 'drag'. Look at Figure 23.8 showing the People Focus behaviour. Examine the bottom left zone – functions in that zone have that behaviour absent for both Place and People, and I am sure you will notice the percentages are by far the highest in that zone for People Focus behaviour. That is what I mean by the most 'drag'.

This quadrant approach helped us to design several investigative workshops and importantly to target these workshops precisely for selected functions based on which behaviours are present or absent, and helped us gain significant insight for the context, the capability as well as the opportunity enablers/inhibitors and motivation. Figures 23.10, 23.11, 23.12 and 23.13 show the output from these workshops for Expressive, Team Focus, People Focus and Conformity behaviours respectively. These outputs are very useful templates that you can use for any intervention pre-design.

The outlined qualitative yet targeted approach derived from the workshops outputs was used for the intervention design. These interventions are listed in Table 23.2 and include the full approach for targeting people, process, communications and technology to drive behavioural change.

In collaboration with the organizational leadership team, a detailed implementation time plan was established to cover 12 months, which included a remeasure after six months. The summary time plan can be seen in Figure 23.14.

FIGURE 23.7 Quadrant distribution for the Team Focus behaviour functionally across the organization

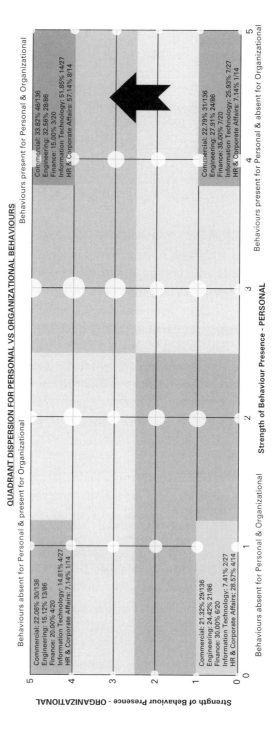

FIGURE 23.8 Quadrant distribution for the People Focus behaviour functionally across the organization

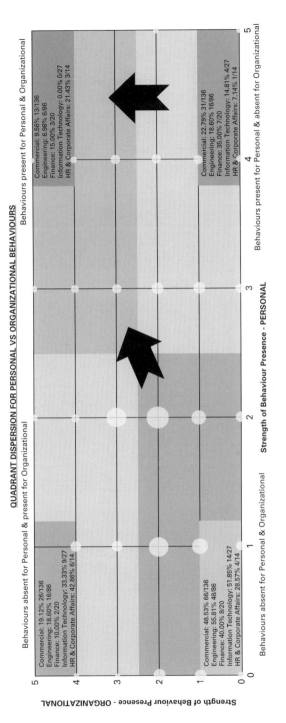

FIGURE 23.9 Quadrant distribution for the Conformity behaviour functionally across the organization

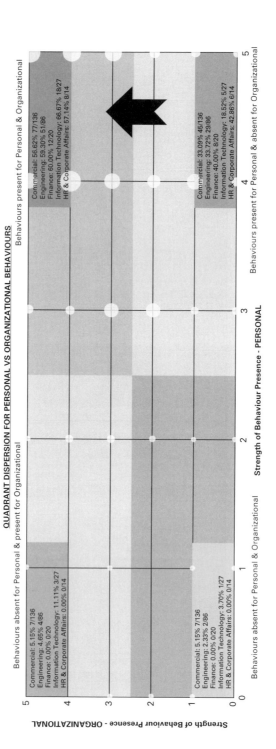

FIGURE 23.10 Workshop output for the Expressive behaviour

Opportunity & Motivation – The Place

Opportunity Inhibitors
- 'Great, now do it and show us the results. You are responsible for that'
- Accountability with no tolerance for mistakes
- HR NOT seeing the employee as the customer
- Governance processes are complicated and based on questioning and mistrust
- Huge work pressures and volumes

Opportunity Enablers
- Internal communication – but rarely used

EXPRESSIVE

Behaviour Manifests

Intent

Partial

Context

Attitudes
Toward the behaviour
- If you raise it, you'll end up doing it
- They hear: 'if you don't like things then you can leave'
- Expressing your thoughts is not safe
- Nothing will change - so people don't speak up

Behavioural Norms
What are others doing?
- Subject matter experts won't listen
- Fear of being seen speaking with staff from other departments
- 'Escalation' is a way of handling a problem between staff
- Tolerance for bad behaviour and bullying

Beliefs
Toward the behaviour
- People can express their thoughts and ideas
- My voice is heard and valued and considered
- Long tenure believe they must keep your head down, stay quiet and just do what needs to be done
- Everyone has easy access to everyone else – regardless of job grade

Capability – The People

BIAS
- Conformity BIAS
- Negativity BIAS
- Authority BIAS
- Status Quo BIAS

Physical Ability
No time: Overload of work. So, people refrain from new ideas or speaking up about things that are going wrong, so they don't increase their load

Psychological Ability
- Shame and blame for making a mistake
- Paralysis. We are walking on eggshells
- People don't take initiatives or express their issues because of 'fear culture'
- HR is seen as the judge and jailor rather than the protector

FIGURE 23.11 Workshop output for the Team Focus behaviour

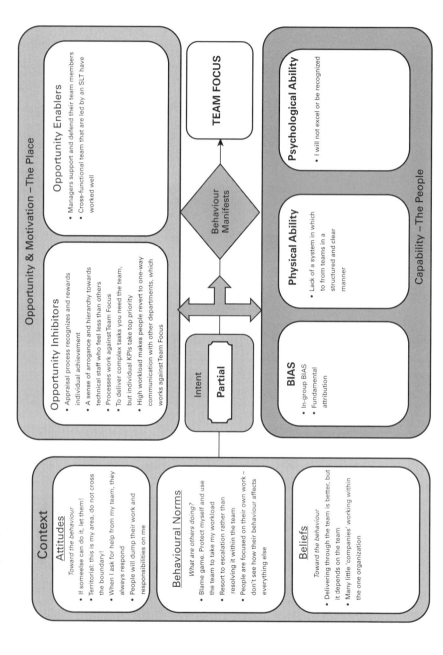

FIGURE 23.12 Workshop output for the People Focus behaviour

Context

Attitudes
Toward the behaviour
- People love the organization and love being part of it
- Casual contracts feel they are a less than others
- If I have a problem with my manager or Director – it is not the end of the world

Behavioural Norms
What are others doing?
- Some managers believe pressure makes people work better
- Managers are supportive and always accessible
- Managers listen to their team and defend them
- Sales are more focused on getting their numbers so less focused on people

Beliefs
Toward the behaviour
- People are very friendly, and we are like a family
- My manager cares about me

Opportunity & Motivation – The Place

Opportunity Inhibitors
- Workloads and pressure leave almost no time to rest and take away from our families.
- Working long hours especially at night causes physical and psychological ailments
- Limited number of staff
- Limited technical and professional skills at Officer and Senior Officer levels
- Work is more important than the people

Opportunity Enablers
- Managers are supportive and flexible with their staff
- HR try to alleviate the pressure with recreational activities
- The 'family' atmosphere
- Everyone has access to everyone regardless of job grade, no questions asked
- Back-stabbing not tolerated

PEOPLE FOCUS

Behaviour Manifests

Intent: **Full**

Capability – The People

BIAS
- Mere urgency BIAS
- Planning Fallacy
- Present BIAS
- Empathy Gap

Physical Ability
- Lack of time
- Not enough staff to support with the workload

Psychological Ability
- Work time is not the time for relationships

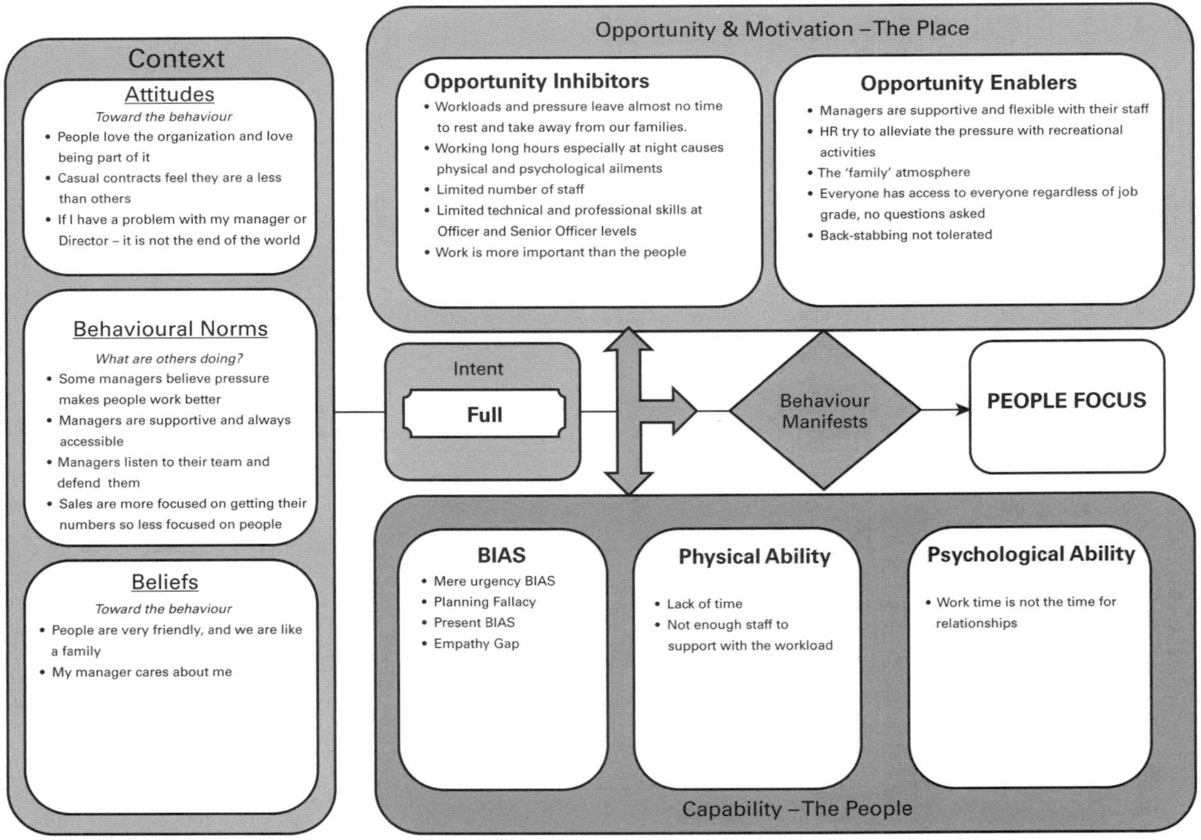

FIGURE 23.13 Workshop output for the Conformity behaviour

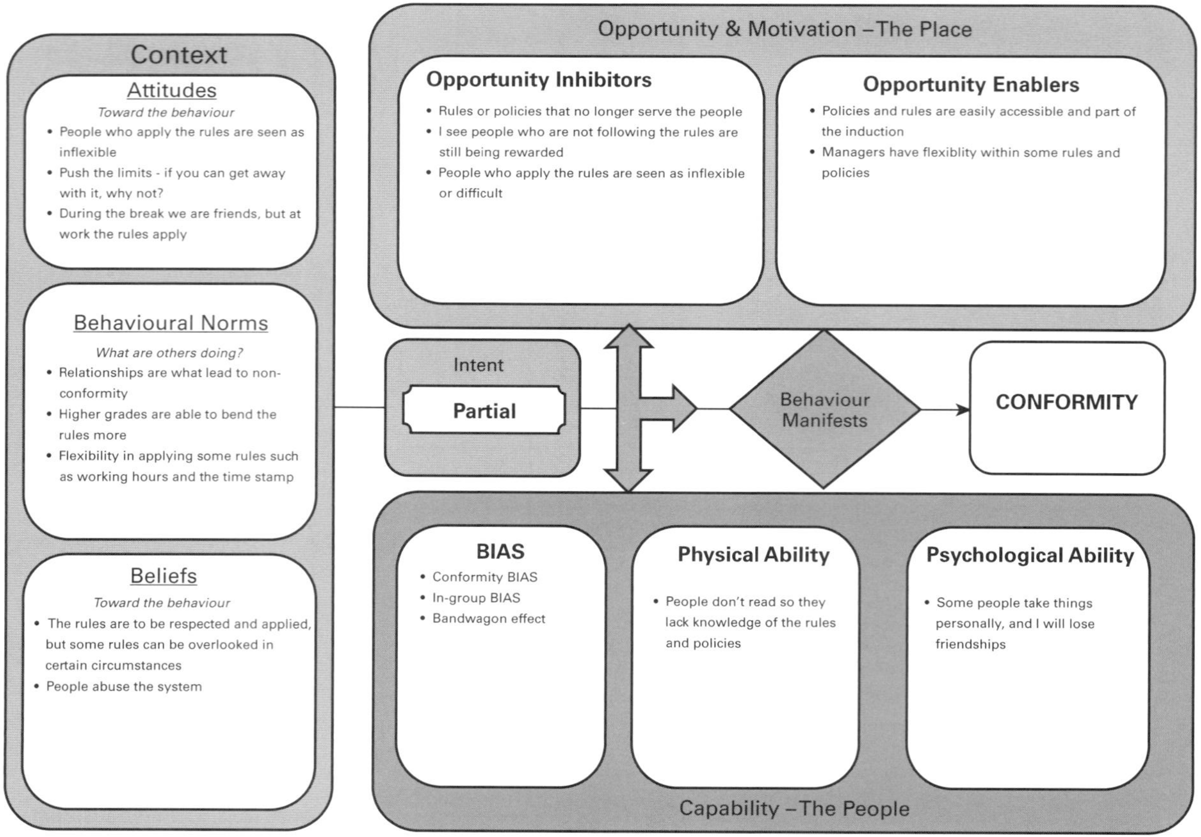

Opportunity & Motivation – The Place

Opportunity Inhibitors
- Rules or policies that no longer serve the people
- I see people who are not following the rules are still being rewarded
- People who apply the rules are seen as inflexible or difficult

Opportunity Enablers
- Policies and rules are easily accessible and part of the induction
- Managers have flexibility within some rules and policies

Context

Attitudes
Toward the behaviour
- People who apply the rules are seen as inflexible
- Push the limits – if you can get away with it, why not?
- During the break we are friends, but at work the rules apply

Behavioural Norms
What are others doing?
- Relationships are what lead to non-conformity
- Higher grades are able to bend the rules more
- Flexibility in applying some rules such as working hours and the time stamp

Beliefs
Toward the behaviour
- The rules are to be respected and applied, but some rules can be overlooked in certain circumstances
- People abuse the system

Intent: Partial

Behaviour Manifests → CONFORMITY

Capability – The People

BIAS
- Conformity BIAS
- In-group BIAS
- Bandwagon effect

Physical Ability
- People don't read so they lack knowledge of the rules and policies

Psychological Ability
- Some people take things personally, and I will lose friendships

TABLE 23.2 All intervention designs

Intervention	Behaviour	People	Process	Technology	Communications	Partners
Employee Continuous Improvement (CI) Tool (Or Online Suggestion Box)	Expressive Team Focus	• Initial training to introduce the tool and how to use it and to drive acceptance	• New Employee continuous improvement process required to embed and promote new CI system • Agenda can be included on all Team meetings	• Implementation of an Employee Continuous Improvement (CI) Tool that has the following features: Easy access by all employees • Rewards inputs at the Team level • Allows for easy evaluation and prioritization of suggestion planning	• CEO communications • Company-wide comms plan to accompany roll-out and training – focus on anonymous participation and TEAM reward • CI Suggestion Nudge • Action taken as a result of a suggestion made must be communicated widely – and particularly to the TEAM that made the suggestion	Need tool provider

(continued)

TABLE 23.2 (Continued)

Intervention	Behaviour	People	Process	Technology	Communications	Partners
TEAM Psychological Safety Training	Expressive Team Focus	• All Level 1 & 2 employees via experiential workshops	• Needs to be added to CORE competencies • Introducing 'Time out' for Team Safety each week	System to provide daily nudges either through email (such as Microsoft Viva) or text-based system using mobile (better fit for company)	• Supporting communications • Daily 'Psychological Safety Nudge' provided via web message or email	Need a trainer – ideally one that provides experiential workshops using situation-based role playing
Active Listening for Leaders	Expressive	• All Level 2 and above leaders • Initial training • Ongoing coaching/ mentoring	• Added to leadership competencies • Coaching provision needs to be written into annual training plans	• Nil	• Nil	Active Listening Trainer Coaching partner to provide ongoing support

Team Reward System	Team Focus	• All Team members need to be rated not just for individual performance but also for Team performance	• Reward/ promotion or bonus structure must recognize Team KPI achievement and results alongside individual performance	• Update to HR system to reflect new process	• This change needs to be rolled out with appropriate communications from the top • Regular Comms Nudge to reinforce the in-group bias towards Team being credited	Internal HR
Time Management Training and Tool	People Focus	• Training on tool use	• This is a self-management tool to provide awareness on where there is time that can be saved. It is not for the manager to track his team	• Time management tool that should: • Accurately track employee hours • Track the tasks • Track the People Focus	• Rollout supported by messaging and follow-on nudges	• Time management tool: Microsoft VIVA

(continued)

TABLE 23.2 (Continued)

Intervention	Behaviour	People	Process	Technology	Communications	Partners
Leadership Communication Around People Being as Important as Task in Team Dynamics	People Focus	CEO & Board	Nil	Nil	• Leadership need to give organization permission to focus on People • Valid use of work time is supporting colleagues	Team dynamics training
Time Out for People – Regular Time Each Day to Focus on the How Not Just the What	People Focus	All – leader led	Daily time out for People Planned, mandatory meeting each week where Teams take stock	Nil	• Needs supporting with regular comms	• Nil

360 Leadership Reviews Concentrating On How Things Get Done Not What	People Focus	• All Leaders	• Clear metrics for the HOW • Integrate this as part of the 360 annual review	• 360 survey tools which: • Collects 360 feedback • Collects data on the HOW as well is the WHAT	• Communication by CEO and HR that explains the HOW metrics and the objective from shifting the focus from only achieving the targets to also how the targets were achieved • Need 360 review partner
Leadership & Ethics Training	Conformity People Focus	• All Leaders	• Workshops concentrating on servant leadership	• Nil	• Examples of great service leaders should be promoted • Servant leadership training provider
Review Core Competency/ Leadership Training	People Focus Expressive Team Focus Conformity	• All	• Review the training for the companies with a focus on the highlighted areas which drive the four desired behaviours	• Nil	• Nil • Internal Training Team/HR

(continued)

TABLE 23.2 (Continued)

Intervention	Behaviour	People	Process	Technology	Communications	Partners
Rules & Responsibilities Comms Campaign	Conformity	• All	• Consequences for not following the rules made very clear • Process reviewed to ensure Conformity	• Nil	• Rules need to be re-stated often • Principles of fairness and ethics published and shared • Issue raised at Team meetings • Incidences of non-compliance can be reported through Employee CI tool	• Nil

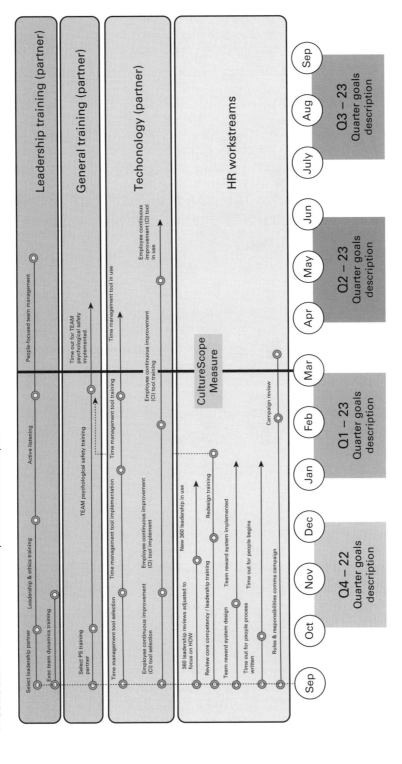

FIGURE 23.14 The interventions implementation time plan

As a key takeaway, when it comes to wellbeing, do take a detailed look at workplace culture first, and before you spend a lot of cash on employee perks that may yield negligible results. These perks may sound like a great idea, but there is limited evidence for how they will work on the root cause of employee wellbeing issues.

Note

1 S S Johnson (2021) The science of teamwork, *American Journal of Health Promotion*, 35 (5), pp. 730–32, https://doi.org/10.1177/08901171211007955a (archived at https://perma.cc/C7BS-DGFD)

24

Can we make organizational culture the hero it deserves to be?

This question sounds so simple, yet it has been the most significant driving force as to why I have dedicated myself, since 2007, to finding a practical and actionable answer to this exact question.

By virtue of the plethora of evidence available through horrific cases, which are still unfortunately happening, the way we have been thinking and actioning workplace culture has not been working.

Why so? Simply, organizations have been badly served with a lack of valid leading indicators measurement and at best the reliance on lagging indicators. Outcomes and employee engagement are important measures, but they are lagging indicators, and by the time the outcome has manifested you are already too late.

I do understand that the definition of workplace culture can be complex, as it includes the shared beliefs, values, attitudes and norms that exist within an organization. However, all of these manifest in behaviours, which is the evidence-based approach to measuring organizational culture and was the result of the initial seven-year research I shared with you in Chapter 4.

This misconception is unsurprising as the narrative peddled by countless consultancies and thought leaders is one that confuses engagement, morale and culture as one and the same. However, this couldn't be further from the truth.

Organizational culture is, in its purest form, 'how we do things around here'. These are the unspoken norms and behaviours that members of an organization instinctively follow. When an individual joins a new company, they quickly learn these, adjusting and adapting, often without even realizing it. We quickly figure out these unwritten behavioural rules and adapt our behaviour to fit in, or we may leave.

Let's look at the three essential revelations every leader must grasp to truly harness the power of culture.

1. To drive success, stop focusing on results alone and focus on the behaviours that drive these

Leaders get so caught up in wanting to drive outcomes such as 'we need to increase performance', 'we need to enhance wellbeing', 'this quarter we are going to drive engagement', etc. All of the focus, intervention planning and resources are put into trying to enhance these outcomes, but little goes into accurate, precise attention and focus on what moulds these outcomes – behaviours.

To steer any vessel effectively, one must understand the difference between the destination and the course. Outcomes, like improved performance or heightened engagement, represent the desired destinations. Behaviours, on the other hand, are the courses charted – patterns of actions or interactions that drive an organization toward these destinations.

Critically, behaviours manifest in two distinct and interconnected ways:

1 **Individual behaviour:** This pertains to how single members of the organization act and respond. It is driven by individual capability and the willingness to act in certain ways. For instance, an employee's dedication to continuous learning or their responsiveness to feedback.

2 **Organizational behaviour:** This reflects the organizational environment. It's the behaviour that employees observe around them and is a powerful driver or inhibitor of individual behaviour. This pertains to organizational processes, systems and established ways of working. For example, the organization's informal reward systems that give accolades to employees who support their colleagues.

Here's why focusing on behaviours is transformative:

- **Behaviours are tangible and modifiable:** Unlike outcomes, behaviours are observable. They can be identified, assessed and directly adjusted. By spotlighting behavioural patterns, organizations can craft actionable strategies to reinforce or rectify them.

- **Predictive power:** Behaviours often serve as leading indicators. Before any outcome materializes – be it good or bad – there's usually a consistent pattern of behaviours leading up to it. Recognizing and addressing these patterns early can help shape desired outcomes.
- **Inclusivity and empowerment:** While outcomes might seem distant and broad, behaviours are immediate and personal. By fostering a focus on behavioural standards, every employee, regardless of their role, has a stake in shaping the culture.

While outcomes present a snapshot of an organization's current state, it's the behaviours that shape its future trajectory. For leaders aiming for sustained success, the formula is straightforward: prioritize behaviours as primary levers and allow outcomes to naturally follow.

In essence, to truly influence results and cultivate a thriving organizational culture, leaders need to shift their gaze from the distant horizon and focus on the steps right in front of them.

2. Off-the-shelf models and values do not work

Delve into any leading management book, white paper or keynote speech and you'll likely stumble upon models or values presented as the universal remedy for organizational challenges. Yet, as my research revealed, the reality that emerged was sobering: every organization's behavioural blueprint to drive success was different.

The idea that universal strategies can be transplanted successfully across varied organizational contexts is a fallacy. Each organization's distinct context, strategy, people and operating model sculpt a unique culture and behavioural ecosystem.

Consider the interplay of behaviours and outcomes as an intricate web, where every thread holds significance. This web isn't manufactured in bulk, but is a unique tapestry for each organization, interwoven with its specific nuances and contextual factors.

The implications of this revelation are two-fold:

- **Avoid copy-paste culture strategies:** Just as a neighbour's key won't fit your front door, their organizational strategies won't necessarily unlock success in your company. Emulating external models without adapting them to your unique context is a misstep.

- **Beware the off-the-shelf consultants:** While external guidance can provide invaluable insights, it's crucial to ensure consultants are tailoring strategies to your organization, rather than deploying a generic playbook.

3. Leaders are the custodians of organizational culture, but every employee is accountable for it

For all leaders, that will mean being behavioural champions; however, it also means creating the workplace environment to enable all employees to champion the pursued behaviours. This is why you should adopt workplace Culture by Design.

If you don't actively set the behavioural standards for your organization, you might end up with negative behaviours which can harm your work environment. But with a clear plan, you can build a culture that matches your goals and ensures success.

To enable you to design the culture you need to drive success and stay out of trouble, follow the six phases outlined as follows.

Phase 1: Review your organizational strategy to derive critical organizational outcomes

Connecting culture to strategy is an obvious first step for most, but it is rarely done with the rigour and precision that is required. Start by reviewing your organizational strategy and mission, highlighting key objectives and goals. Ask questions like, 'What tangible results are we aiming for in the next year?', 'What employee or customer experiences do we want to drive?' and 'What do we want to control and minimize around risk, disruption and change?'

From this, outline and populate the specific outcomes you wish to achieve, such as increased sales, improved psychological safety, enhanced customer satisfaction or high compliance with safety processes.

Phase 2: Assess desired outcomes and identify key behaviours to achieve them

As you progress, identify the specific behaviours – individual behaviour (capability and willingness) and organizational behaviour (the systems, processes and ways of working) – that may be needed to achieve these outcomes. Keep these behaviours specific and actionable. For every individual behaviour, there should be a corresponding organizational behaviour to drive and reinforce it.

For example, to drive the outcome of psychological safety, instead of 'employees speaking up' as the behaviour needed to drive this outcome, more specific and actionable behaviours would be 'capability and willingness to work with others to achieve goals' (individual behaviours) and 'rewarding those who speak up and voice concerns' (organizational behaviour).

This direct approach ensures that every strategic element has corresponding outcomes and behaviours, setting the stage for a culture that is both purposeful and aligned with your core objectives.

Phase 3: Measure the outcomes and behaviours to connect the dots

Achieving great things is always the result of various behaviours and outcomes working together. Almost like a web. If you want to achieve excellent risk management, you will need to drive multiple behaviours and outcomes to get there.

Every organization is unique and so the behavioural roadmap to desired outcomes will be unique to you. Therefore, it is critical to understand your own behavioural roadmap. This requires robust measurement of the outcomes and behaviours. From this data, you can start to understand how specific behaviours predict outcomes, and you can strategically focus your interventions to maximum impact.

Phase 4: Plan and implement impactful interventions and organizational changes

To achieve meaningful change within an organization, interventions need to be meticulously planned and executed. Below we outline the essential ingredients for effective intervention planning.

OWNERSHIP FROM SENIOR LEADERS

Any intervention, regardless of how well-crafted, will only be as effective as the support it receives. It's essential that senior leaders not only endorse but actively participate in the intervention design process. Their involvement underscores the intervention's importance, ensuring broader organizational buy-in.

ACCOUNTABILITY FROM KEY STAKEHOLDERS

Ownership ensures endorsement, but for an intervention to truly take off, key stakeholders must be accountable for driving it forward. These stakeholders act as torchbearers, ensuring that the interventions are implemented and maintained as intended, and that feedback loops are in place to measure progress and make necessary adjustments. These could be from relevant departments or identified change champions.

THE THREE PILLARS OF FOCUS – CAPABILITY, OPPORTUNITY AND MOTIVATION

For individuals to adopt new behaviours or ways of working, they require three essential elements:

1 **Capability**: This refers to an individual's ability to enact the desired behaviour. Does the person possess the necessary skills, knowledge and physical ability? When planning interventions, it's vital to ensure that people have the requisite capabilities or that training is provided to equip them with those capabilities. For example, if you're looking to shift your team from tactical thinking to a more innovative mindset, it's not enough to simply tell them to 'think outside the box'. Practical steps might involve offering workshops in creative problem-solving or bringing in guest speakers from industries known for innovation. By doing this, you are building their capability to think innovatively.

2 **Opportunity**: This pertains to the workplace factors – the environment, resources and circumstances – that make a behaviour possible. Organizational systems, processes and ways of working can either facilitate or hinder these opportunities. Interventions must address these organizational aspects to pave the way for desired behaviours. For instance, if an organization wants to promote collaborative work instead of teams working in silos, the environment should be conducive to that. This could mean reconfiguring office spaces to have more open-plan areas or shared workstations, introducing software that facilitates teamwork, or establishing regular inter-departmental brainstorming sessions. These interventions create opportunities for collaboration.

3 **Motivation**: This is the driving force behind behaviour. It encompasses the intrinsic and extrinsic incentives that drive people to act in a certain way. When planning interventions, consider both the personal motivations of employees and the broader organizational incentives that can be leveraged. Consider a scenario where you want to shift the reward system

from one that values status to one that celebrates achievement. Instead of providing perks based on seniority or titles, you could introduce an 'Innovator of the Month' award. This recognizes and rewards individuals who have come up with groundbreaking ideas, irrespective of their position in the company hierarchy. By aligning rewards with achievement, you're bolstering motivation to act in the desired way.

It's paramount to direct interventions where they're most needed. This means ensuring that efforts targeting individuals build capability, while those addressing the organizational framework enhance opportunity and motivation. The precision of these targeted interventions maximizes their effectiveness and ensures that resources are utilized optimally.

By integrating leadership ownership, stakeholder accountability, a deep understanding of capability, opportunity and motivation and the insights from detailed measurements, you'll be well-positioned to drive impactful, lasting change within your organization.

Phase 5: Seeing your interventions in action

Designing an intervention is only half the journey. The real test lies in implementing these strategies effectively. Here's how to move forward with this crucial phase:

- **Strategic roll-out**: Before introducing any interventions, ensure there's a comprehensive roll-out strategy in place. This includes setting clear timelines, designating responsible teams or individuals and defining milestones. Communication is key during this phase: inform all relevant stakeholders about the impending changes, the reasons behind them and the benefits they're expected to bring.
- **Offer support**: Especially if your interventions involve new ways of working or changes in behaviour, it's essential to offer training sessions, workshops or resources. These provide individuals with the tools and understanding they need to adapt and thrive.
- **Foster open communication**: Encourage feedback loops by encouraging teams and individuals to voice their experiences, challenges and suggestions regarding the intervention. This not only fosters a sense of involvement and ownership but also provides valuable insights that can help refine the intervention.

Phase 6: Re-measure behaviours and outcomes to refine your culture transformation efforts

After a set period post-implementation (this could range from a few months to a year, depending on the intervention and expected results), it's critically important to measure again.

Assess both behaviours and outcomes using the same metrics and methodologies you employed initially. With the new data in hand, compare the post-intervention results to the baseline measurements. This will offer a clear picture of the shifts that have occurred, whether positive or negative.

Are the changes in line with your goals? If so, celebrate the success and consider how to further amplify or sustain these results. If the results aren't as expected, delve deeper to understand why. Perhaps there are external factors at play, or maybe certain aspects of the intervention need tweaking.

Based on the insights from the re-measurement, it's time to refine your interventions if necessary and make adjustments based on feedback and the data you've collected. Once refinements are in place, continue the cycle of implementation and measurement to ensure continuous improvement.

In essence, the process of implementing interventions and subsequently measuring their impact is iterative. It's about creating a feedback loop where interventions are continuously improved upon based on real-world results. This cyclical approach ensures that your strategies are always in alignment with the ever-evolving needs and dynamics of your organization.

The next time you're tempted to simply copy a value from a high-performing competitor, or when someone insists that engagement surveys are the true reflection of your organizational culture, or when you're about to green-light a wellbeing initiative without deeper insights, remember this book! This book has equipped you with the unique lessons that I have humbly learnt and shared with you. I truly hope you are now better positioned to cultivate a resilient, purposeful and thriving organizational culture.

It's your choice now – make your workplace culture your organizational hero.

INDEX

Page numbers in *italic* denote information within a figure or table.

accountability 262, 264, 269–72, 330
achievement 26, 52, *132*, 219, 240
acquisitions 150–53
act first culture types 124, *127*
actionable insights 15, 35–42, 287–91, 299–301
active learning 26, 105–20, *131*, 173, 218
active listening *318*
adaptability 150, 279–82
Adaptive Computer Testing 30
adjusted R square 45, *46*, 103
agility 164, 279–96
airline industry 8, 24, 154–55
APEASE intervention design 135
  see also equity
Apple 245
apply type culture 122
automatic motivation (system 1 thinking) 11, 14, 140, *141*
average mean correlation 79, *83*, *92*, 97

Bandura, Albert 12
banking sector 165, 166–77, 247–59
  challenger banks 171
behaviour 18–19, 19–22, 24, 326–27, 328–29
  individual 27
  organizational 13, 27
behaviour change 13–17, 140–42
behaviour interventions (culture by design) 15–17, 135–48, 260
behaviour mapping 30–34, 58–61
behavioural clusters 42, 121–34, *174*
behavioural economics 13
behavioural factors descriptors 25–26, *31*, 38–39
behavioural measurement (diagnostics) 26–30, 69–72, 151–53, *156*, *157*
behavioural nudges 12, 144, 147–48
behavioural research studies 24–26
behavioural roadmaps 183–84, 194–202, 329
behavioural science 10–17
behavioural selection 135, 136–40

beta coefficient 47, *50*, 52, 103
between-cluster differences 190
bias 12, 13, 159, 216
big data 156–57, 245
Black employees 226–27, 231
Boeing 737 Max 8
briefings 264

capability (people focus) 14, 26, 35–42, 54–61, 132–34, 136–40, 166–67
  change management *186*, 195–202
  risk management 275, 276, 277
  wellbeing 302, 307, 309, *311*, *315*, *320*, 330
challenger banks 171, 247, 254–59
change
  behavioural 13–17, 140–42
  commitment to 184–88
  transformational 180–204
change champions 54, 57, 181–88, 197, 202, 306–07, 328
change management 180–204
change programme success/ failure rate 181, 188, 202
Chernobyl disaster 278
classical conditioning 11
cluster analysis 75, 190–93
  behavioural 42, 121–34, *174*
cluster maps 33, *199*
coefficients 45, 47, *48*, 75
  beta *50*, 52, 103
  see also correlation coefficient tables
cognitive behavioural therapy 12
collaboration 251, 263, 280, *281–82*, 284–86
collectivity (partnerships) 26, 122, *132*, 175, 212–13, 218, 276, 280
collegial relationships 256–57
COM-B model 13–17, 140–42
  see also capability (people focus); motivation; opportunity
communication 7, 147, 150, 237, 239, 262–64, 267–68, *320*, 331
  see also listening skills
competition (competitive edge) 251, 282

INDEX

compliance 70, 124, 125, 278, 328
compound annual growth rate 245
conformity (non-conformity) 26, *130*, 175, 212–13
   diversity 222–27, 229–36, 239–40
   innovation 249, 259–60
   safety culture 266–71, 275
   wellbeing 299–301, 302–05, 307, 309, *312*, *316*
consent 158
consider first culture types 124, 126, *127*
consistency (moderation) 26, 76, *130*, 248, 252, 280, 281
consolidation (risk avoidance) 26, 52, 59, 116–17, *131*, 212–13, 248
consultants 220–21
context 135, 136–40, 189
continuous improvement (radical behaviour) 26, 52, 60, *130*, 248, 280, 281, *317*
continuous learning 262, 264, 268–69
correlation coefficient tables 77–84, 89
   see also multiple R
creativity 282
criterion (dependent) variables 25, 44, 50, 103, 177
cross-functional teams 280, *281–82*
culture 216
   see also social norms
culture analytics function 157
culture by design 15–17, 135–48, 260
culture champions 54, 57, 181–88, 197, 202, 306–07, 328
customer experience 254–56
customer satisfaction 68, 70, *71*, 282
customer service 171, 200, 254
cybersecurity 251

data privacy 158
data sampling 159, 176, 276, 283, 287, 299
data security 251, *252*
DE&I 215–44
   see also diversity; inclusion
decision making 5, 11, 250
   see also empowerment (delegation); system 1 thinking (automatic motivation); system 2 thinking
defaults 147
define the answer culture types 125, *128*
delegation (empowerment) 26, 36–40, 42, 52, *130*, 137–38, *139–41*, 148, 218, 327
   agility 289–91

safety culture 262, 275
wellbeing 302
delivery centric (focus) 26, *132*, *186*, 212–13
dependent variables 25, 44, 50, 103, 177
descriptive statistics 43–44
df 46
'dieselgate' 8
digital transformation 154–59
disenfranchisement 26, 39, *122–30*, *133*, *139–41*, 212–13, 224–27, 285, 293
diversity 150, 159, 215, 217
double negative *170–71*, 172, 207, 209, *210*, 211, 212

effect size 49, *51*, 52, 157, 177, 222, 229, 291, 299
electronics sector 245
'emissionsgate' 8
employee silence 164–65
employee voice 163–79
employees 5, 6–9, 328–32
   commitment to change 184–88
   engagement 5, 8, 64, 219, 221, 283
   retention 5, 68, 71–72, 208, 209–13, 219–20
   sentiment analysis 157, 163–79, 184
   surveys 8, 64, 167–70, 176, 219, 221–22
empowerment (delegation) 26, 36–40, 42, 52, *130*, 137–38, *139–41*, 148, 218, 327
   agility 289–91
   safety culture 262, 275
   wellbeing 302
endogenous variables 75
engagement 5, 8, 64, 219, 221, 283
ensure safety culture 125, *126*, *127*, *129*
Environmental Protection Agency 8
envision type culture 122, 123, *124–29*, *131*, 134
equity 135, 217
ethics 158–59, *321*
ethnicity 226–37, 240–41
ethnography 155
exam performance analysis 44–45
Excel tracking sheets 142, 144, *146*
executive committees 142–44, *145*, 237, 239
exogenous variables 75
experimentation 173, 196, 250, *251*, 252, 258, 282
explanatory variables 44
exploratory multivariate analysis 75
explore type culture 122, *123–29*, *130*

expressiveness 26, 36, *130*, 173, *186*, 197, 302, 306–09, *313*
  DE&I 218, 223, 224–27, 229–37, 239–40
external (outer) focus 26, *131*, 248–49, 275, 280, 281
external perceptions 257–58

F-test 46
factor analysis 23, 25, 73, 74, 75, 176, 228
factors 25
fairness 159, 165, 222
false positives 63, 64
fatigue effect 28
fear 164–65, 278
feedback 30, *32*, 147, 254, *256*, 280, 281, 282, *284*
feedback loops 17, 263, 330, 331, 332
finance sector 166–77, 184–88, 189–94, 219–42
Financial Conduct Authority (FCA) 216, 219–20, 241
financial performance indicators 68–69, 71
first level modelling 49
fit 45, 167
five participant rule 49–50, 158
flexibility 26, *130*, *186*, 197, 248, 258, 279–80
front office functions 222, 223, *225*–26, 231, *236*, 237, 241

gas industry 283–96
gender 209, 219–20, 222–26, 230–33, 239–41
geographical context 135, 155, 167
'get-me-there-it is' 66
goal setting 182, 183, 218
good practice 21, 183, 221
goodness of fit 45–46
growth 149–53, 205
growth mindset 288–89

health sector 13
heatmaps 35–36, 37–38, 40, 43, 54–55, 62–63
hiring (recruitment) 5, 149–50, 208–13
HR processes 205–14
humility 30, *32*–33, 35, 36, 37, 39, 59

IBM 246–47
identification strategy 76
implementation plans 144, *146*
impression management 28

inclusion 155, 159, 217–19, 222–27, 230–35, 263, 266, 327
incremental change 280–81
independence tension 130, *132*, 134
independent variables 44
individual behaviour 27, 326
individualism 26, *132*, 280, *284–85*
information exclusivity 250
information technology sector 245
innovation 26, 36, 37, 59–60, 99, *131*, 245–49, 282, 302
innovation centres 248, 249
innovation indexes 247, 248–49, 252–55, 258–59
innovation showcases 251
internal (inner) focus 26, *131*, 249, 280, 281
Internet of Things 245
intervention design 135, 140–42
intervention plans 135, 142–48, 306–24, 329–31
interviews 248, 249–52
iPhone 245
ipsative diagnostics 27, 28–29, 30
Item Response Theory model 27, 29–30
iteration 280–81

K-means clustering 190
key behaviour identification 328–29
known knowns 63, 216
known unknowns 63, 65–66, 216

lagging indicators 20–22, 67
latent constructs 23, 74, 75
leadership 5, 6–9, 150, 155, 173, 262, 263, *318*, *320*–21, 328–32
  team interventions 143–44
  training reviews *321*
  see also executive committees
leading indicators 20–22, 25, 67–72, 327
learning 117–18
  active 26, 105–20, *131*, 173, 218
  continuous 262, 264, 268–69
  see also training
least squares regression models 187–88
life sciences sector 245
Likert scale 27, 157, 287
line graphs 57–59
linear regression 49, 50, 103, 187–88
listening skills *318*
logistic regression 49, 187–88

mean 43
  see also average mean correlation
measurement error 23, 74

measurement (metrics) 6, 15, 75,
    184–88, 329
  behavioural 26–30, 69–72, 151–53,
    156, 157
  financial 68–69, 71
  HR 206, 208
  outcomes 19
  retention 68, 71–72
  safety 20–21, 22, 68, 69–70
  see also lagging indicators; leading
    indicators; re-measurement;
    validation
measurement model 75
median 43–44
mediation analysis 76
mergers 150–53
Microsoft Teams 239
mindset 288–89
Mixed race employees 226–27
model coefficient 103
model fit assessment 46, 76, 103, 187–88
moderation 26, 130, 248, 252, 280, 281
moderation analysis 76
motivation 11, 14, 139, 140, 141, 195, 208,
    211, 330–31
MS 46
multi-traits multi-methods analysis 25
multiple R 45, 49, 50, 102–03, 177,
    188, 299
multiple regression analysis 25, 44–53, 71,
    102–03
multivariate analysis 74–75
multivariate analysis of variance 25

navigate possibility culture 125, 126,
    127, 129
negative reinforcement 12
nested behavioural model 49, 52, 187–88
neutrality 26, 130, 186, 224–26, 227,
    232–35
non-conformity (conformity) 26, 130, 175,
    212–13
  diversity 222–27, 229–36, 239–40
  innovation 249, 259–60
  safety culture 266–71, 275
  wellbeing 299–301, 302–05, 307, 309,
    312, 316
normative diagnostics 27–28
norms 147, 166
Nuclear Leadership Effectiveness
    Attributes 263
nuclear power industry 262–78
nudges 12, 144, 147–48

objectivity 159

observations 46, 50
odds ratio 103–20, 228–30, 265–70, 274,
    287–91, 295, 300–01
off-the-shelf frameworks 21, 65, 327–28
oil industry 283–96
onboarding 208, 211
one-size-fits-all 183, 191–92
open communication 237, 262–63, 331
operant conditioning 12
operational efficiency 44, 68, 71
operational systems (processes) 151,
    165–66, 282
opportunistic modelling 38
opportunity 14, 139–41, 195–96, 280, 330
opt-out mechanisms 147
organizational behaviour 13, 27, 326
organizational change 180–204
organizational culture 4–5, 6, 65–66,
    149–53
  and outcomes 43–53
organizational development 220, 221, 296
organizational growth 149–53
organizational strategy 15, 328
organizational values 4–5, 7–8, 14–15,
    107–08, 128, 150
  behaviour mapping 30–34, 58–61
orthogonal rotation 25
outcome (dependent) variables 25, 44, 50,
    103, 177
outcomes 18, 19–22, 24, 25, 43–53, 328–29
outer (external) focus 26, 131, 248–49, 275,
    280, 281
own type culture 122
ownership 257, 329

parsimonious model 45, 49, 70, 77, 190,
    265, 287, 299
partnerships (collectivity) 26, 122, 132, 175,
    212–13, 218, 276, 280
passive learning 26, 131
path analysis 22–23, 72–101, 168–69, 177,
    271–78, 291–96, 301–06
path coefficients 75
Pavlov, Ivan 11
people focus (capability) 14, 26, 35–42,
    54–61, 132–34, 136–40, 166–77
  change management 186, 195–202
  risk management 275, 276, 277
  wellbeing 302, 307, 309, 311, 315,
    320, 330
perceptions 257–58
performance 5, 55–59, 68–69, 71, 223
personality questionnaires 27–30, 150
persuasive design 195–96
pharmaceutical sector 245

physical capability 14
physical opportunity 14
'place' (workplace environment) 5–6, 133–34, 166–68, 182–83, 188–94, 197–202, 297–324
positivity 30, *33*, *35*, 36, *39*, 60–61
predictive analytics 25, 44–61
    see also multiple regression analysis
predictor variables 44
primary behavioural clusters 121–23
principal component analysis 25, 75
proactive safety management 272–73
process management 151, 165–66, 282
professional services sector 208–13
progressive tension 130, *131*, 134
prohibitive cultures 169, 306
promotive cultures 169, 306
psychological capability 14
psychological safety 91–96, 101, 111–12, 237, 263, 265, 278, 294, 329
    wellbeing 297, 302–06, *318–19*
psychometric testing 27–30
public health 13
purpose 109–10

quadrant distribution method 40, *41*, 54–57, 62–63, 64, 136, 171–76, *236*, *238*, *308–12*
qualitative data 157, 249–52, 254–58
quality indicators 68, 70
quantitative behavioural research studies 24–26
quantitative behavioural science 10–11
quantitative data 157, 252–54, 258–59
question and listen culture 125, 126, *128*
questioning 266–67

R 45–46, 272, 273
R&D investment 245–61
    see also innovation
R square 45–46
    see also adjusted R square
racial discrimination 226–37
radar graphs 222, 223–27, 232–35, 252, *253*, *255*, *259*
radical behaviour (continuous improvement) 26, 52, 60, *130*, 248, 280, 281, *317*
re-measurement 17, 332
recognition 91–96, 101, 108–09
recruitment 5, 149–50, 208–13
reflective motivation (system 2 thinking) 11, 14
regression analysis 104, *229*, *230*

linear 40, 50, 103, 187–88
logistic 49, 187–88
multiple regression 25, 44–53, 71, 102–03
regressor variables 44
regulation 251, 263
    see also Financial Conduct Authority (FCA)
reinforcement theory 12
relationship building 26, *132*, 276
    collegial 256–57
residual plots (model fit) 46, 76, 103, 187–88
resilience 94, 110–11
resource implementation plans 144, *146*
respect 30, *32*, *33*, *35*, *36*, *37*, *39*
retention 5, 68, 71–72, 208, 209–13, 219–20
return on investment 102–20, 245, 274–75, *295*
reward systems *319*
risk 117–18
risk anticipation 115–16
risk aversion 257, *258*
risk avoidance 116–17
risk avoidance (consolidation) 26, 52, 59, 116–17, *131*, 212–13, 248
risk management 5, 114–15, *251*, 262–78
risk ownership 113–14
risk path analysis 84–91
risk tension 129, *130*, 134
roadmaps 183–84, 194–202, 329
role modelling 6, 7
roll-out strategy 331
'roll up your sleeves' attitude 256
Romerty, Ginni 246
rules and responsibilities campaigns 322
Rumsfeld, Donald 216

safety culture 125, *126*, 127, *129*, 262–78
safety indicators 20–21, 22, 68, 69–70
sample size 43, 46, *55*, *64*, 176, 208, 276, 277, *283*, 299
sampling 159, 176, 276, 283, 287, 299
Schein's culture model 4
second level modelling 49
secondary behavioural clusters 124–29
secondary regression output 46–47
security 251, *252*
self focus 70, *132*, *133*, 186, 224–27, 232–35, 280, *285*
semi-structured interviews 248, 249–52
senior leaders 329
sentiment analysis 157, 163–79, 184

sequential ordering 26, 36, 37, 71, *131*, 248, 281
short-termism 26, *131*, 249, 281
significance F 46, *50*, 52, 103
simultaneous analysis 76
Skinner, B F 12
social desirability 28
social learning theory 12
    see also role modelling
social norms 147, 166
social opportunity 14
spurious model 45
SS 46
stakeholders 330, 331
    see also employees
standard deviation 44
standard error 45–46, *48*, *50*, 52, 103
standardization 26, *130*, *186*, 248, 279
statistical validity 49
status 26, *132*
strategic alignment 205–14
strategic thinking 26, *131*, 249, 281
strategy 15, 328
    roll-out 331
strong foundation quadrant 170–72, 173, 207, 209, *210*
structural equation modelling 22–23, 73–101, 271–78
structural model 75
suppressed talent quadrant 173, 207, 209, *210*
surveys 8, 64, 167–70, 176, 219, 221–22
synchronous working 26, *131*, 248, 258, 281
system 1 thinking (automatic motivation) 11, 14, 140, *141*
system 2 thinking 11, 14

tactical focus 26, *131*, 249, 281
target (dependent) variables 25, 44, 50, 103, 177
team focus 26, 52, 71–72, *132*, *186*, 197, 275, 280, *319*
    DE&I 218, 222–27, 229–36, 239, 240
    wellbeing 299–301, 302, 307, *310*, *314*
    see also cross-functional teams
tech fests 251
tech stacks 258
technology 154–59, 245, 256, 257, 258

telecommunications sector 298–324
test-retests 25
thematic maps 249–50, 254–58
time and resource implementation plans 144, *145*, *146*
time management *319*
'tone from the top' (role modelling) 6, 7
top-down decision making 250
toxic cultures 8
tradition 250
traditional banks 249–54
train industry 154–55
training 165, 215, *318*, *319*, *321*, 331
training analysis 105–20
training reviews *321*
transaction focus 26, *132*
transformation consultants 220–21
transformational change 180–204
transparency 257, 262, *284*, 287–88
trust 7, 158, 167, 168–75

unconscious bias 216
univariate analysis 74
universal truths 21–22
unknown unknowns 216

validation 135–36, 148
    see also feedback loops
validity 25, 49
values 4–5, 7–8, 14–15, 107–08, 128, 150
variables 25, 44, 50, 75, 103, 177
varimax rotation 25
verify type culture 122, *130*
virtuous alignment quadrant 170–73, 207, 209, *210*
Volkswagen emissions scandal 8

WebMD Health Services 215–16, 242
wellbeing 167, 168–70, 171–74, 297–324
Wells Fargo 8
White employees 226–27
within-cluster differences 190
workplace culture 154–55
workplace environment 5–6, 133–34, 166–68, 182–83, 188–94, 197–202, 297–324
workshops 189, 215, *313–16*
World Association of Nuclear Operators 263, 276–78

Looking for another book?

Explore our award-winning books from global business experts in Human Resources, Learning and Development

Scan the code to browse

www.koganpage.com/hr-learning-development

More from Kogan Page

ISBN: 9781398614567

ISBN: 9781398610040

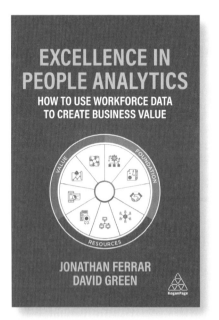

ISBN: 9780749498290

ISBN: 9781398615786

www.koganpage.com